THE
BUTCHER
OF PARIS
™

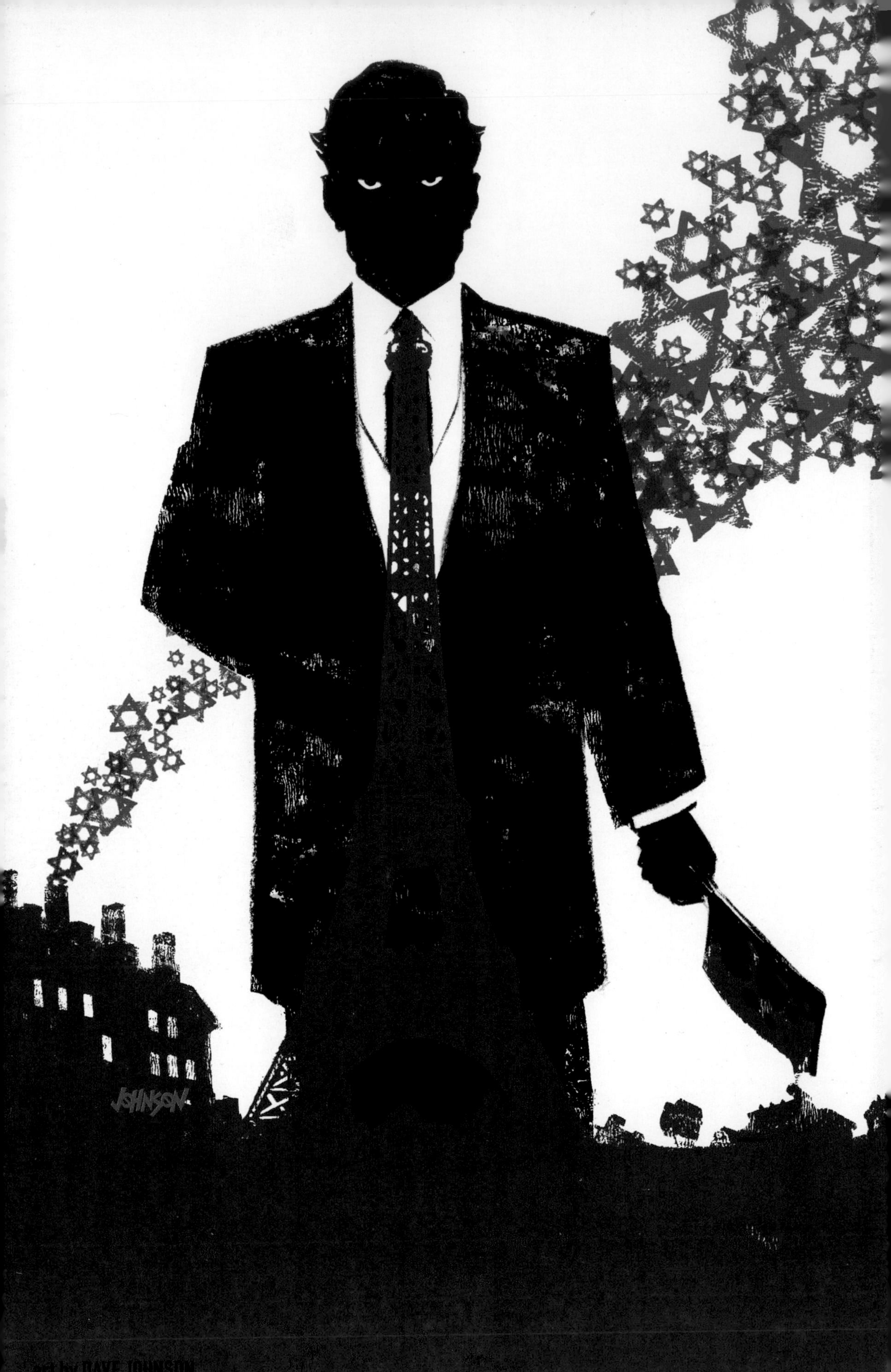
JOHNSON

art by DAVE JOHNSON

THE BUTCHER OF PARIS

script
STEPHANIE PHILLIPS

art
DEAN KOTZ

coloring
JASON WORDIE

lettering
TROY PETERI

cover and back cover art
DAVE JOHNSON

dark horse books

president and publisher MIKE RICHARDSON

editor RANDY STRADLEY

assistant editor JUDY KHUU

designer PATRICK SATTERFIELD

digital art technician JOSIE CHRISTENSEN

THE BUTCHER OF PARIS

This volume collects the Dark Horse comic book series *The Butcher of Paris* #1–#5, originally published December 2019–May 2020.

Published by Dark Horse Books
A division of Dark Horse Comics LLC
10956 SE Main Street
Milwaukie, OR 97222

DarkHorse.com

To find a comics shop in your area, visit comicshoplocator.com

First edition: December 2020
Ebook ISBN: 978-1-50671-586-5
Trade Paperback ISBN: 978-1-50671-569-8

1 3 5 7 9 10 8 6 4 2
Printed in China

Library of Congress Cataloging-in-Publication Data

Names: Phillips, Stephanie, author. | Kotz, Dean, artist. | Wordie, Jason,
    colourist. | Peteri, Troy, letterer.
Title: The Butcher of Paris / script, Stephanie Phillips ; art, Dean Kotz ;
    colors, Jason Wordie ; lettering, Troy Peteri.
Description: Milwaukie, OR : Dark Horse Books, 2020. | Summary: "In 1944,
    as Swastikas flew over Paris, one of the most notorious and prolific
    serial killers in history turned the occupied city into his personal
    hunting ground"-- Provided by publisher.
Identifiers: LCCN 2020001959 | ISBN 9781506715698 (paperback)
Subjects: LCSH: Comic books, strips, etc.
Classification: LCC PN6728.B885 P48 2020 | DDC 741.5/973--dc23
LC record available at https://lccn.loc.gov/2020001959

WHEN A CITY GOES DARK

Almost three years ago, I was reading a book about the Nazi occupation of France (yes, I am a big giant nerd) when I came across a throwaway line in the book about the trial of a man named Marcel Petiot. Without much more information than that, I started to research Petiot (did I mention I'm a nerd?) and found *The Butcher of Paris*: a man responsible for an estimated 60–200 murders in a four-year span. The vast majority of Petiot's victims were Jews seeking safe passage out of the city. Beginning in 1942, over 13,000 French Jews were forcibly collected and sent to Auschwitz concentration camp. That was only the beginning. Until the liberation of Paris in 1944, Jews were targeted, harassed, sent to concentration camps, and murdered on a weekly basis. Truly, the Nazis are the worst serial killers the world has ever seen. Yet, within their midst was a man who saw these heinous actions as an opportunity to prey on the scared and the desperate. Posing as a French resistance fighter, Petiot was able to lure unsuspecting Jews to their deaths inside his townhome on 21 Rue le Sueur.

I have to be honest with you – even now, writing about the history of Petiot that I have read and studied for years in preparation to write this comic, I am stunned by this story. A city devastated by war and occupied by Nazis became the hunting ground for one of the most prolific serial killers I had (at the time) never even heard of. How could someone see such horror and devastation as an *opportunity*? Just what kind of person . . . No . . . what kind of *monster* was Marcel Petiot?

Thus, the idea of this series, *The Butcher of Paris*, was born from my horror that something so truly vile had actually happened. I couldn't have made this up . . . . Coming from a Jewish family with relatives that fought in both WWI and WWII, elements of this story have also felt very personal.

There have been times where I have needed space from the scripts for *Butcher* because the weight of this story became too heavy. Couple that with the rhetoric regarding fascism and Nazism today and the story almost becomes somehow *more* heinous because there is a need to continue discussing it in 2019. In Pittsburgh in October 2018, eleven lives were

Ms. Phillips's great great uncle William "Buzz" Wightman, a B-25 pilot during WWII who was killed in action in 1943.

lost when a shooter opened fire in a synagogue during the Shabbat morning services. In August of this year, both a Connecticut and New York synagogue were vandalized with anti-Semitic graffiti. Before that it was an Indiana synagogue, and Los Angeles, and Chicago . . . the list goes on. I knew this story needed to be told.

The monsters that appear in *The Butcher of Paris* were not exorcised in the 1940s.

I remember reading some transcripts from Petiot's court case and I came across an interesting line from the prosecutor. The crowd at the trial *loved* Petiot. Keep in mind, the trial was happening at the close of WWII. Paris had been liberated following the invasion of Normandy Beach. The audience came to the Petiot trial for a show, and he was more than happy to give it to them. Petiot harassed the prosecutors and titillated the audience. In a very Bundy-esque fashion, it is believed that Petiot also had many female admirers in the audience. At some point during the trial, Petiot made the crowd laugh. The prosecutor turned to them wildly and yelled, "Does the sanctity of life mean nothing to you?!" The audience just laughed harder.

WWII is still the deadliest military conflict in history with a death toll sitting at 85 million. Let's break down some of these numbers for a minute. The Normandy campaign of 1944 saw 226,386 casualties for the Allies, and another 240,000 German losses. From 1941-1945 six million Jews were killed as part of the Holocaust. How, then, could the prosecutor in the Petiot trial believe anyone in attendance could still feel empathetic when discussing the loss of life? The entire world just watched 85 million people die. Petiot was but a blip in comparison, right?

The problem, of course, is when we devalue the lives of the individual 85 million lost to war and genocide, we lose the empathy that makes us human—that helps us relate and care about one another. Petiot is a fascinating case of what happens when a person is more monster than man

and, to a larger extent, when an entire nation is complicit in the deaths of six million Jews.

In actuality, both the Gestapo and the French police were invested in catching Petiot (how bad does it have to be when the *Nazis* want you arrested . . . ?). As such, I really wanted to tell a story about the tensions of war and occupation, about a city once known as "The City of Light" going dark. Petiot happens to be in this city and in this story, but this is a story about victims, about a struggling city, and about complicity. While the entire creative team has attempted to be as faithful to the historical material as possible, our larger goal was to tell a story that holds a mirror to those who are *complicit* and provide a reminder about the dangers of silence.

Stephanie Phillips
September, 2019

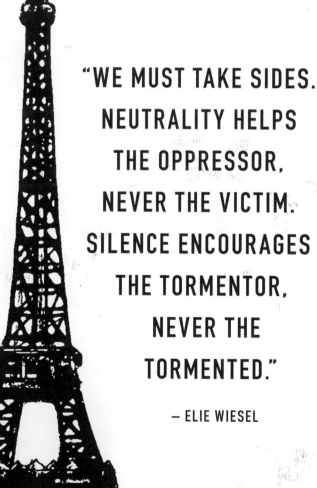

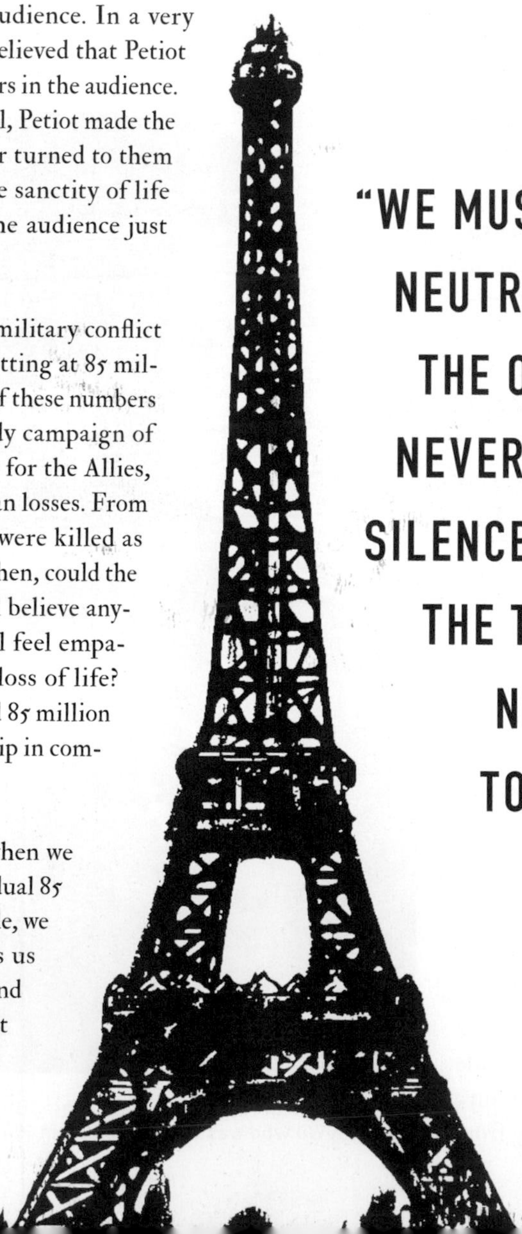

"WE MUST TAKE SIDES. NEUTRALITY HELPS THE OPPRESSOR, NEVER THE VICTIM. SILENCE ENCOURAGES THE TORMENTOR, NEVER THE TORMENTED."

— ELIE WIESEL

art by DAVE JOHNSON

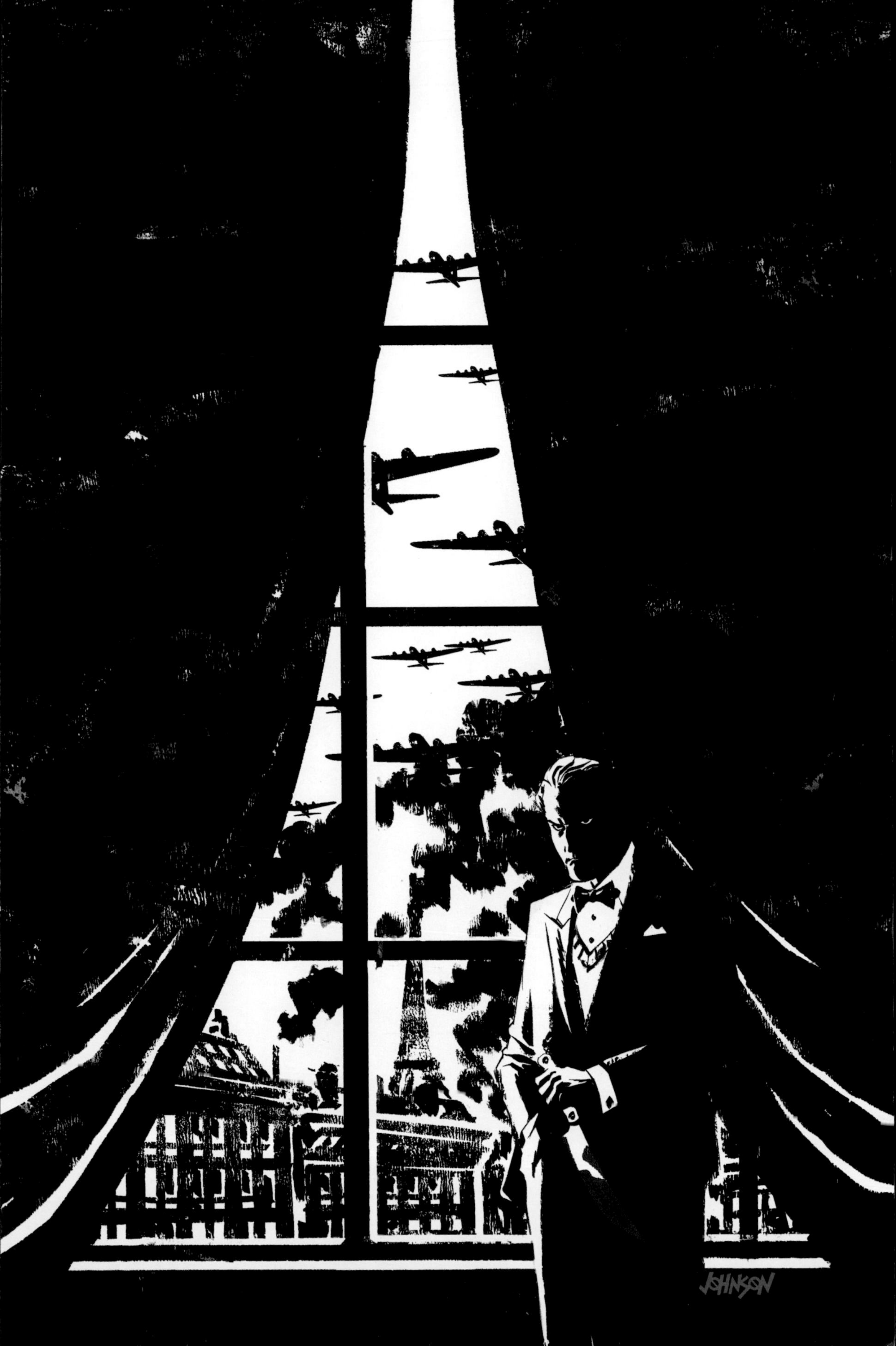
JOHNSON

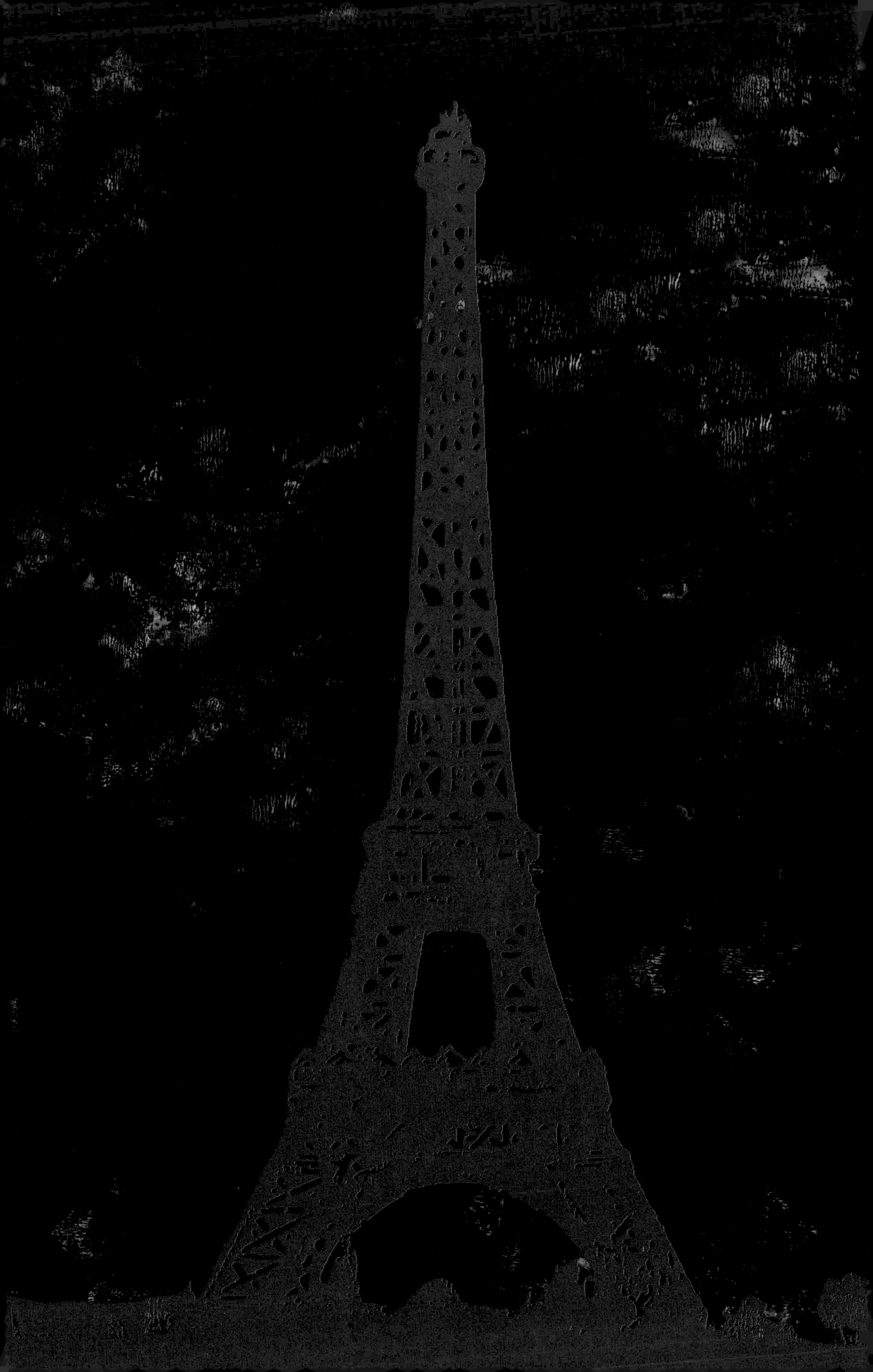

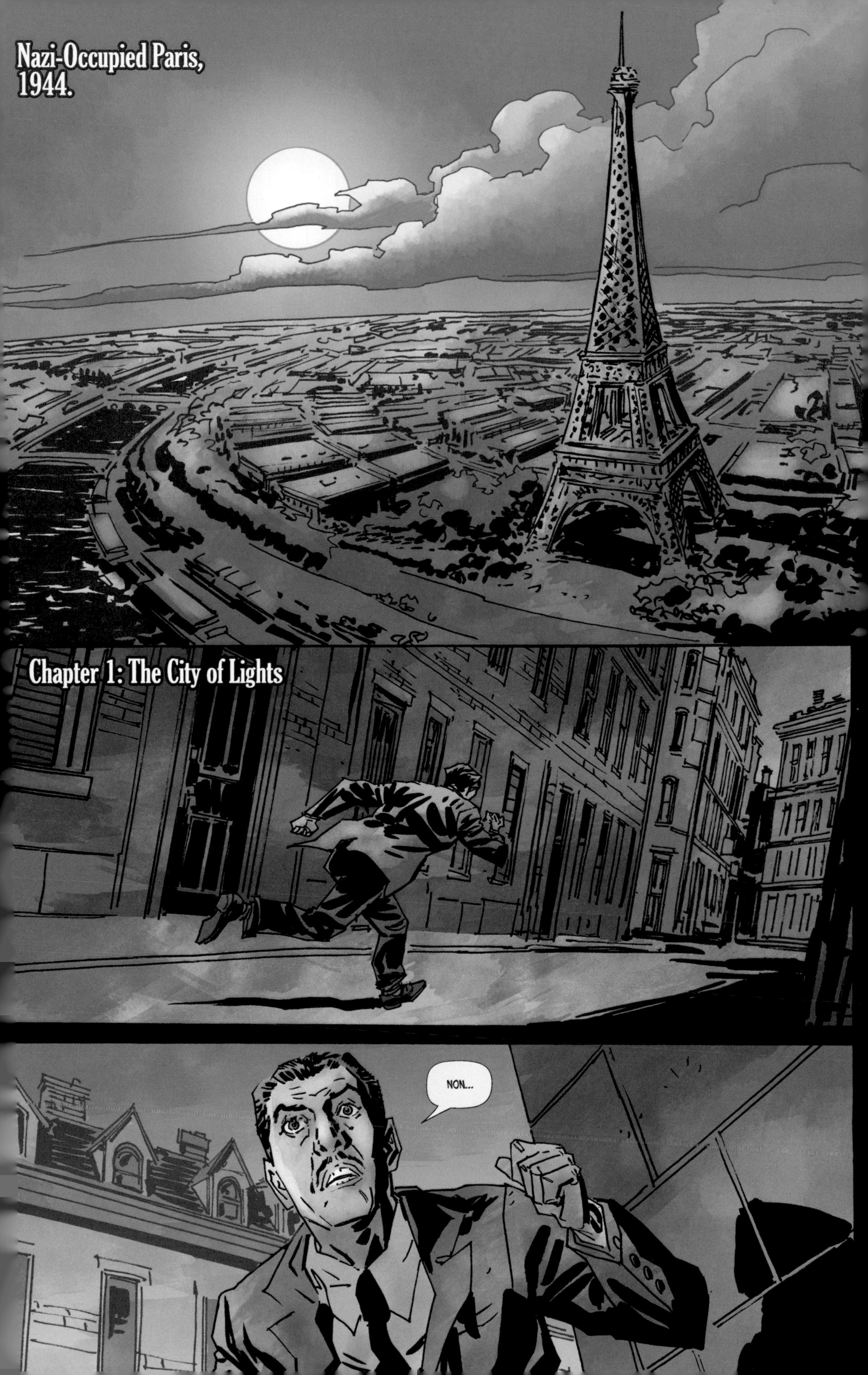
Nazi-Occupied Paris, 1944.
Chapter 1: The City of Lights
NON...

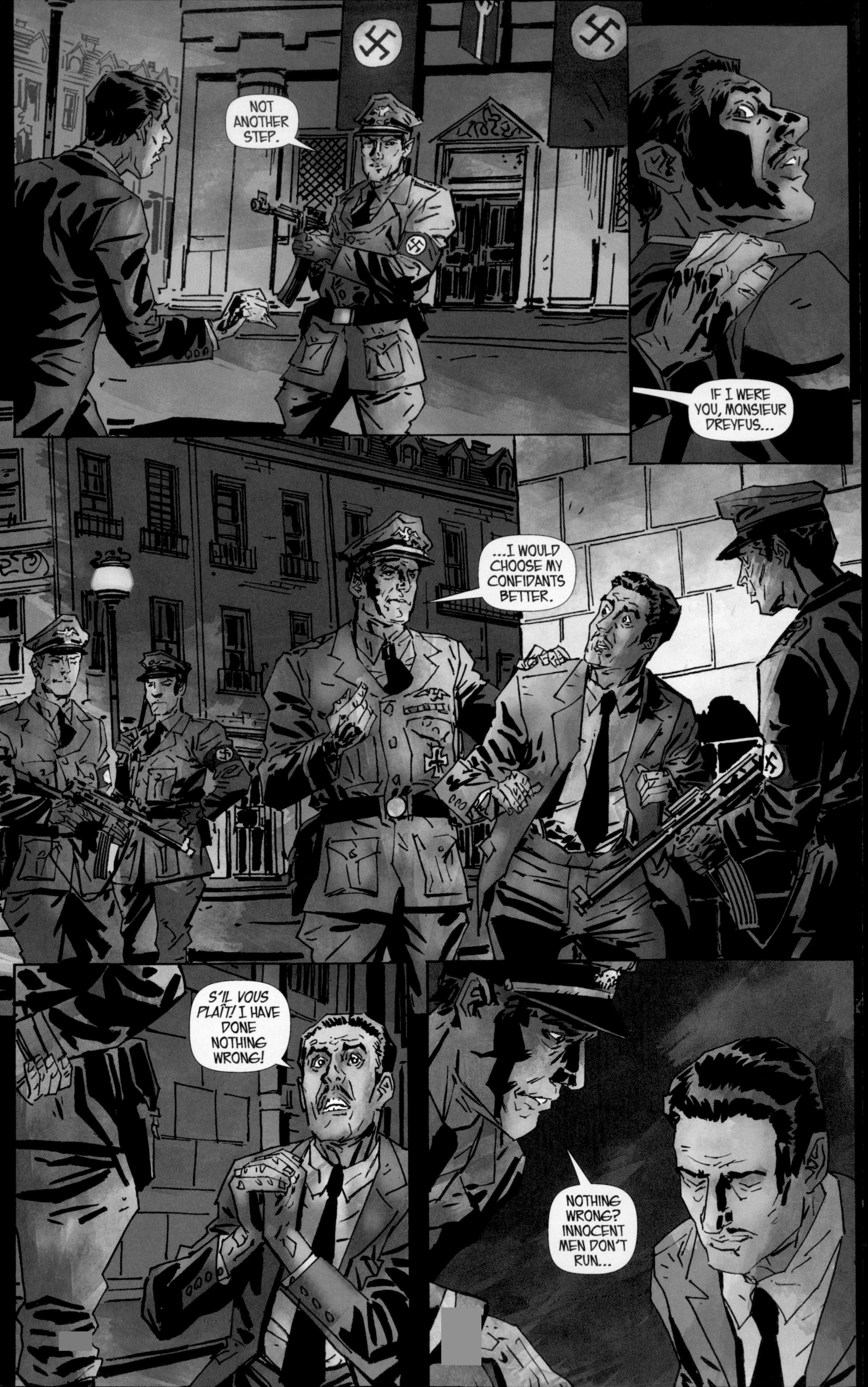
NOT ANOTHER STEP.
IF I WERE YOU, MONSIEUR DREYFUS...
...I WOULD CHOOSE MY CONFIDANTS BETTER.
S'IL VOUS PLAÎT! I HAVE DONE NOTHING WRONG!
NOTHING WRONG? INNOCENT MEN DON'T RUN...

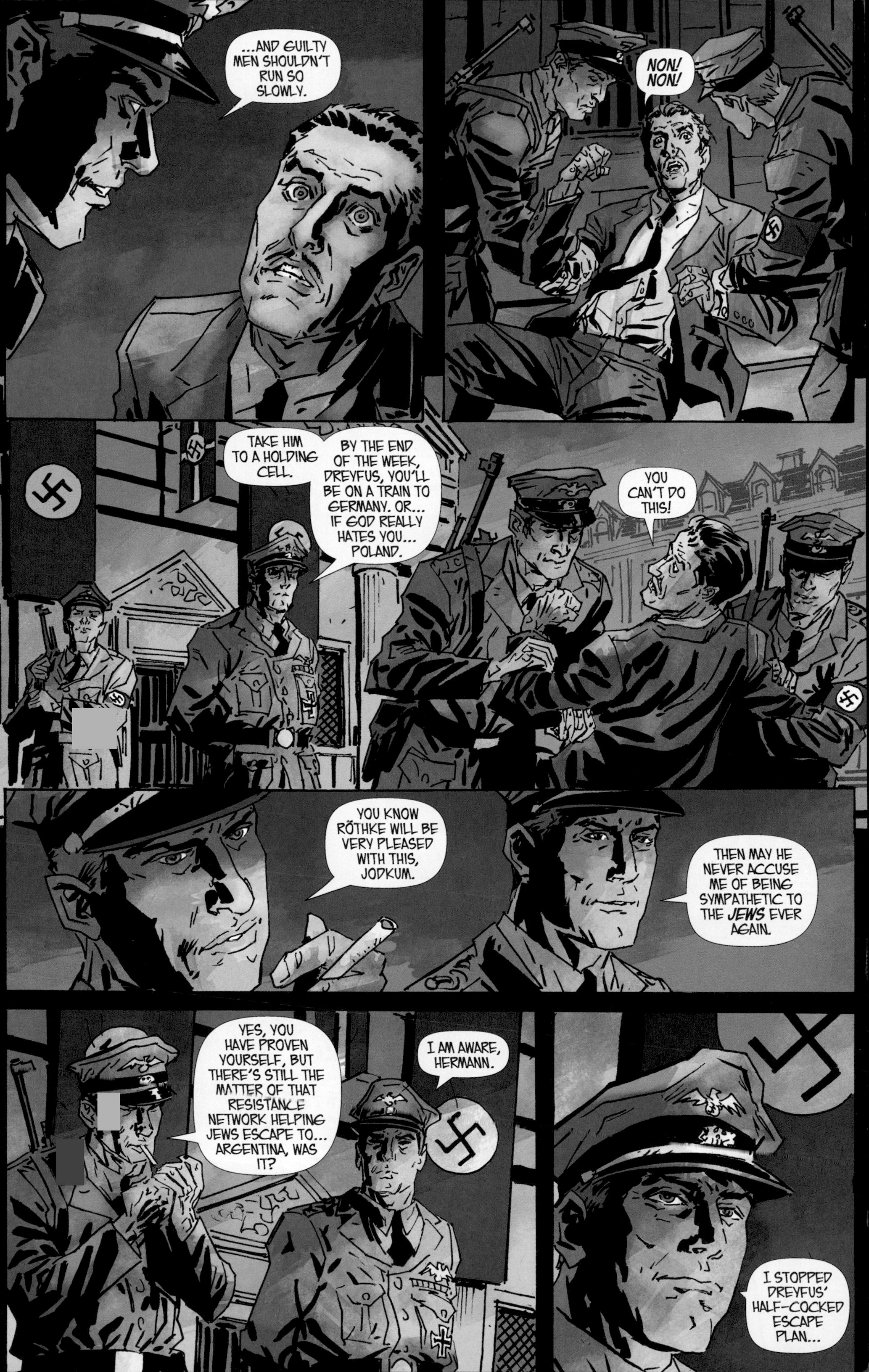
...AND GUILTY MEN SHOULDN'T RUN SO SLOWLY.
NON! NON!
TAKE HIM TO A HOLDING CELL.
BY THE END OF THE WEEK, DREYFUS, YOU'LL BE ON A TRAIN TO GERMANY. OR... IF GOD REALLY HATES YOU... POLAND.
YOU CAN'T DO THIS!
YOU KNOW RÖTHKE WILL BE VERY PLEASED WITH THIS, JODKUM.
THEN MAY HE NEVER ACCUSE ME OF BEING SYMPATHETIC TO THE JEWS EVER AGAIN.
YES, YOU HAVE PROVEN YOURSELF, BUT THERE'S STILL THE MATTER OF THAT RESISTANCE NETWORK HELPING JEWS ESCAPE TO... ARGENTINA, WAS IT?
I AM AWARE, HERMANN.
I STOPPED DREYFUS' HALF-COCKED ESCAPE PLAN...

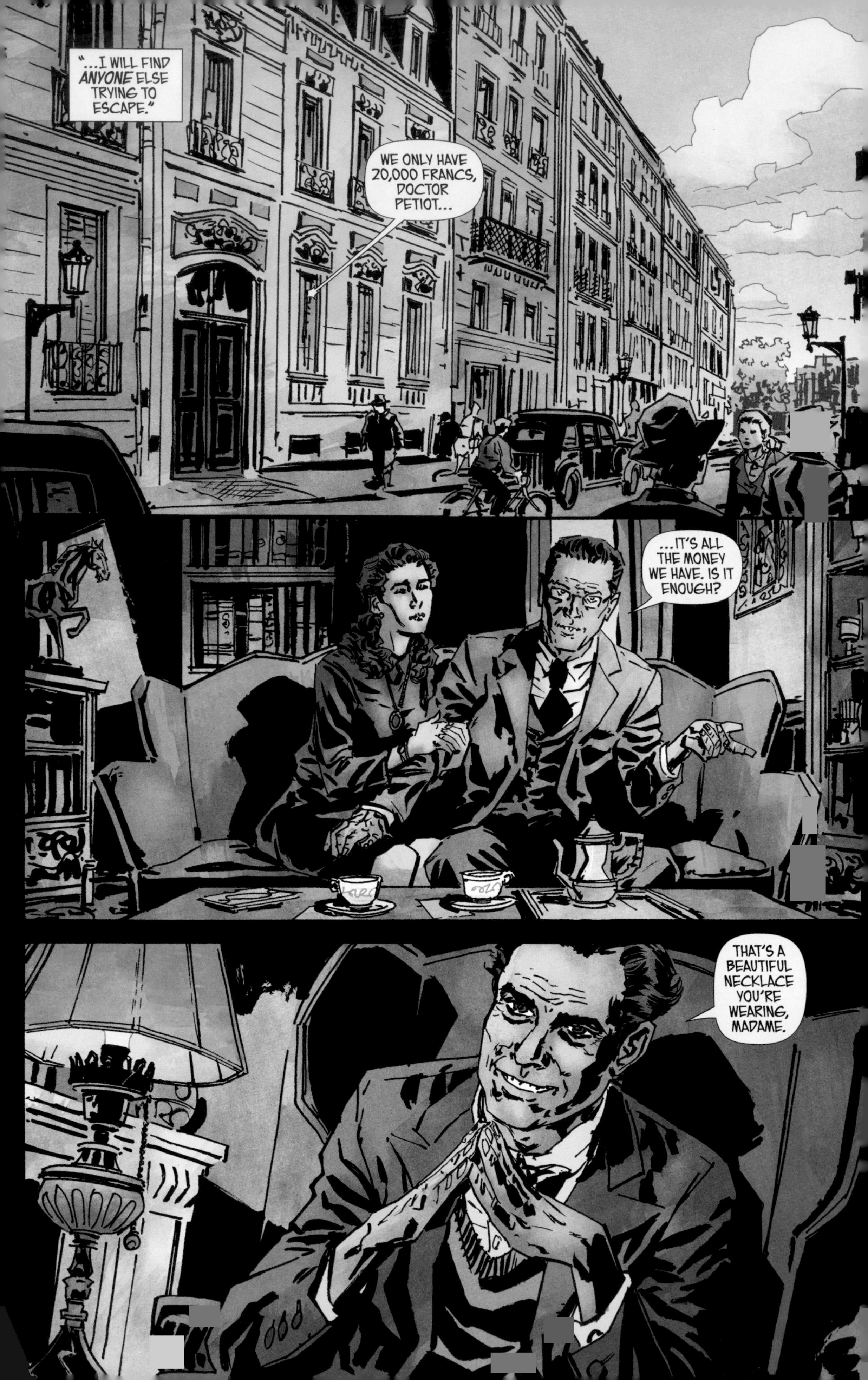
"...I WILL FIND ANYONE ELSE TRYING TO ESCAPE."
WE ONLY HAVE 20,000 FRANCS, DOCTOR PETIOT...
...IT'S ALL THE MONEY WE HAVE. IS IT ENOUGH?
THAT'S A BEAUTIFUL NECKLACE YOU'RE WEARING, MADAME.

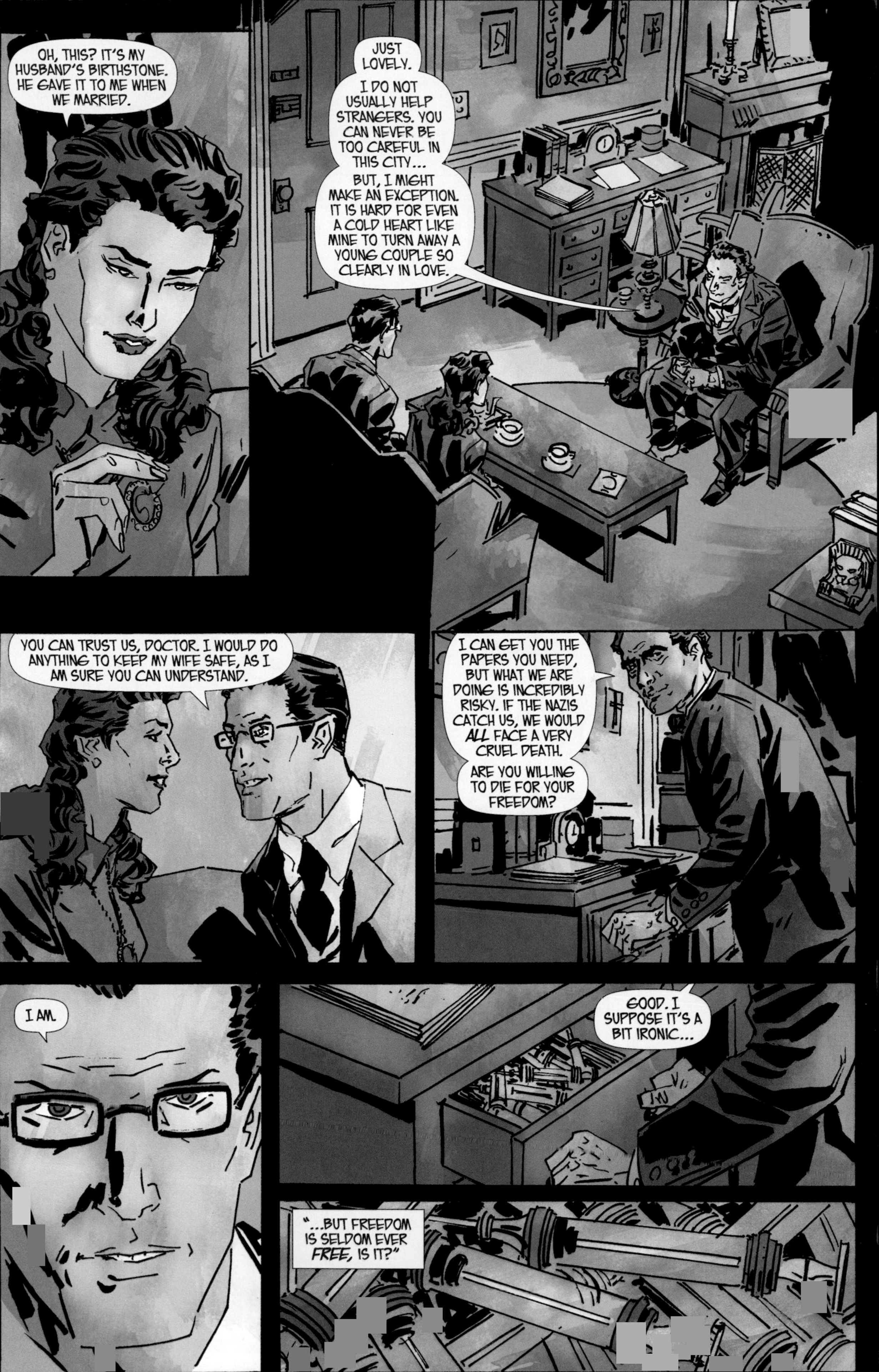
OH, THIS? IT'S MY HUSBAND'S BIRTHSTONE. HE GAVE IT TO ME WHEN WE MARRIED.
JUST LOVELY.
I DO NOT USUALLY HELP STRANGERS. YOU CAN NEVER BE TOO CAREFUL IN THIS CITY...
BUT, I MIGHT MAKE AN EXCEPTION. IT IS HARD FOR EVEN A COLD HEART LIKE MINE TO TURN AWAY A YOUNG COUPLE SO CLEARLY IN LOVE.
YOU CAN TRUST US, DOCTOR. I WOULD DO ANYTHING TO KEEP MY WIFE SAFE, AS I AM SURE YOU CAN UNDERSTAND.
I CAN GET YOU THE PAPERS YOU NEED, BUT WHAT WE ARE DOING IS INCREDIBLY RISKY. IF THE NAZIS CATCH US, WE WOULD ALL FACE A VERY CRUEL DEATH.
ARE YOU WILLING TO DIE FOR YOUR FREEDOM?
I AM.
GOOD. I SUPPOSE IT'S A BIT IRONIC...
"...BUT FREEDOM IS SELDOM EVER FREE, IS IT?"

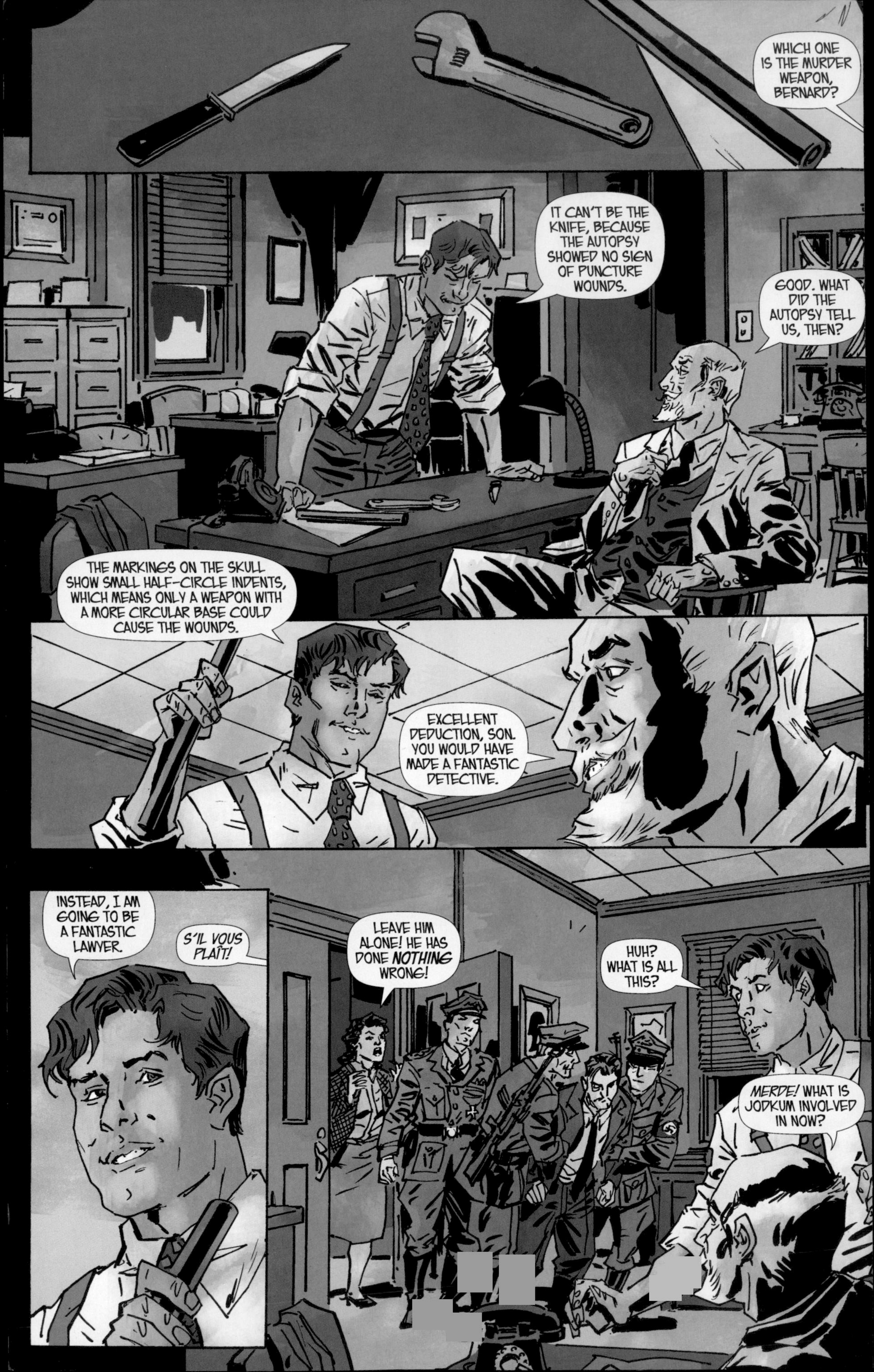

WHICH ONE IS THE MURDER WEAPON, BERNARD?
IT CAN'T BE THE KNIFE, BECAUSE THE AUTOPSY SHOWED NO SIGN OF PUNCTURE WOUNDS.
GOOD. WHAT DID THE AUTOPSY TELL US, THEN?
THE MARKINGS ON THE SKULL SHOW SMALL HALF-CIRCLE INDENTS, WHICH MEANS ONLY A WEAPON WITH A MORE CIRCULAR BASE COULD CAUSE THE WOUNDS.
EXCELLENT DEDUCTION, SON. YOU WOULD HAVE MADE A FANTASTIC DETECTIVE.
INSTEAD, I AM GOING TO BE A FANTASTIC LAWYER.
S'IL VOUS PLAÎT!
LEAVE HIM ALONE! HE HAS DONE *NOTHING* WRONG!
HUH? WHAT IS ALL THIS?
MERDE! WHAT IS JODKUM INVOLVED IN NOW?

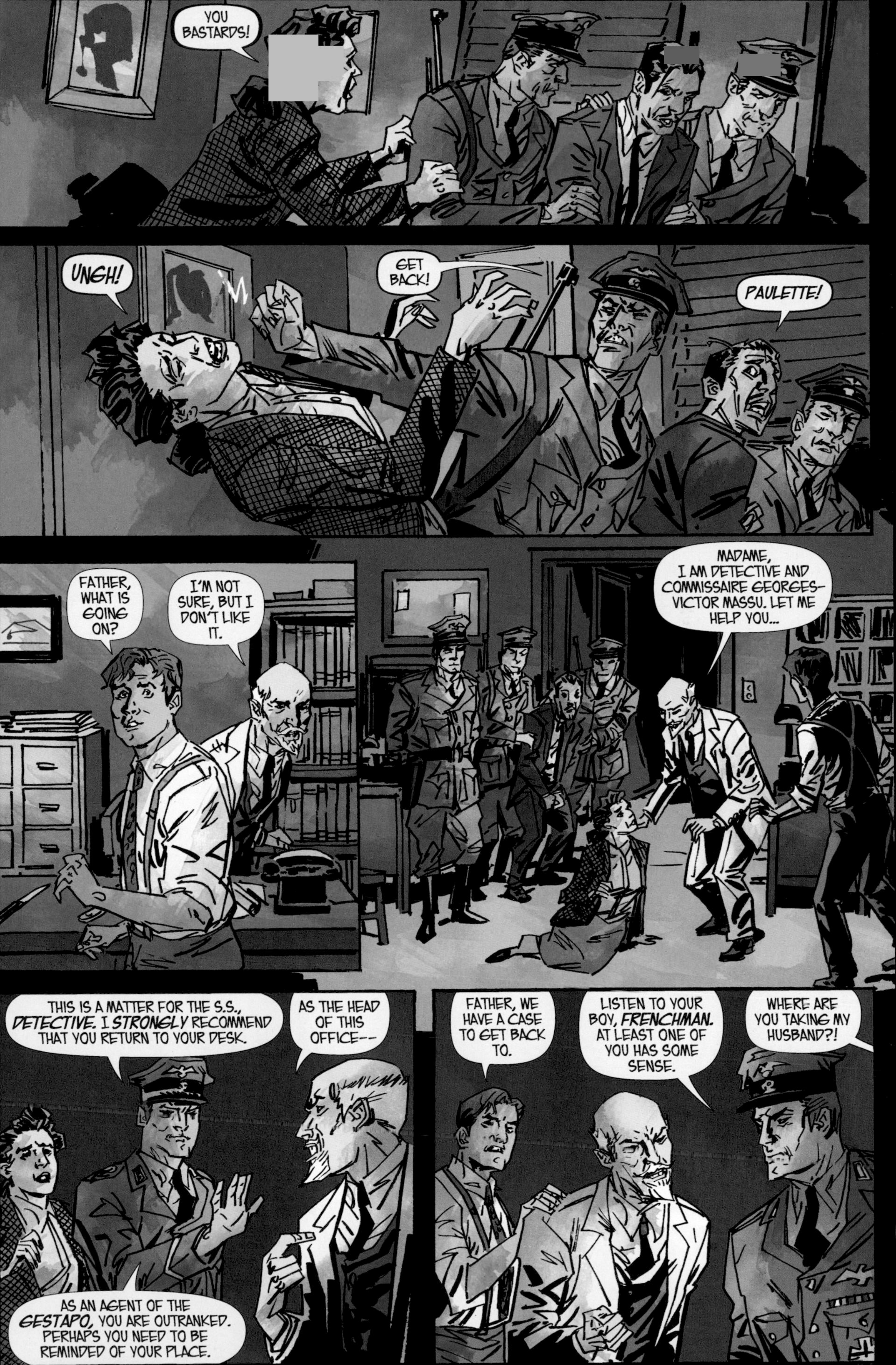
YOU BASTARDS!
UNGH!
GET BACK!
PAULETTE!
FATHER, WHAT IS GOING ON?
I'M NOT SURE, BUT I DON'T LIKE IT.
MADAME, I AM DETECTIVE AND COMMISSAIRE GEORGES-VICTOR MASSU. LET ME HELP YOU...
THIS IS A MATTER FOR THE S.S., *DETECTIVE.* I *STRONGLY* RECOMMEND THAT YOU RETURN TO YOUR DESK.
AS THE HEAD OF THIS OFFICE--
AS AN AGENT OF THE *GESTAPO,* YOU ARE OUTRANKED. PERHAPS YOU NEED TO BE REMINDED OF YOUR PLACE.
FATHER, WE HAVE A CASE TO GET BACK TO.
LISTEN TO YOUR BOY, *FRENCHMAN.* AT LEAST ONE OF YOU HAS SOME SENSE.
WHERE ARE YOU TAKING MY HUSBAND?!

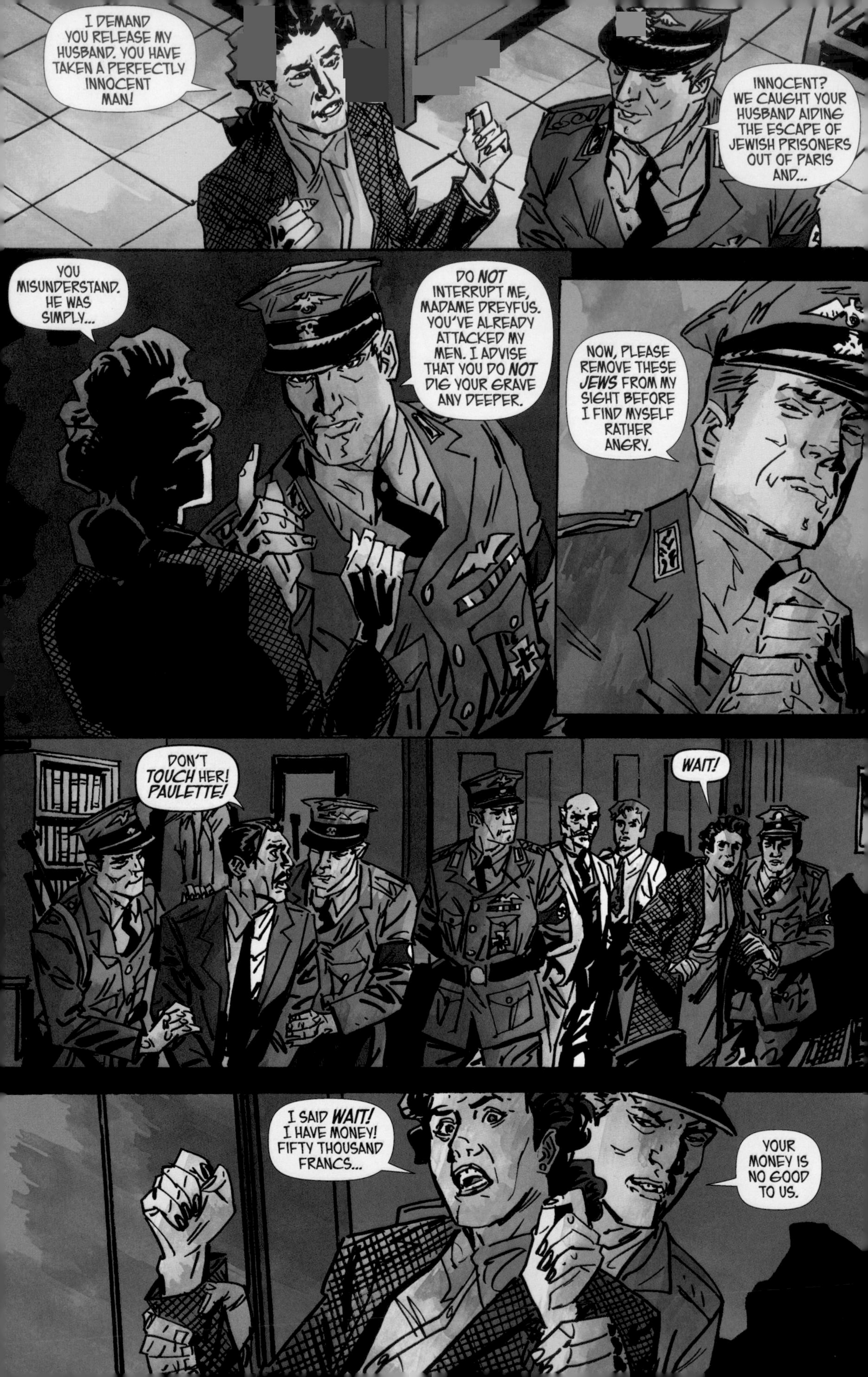
I DEMAND YOU RELEASE MY HUSBAND. YOU HAVE TAKEN A PERFECTLY INNOCENT MAN!
INNOCENT? WE CAUGHT YOUR HUSBAND AIDING THE ESCAPE OF JEWISH PRISONERS OUT OF PARIS AND...
YOU MISUNDERSTAND. HE WAS SIMPLY...
DO NOT INTERRUPT ME, MADAME DREYFUS. YOU'VE ALREADY ATTACKED MY MEN. I ADVISE THAT YOU DO NOT DIG YOUR GRAVE ANY DEEPER.
NOW, PLEASE REMOVE THESE JEWS FROM MY SIGHT BEFORE I FIND MYSELF RATHER ANGRY.
DON'T TOUCH HER! PAULETTE!
WAIT!
I SAID WAIT! I HAVE MONEY! FIFTY THOUSAND FRANCS...
YOUR MONEY IS NO GOOD TO US.

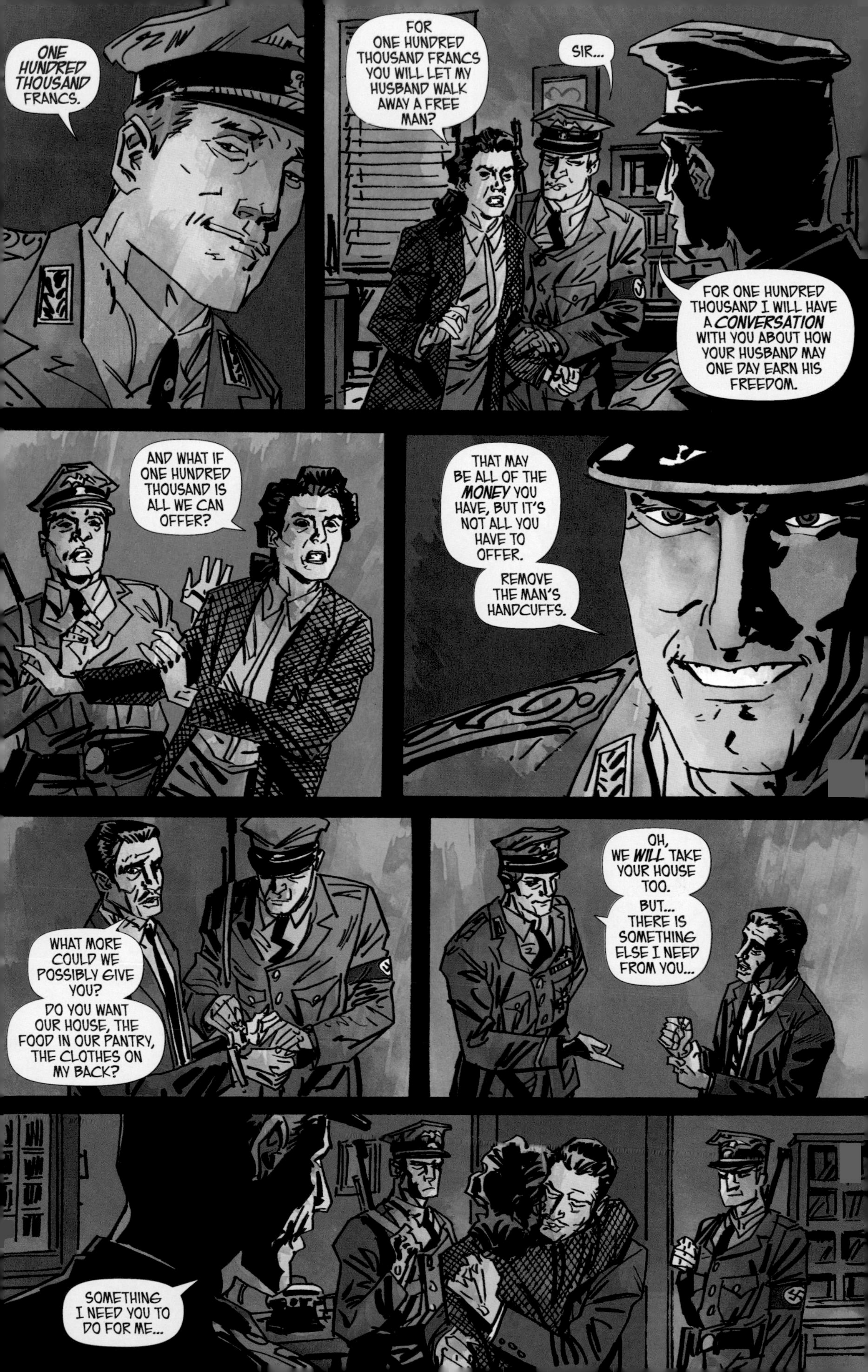
ONE HUNDRED THOUSAND FRANCS.
FOR ONE HUNDRED THOUSAND FRANCS YOU WILL LET MY HUSBAND WALK AWAY A FREE MAN?
SIR...
FOR ONE HUNDRED THOUSAND I WILL HAVE A CONVERSATION WITH YOU ABOUT HOW YOUR HUSBAND MAY ONE DAY EARN HIS FREEDOM.
AND WHAT IF ONE HUNDRED THOUSAND IS ALL WE CAN OFFER?
THAT MAY BE ALL OF THE MONEY YOU HAVE, BUT IT'S NOT ALL YOU HAVE TO OFFER.
REMOVE THE MAN'S HANDCUFFS.
WHAT MORE COULD WE POSSIBLY GIVE YOU?
DO YOU WANT OUR HOUSE, THE FOOD IN OUR PANTRY, THE CLOTHES ON MY BACK?
OH, WE WILL TAKE YOUR HOUSE TOO.
BUT... THERE IS SOMETHING ELSE I NEED FROM YOU...
SOMETHING I NEED YOU TO DO FOR ME...

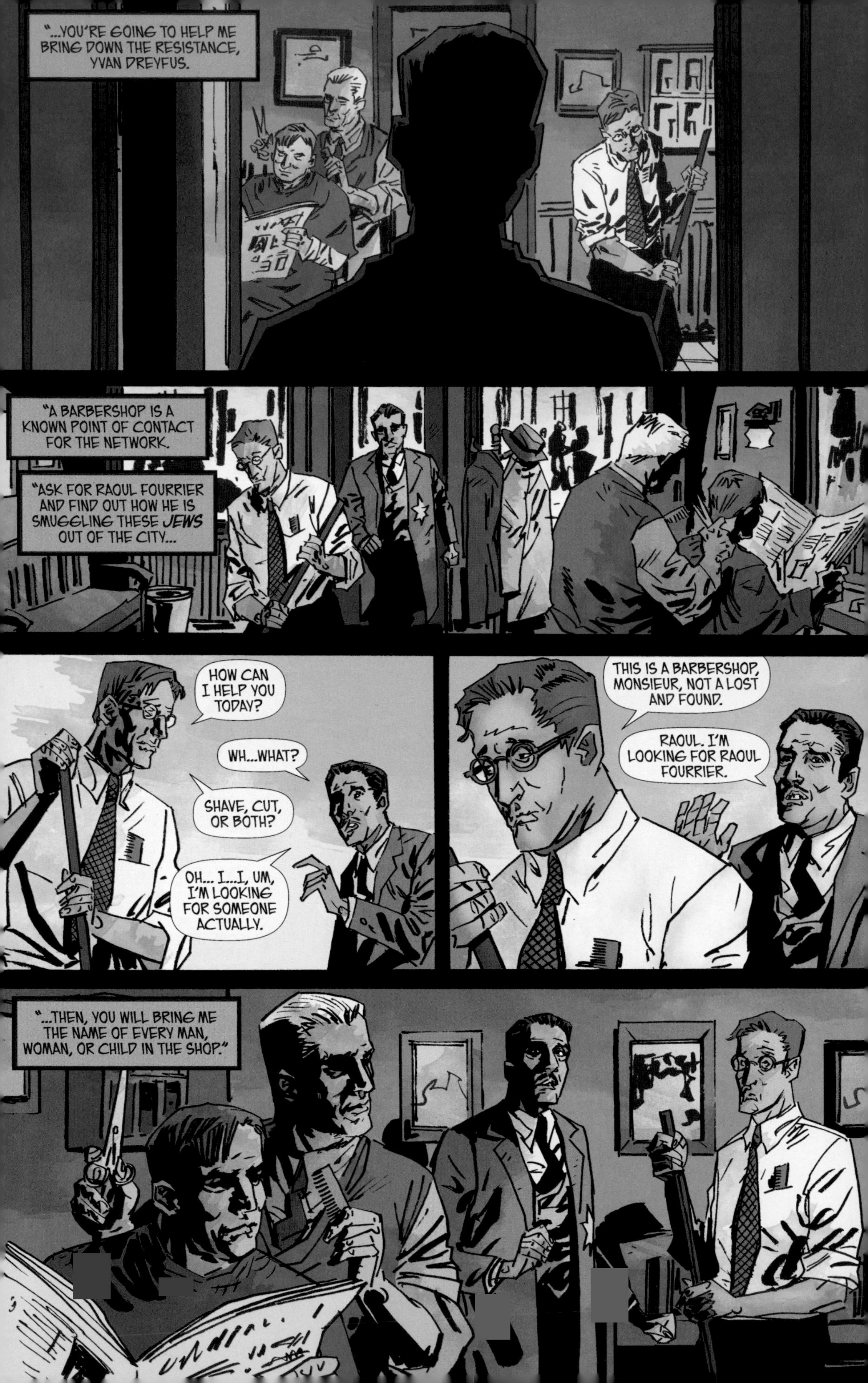
"...YOU'RE GOING TO HELP ME BRING DOWN THE RESISTANCE, YVAN DREYFUS.
"A BARBERSHOP IS A KNOWN POINT OF CONTACT FOR THE NETWORK.
"ASK FOR RAOUL FOURRIER AND FIND OUT HOW HE IS SMUGGLING THESE JEWS OUT OF THE CITY...
HOW CAN I HELP YOU TODAY?
WH...WHAT?
SHAVE, CUT, OR BOTH?
OH... I...I, UM, I'M LOOKING FOR SOMEONE ACTUALLY.
THIS IS A BARBERSHOP, MONSIEUR, NOT A LOST AND FOUND.
RAOUL. I'M LOOKING FOR RAOUL FOURRIER.
"...THEN, YOU WILL BRING ME THE NAME OF EVERY MAN, WOMAN, OR CHILD IN THE SHOP."

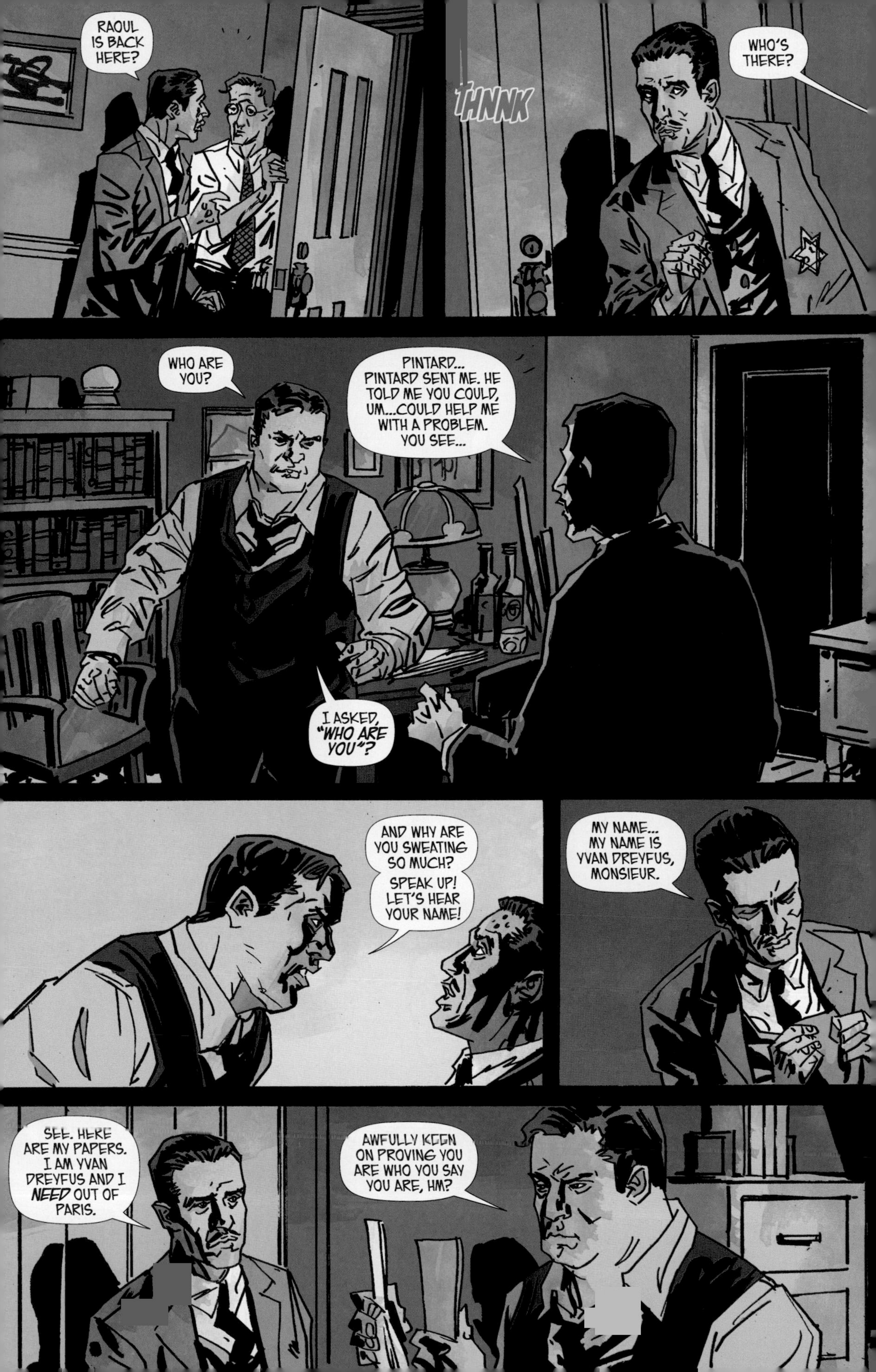
RAOUL IS BACK HERE?
THNNK
WHO'S THERE?
WHO ARE YOU?
PINTARD... PINTARD SENT ME. HE TOLD ME YOU COULD, UM...COULD HELP ME WITH A PROBLEM. YOU SEE...
I ASKED, *"WHO ARE YOU"*?
AND WHY ARE YOU SWEATING SO MUCH?
SPEAK UP! LET'S HEAR YOUR NAME!
MY NAME... MY NAME IS YVAN DREYFUS, MONSIEUR.
SEE. HERE ARE MY PAPERS. I AM YVAN DREYFUS AND I *NEED* OUT OF PARIS.
AWFULLY KEEN ON PROVING YOU ARE WHO YOU SAY YOU ARE, HM?

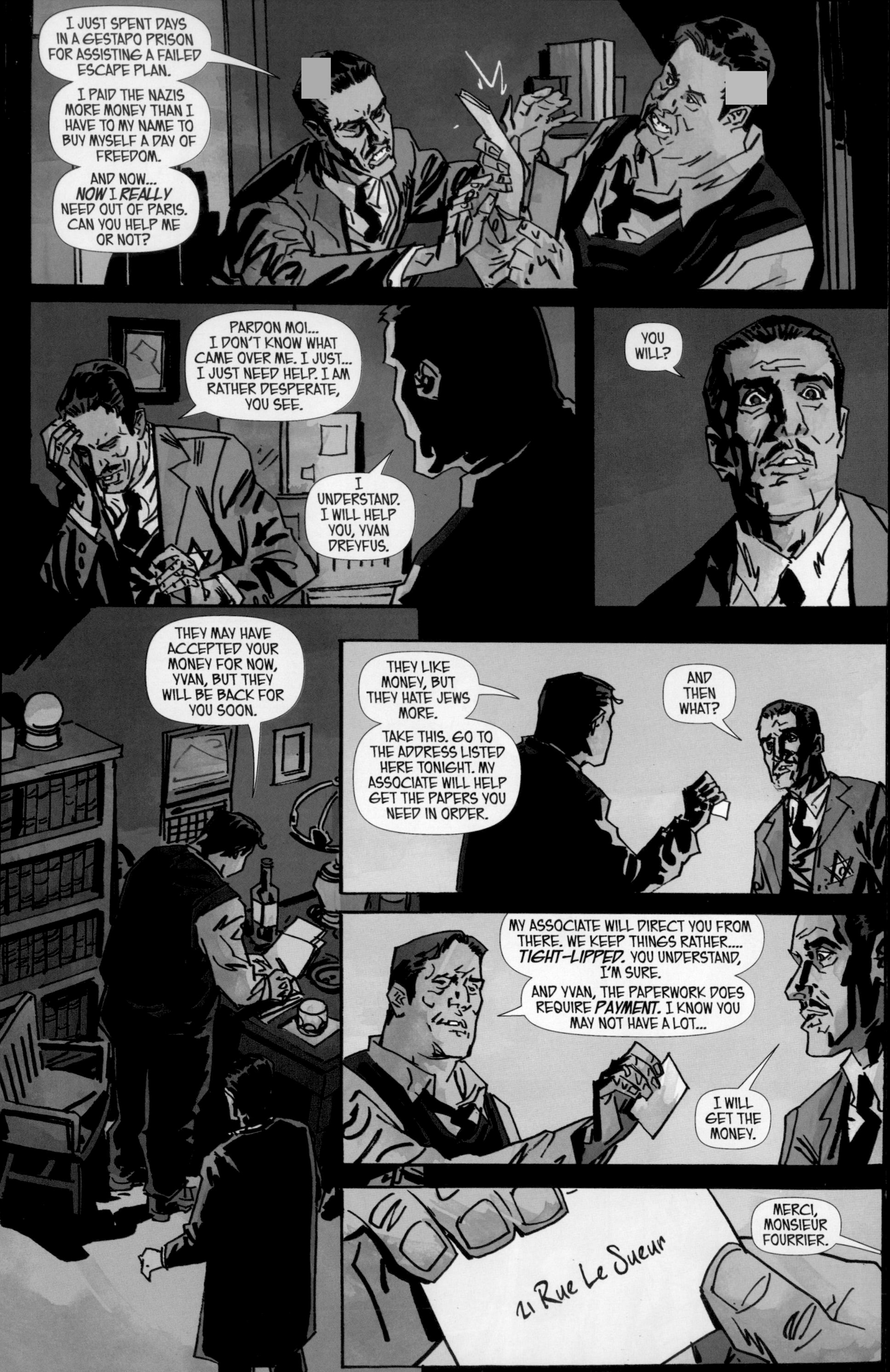
I JUST SPENT DAYS IN A GESTAPO PRISON FOR ASSISTING A FAILED ESCAPE PLAN.
I PAID THE NAZIS MORE MONEY THAN I HAVE TO MY NAME TO BUY MYSELF A DAY OF FREEDOM.
AND NOW... NOW I REALLY NEED OUT OF PARIS. CAN YOU HELP ME OR NOT?
PARDON MOI... I DON'T KNOW WHAT CAME OVER ME. I JUST... I JUST NEED HELP. I AM RATHER DESPERATE, YOU SEE.
I UNDERSTAND. I WILL HELP YOU, YVAN DREYFUS.
YOU WILL?
THEY MAY HAVE ACCEPTED YOUR MONEY FOR NOW, YVAN, BUT THEY WILL BE BACK FOR YOU SOON.
THEY LIKE MONEY, BUT THEY HATE JEWS MORE.
TAKE THIS. GO TO THE ADDRESS LISTED HERE TONIGHT. MY ASSOCIATE WILL HELP GET THE PAPERS YOU NEED IN ORDER.
AND THEN WHAT?
MY ASSOCIATE WILL DIRECT YOU FROM THERE. WE KEEP THINGS RATHER.... TIGHT-LIPPED. YOU UNDERSTAND, I'M SURE.
AND YVAN, THE PAPERWORK DOES REQUIRE PAYMENT. I KNOW YOU MAY NOT HAVE A LOT...
I WILL GET THE MONEY.
21 Rue Le Sueur
MERCI, MONSIEUR FOURRIER.

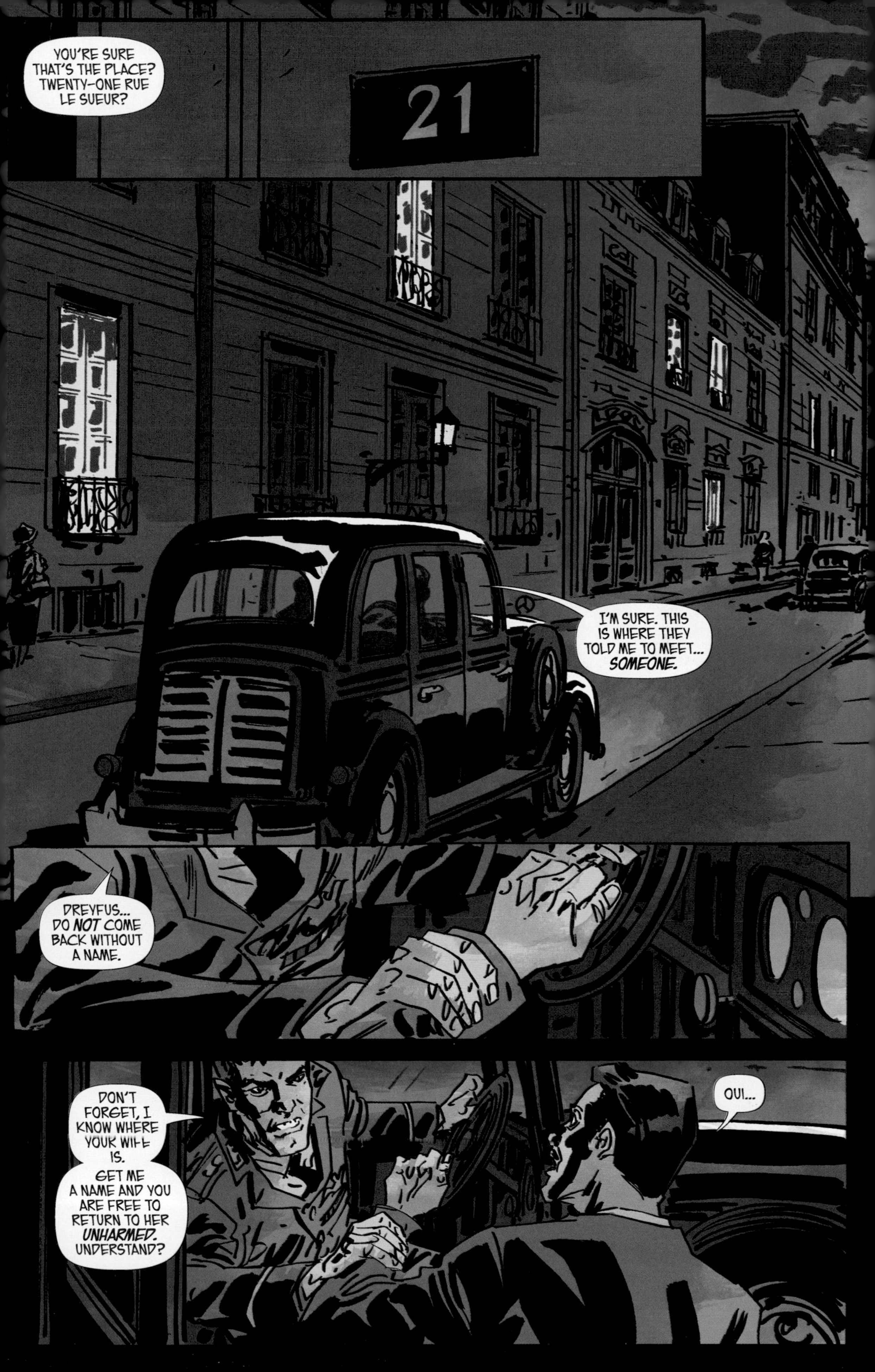

YOU'RE SURE THAT'S THE PLACE? TWENTY-ONE RUE LE SUEUR?
21
I'M SURE. THIS IS WHERE THEY TOLD ME TO MEET... SOMEONE.
DREYFUS... DO NOT COME BACK WITHOUT A NAME.
DON'T FORGET, I KNOW WHERE YOUR WIFE IS.
GET ME A NAME AND YOU ARE FREE TO RETURN TO HER UNHARMED. UNDERSTAND?
OUI...

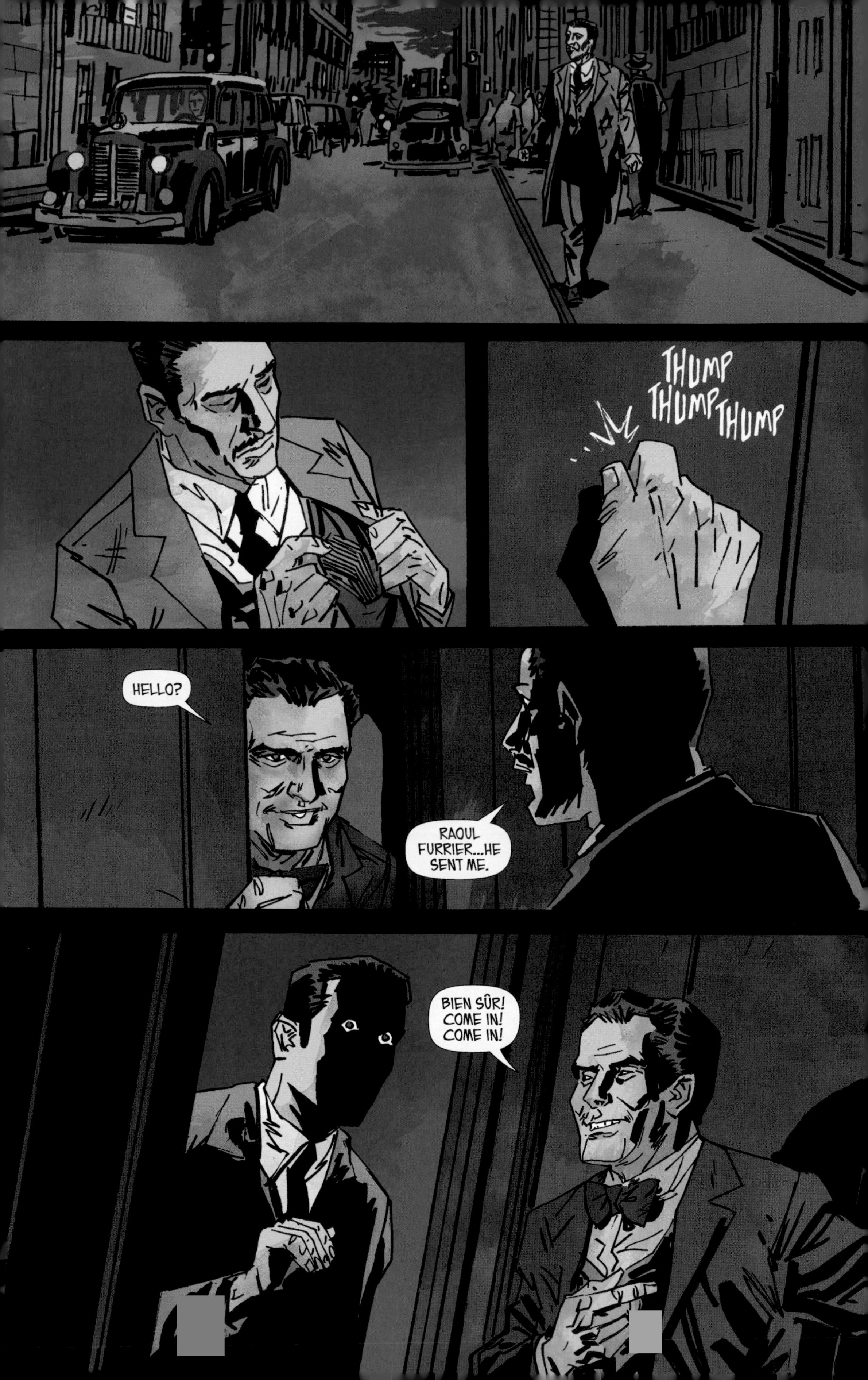
THUMP THUMP THUMP
HELLO?
RAOUL FURRIER...HE SENT ME.
BIEN SÛR! COME IN! COME IN!

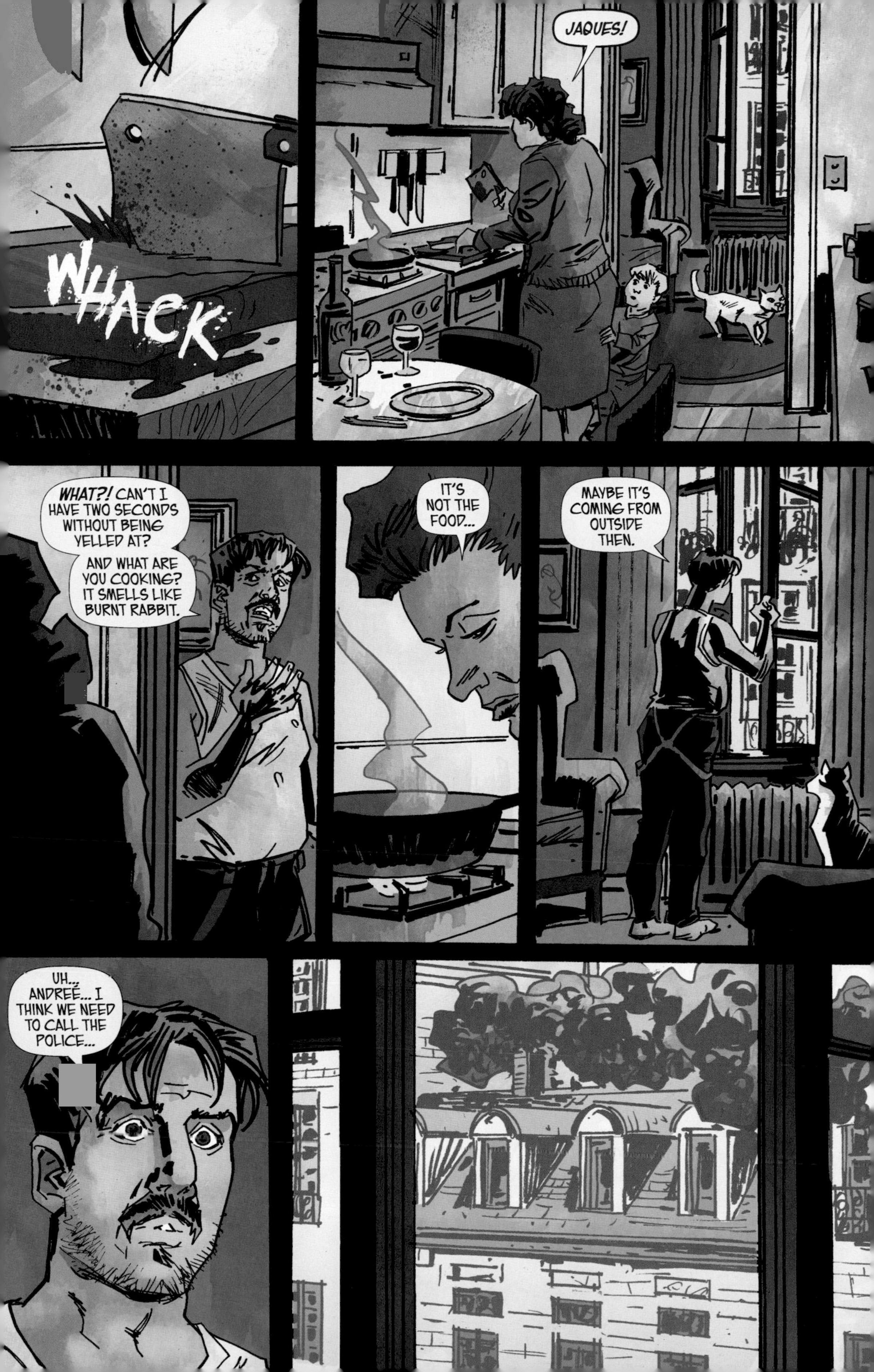

WHACK
JAQUES!
WHAT?! CAN'T I HAVE TWO SECONDS WITHOUT BEING YELLED AT?
AND WHAT ARE YOU COOKING? IT SMELLS LIKE BURNT RABBIT.
IT'S NOT THE FOOD...
MAYBE IT'S COMING FROM OUTSIDE THEN.
UH... ANDREÉ... I THINK WE NEED TO CALL THE POLICE...

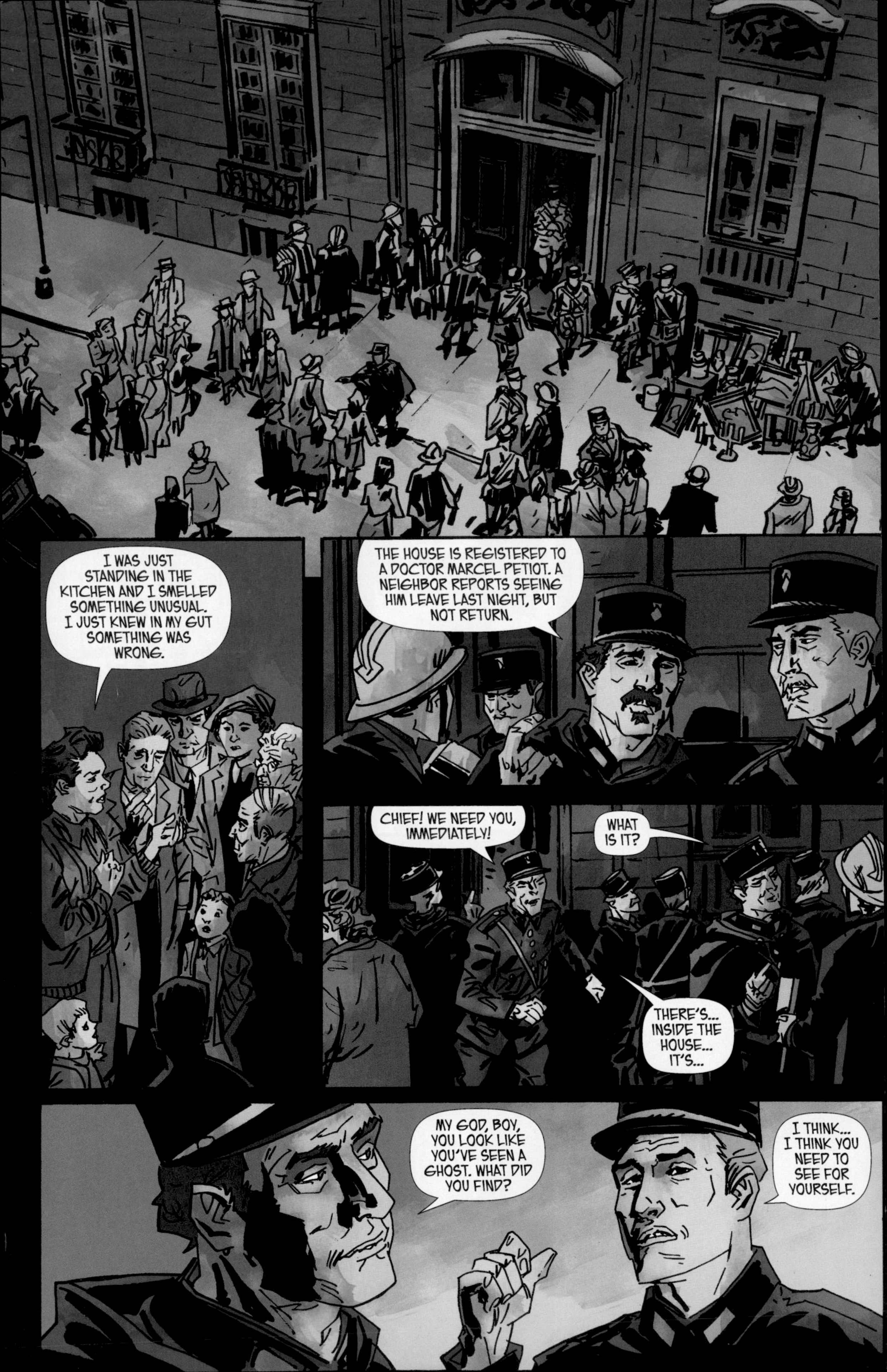
I WAS JUST STANDING IN THE KITCHEN AND I SMELLED SOMETHING UNUSUAL. I JUST KNEW IN MY GUT SOMETHING WAS WRONG.
THE HOUSE IS REGISTERED TO A DOCTOR MARCEL PETIOT. A NEIGHBOR REPORTS SEEING HIM LEAVE LAST NIGHT, BUT NOT RETURN.
CHIEF! WE NEED YOU, IMMEDIATELY!
WHAT IS IT?
THERE'S... INSIDE THE HOUSE... IT'S...
MY GOD, BOY, YOU LOOK LIKE YOU'VE SEEN A GHOST. WHAT DID YOU FIND?
I THINK... I THINK YOU NEED TO SEE FOR YOURSELF.

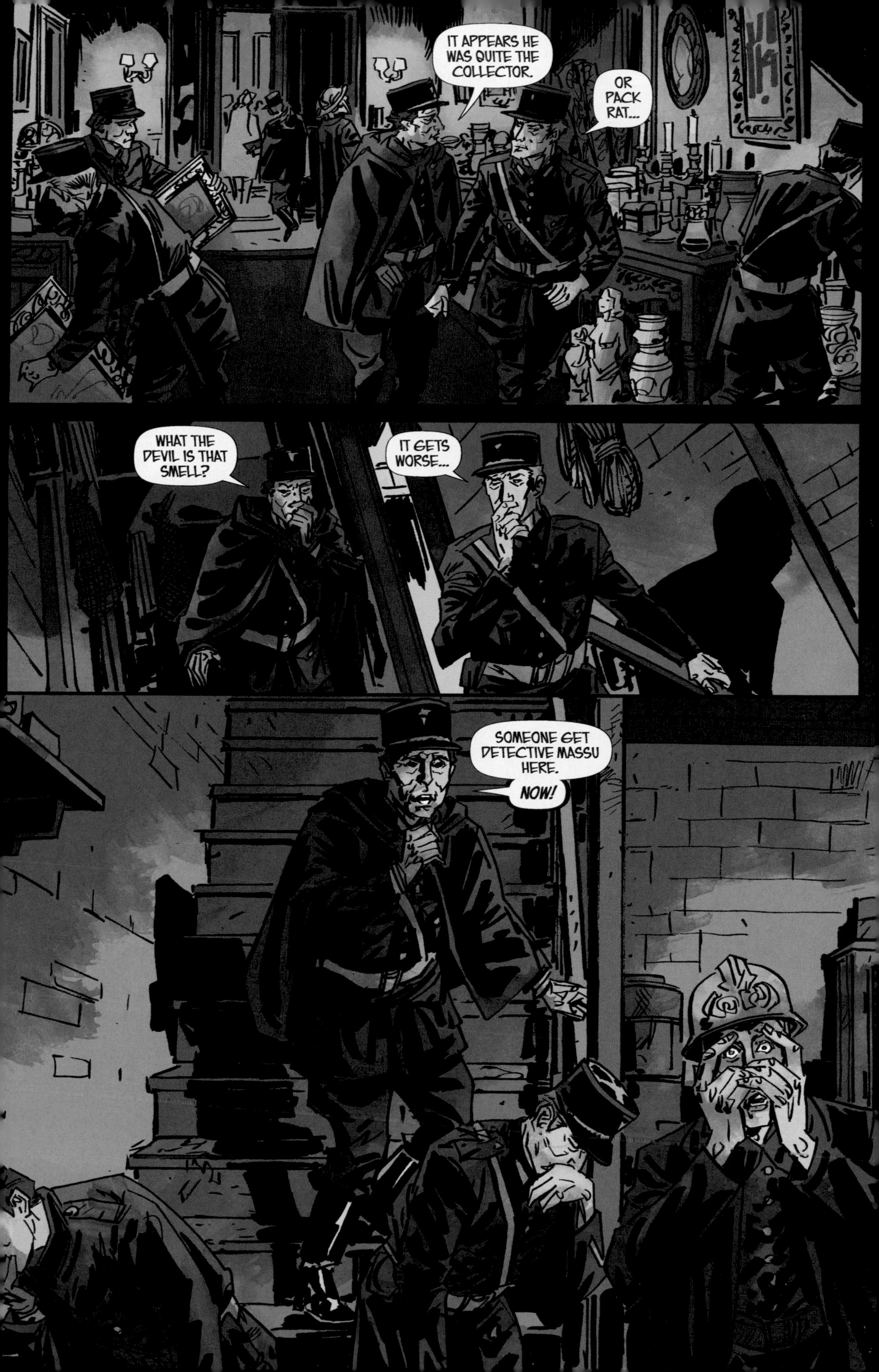
IT APPEARS HE WAS QUITE THE COLLECTOR.
OR PACK RAT...
WHAT THE DEVIL IS THAT SMELL?
IT GETS WORSE...
SOMEONE GET DETECTIVE MASSU HERE. NOW!

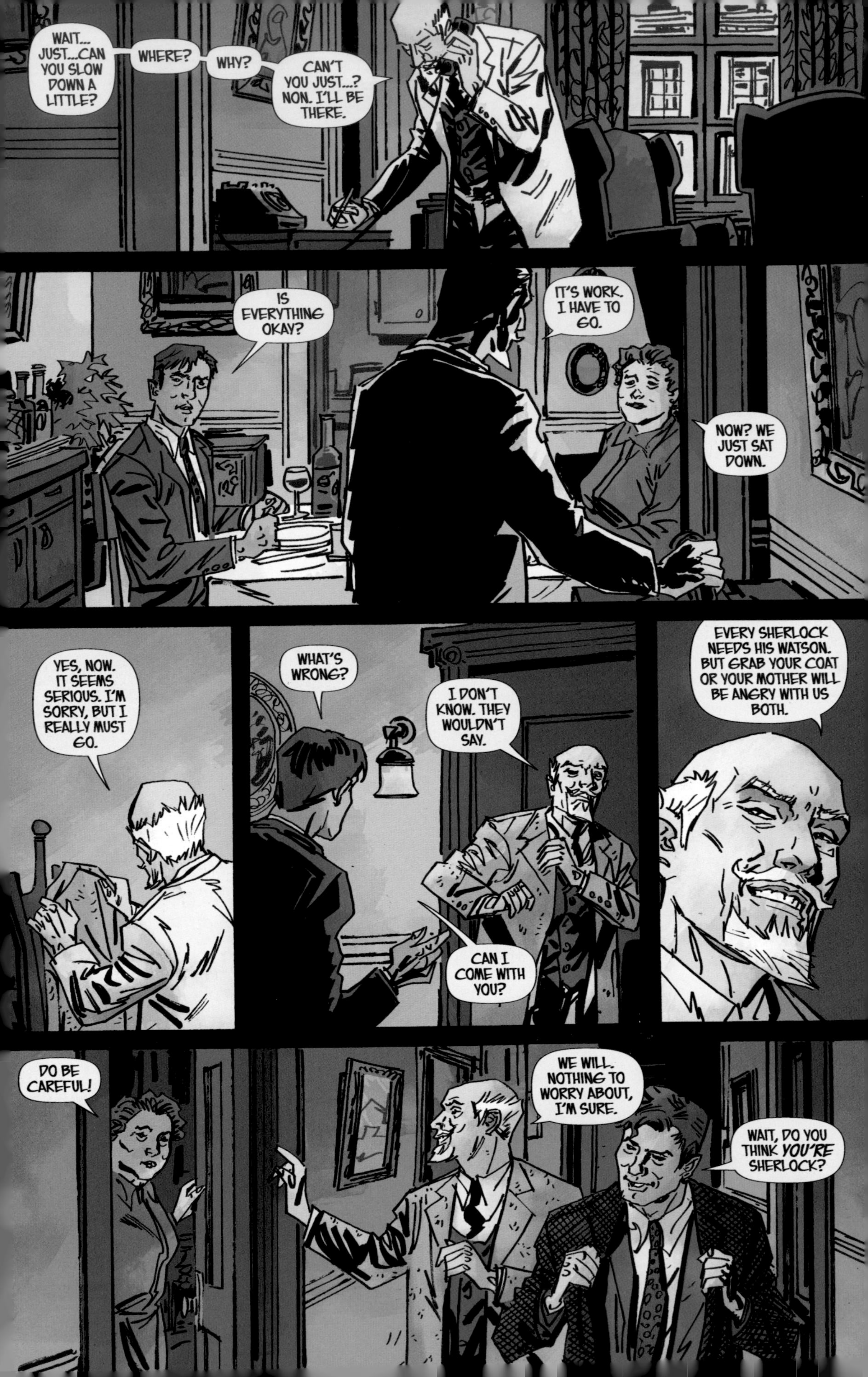
WAIT... JUST...CAN YOU SLOW DOWN A LITTLE?
WHERE?
WHY?
CAN'T YOU JUST...? NON. I'LL BE THERE.
IS EVERYTHING OKAY?
IT'S WORK. I HAVE TO GO.
NOW? WE JUST SAT DOWN.
YES, NOW. IT SEEMS SERIOUS. I'M SORRY, BUT I REALLY MUST GO.
WHAT'S WRONG?
I DON'T KNOW. THEY WOULDN'T SAY.
CAN I COME WITH YOU?
EVERY SHERLOCK NEEDS HIS WATSON. BUT GRAB YOUR COAT OR YOUR MOTHER WILL BE ANGRY WITH US BOTH.
DO BE CAREFUL!
WE WILL. NOTHING TO WORRY ABOUT, I'M SURE.
WAIT, DO YOU THINK *YOU'RE* SHERLOCK?

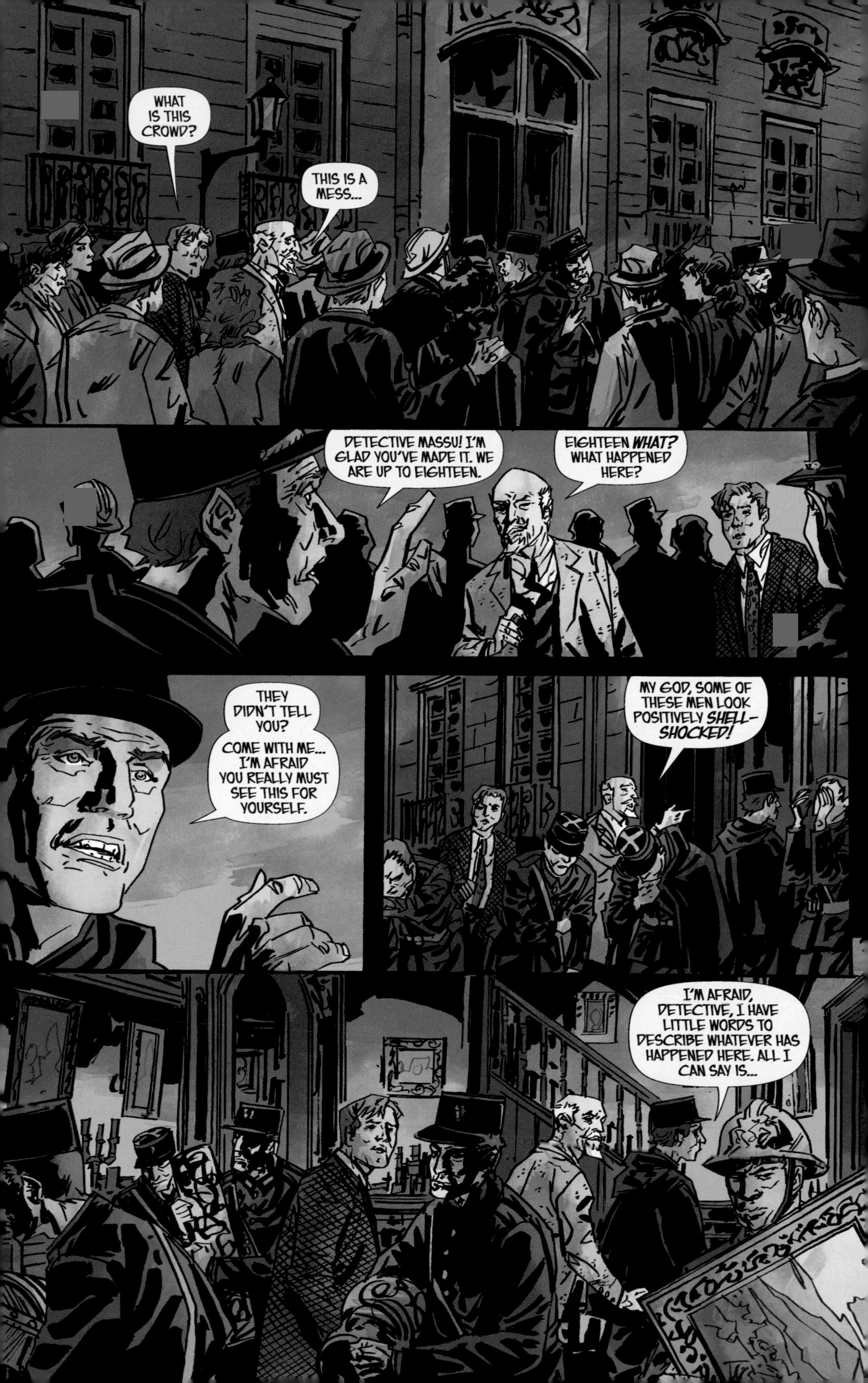
WHAT IS THIS CROWD?
THIS IS A MESS...
DETECTIVE MASSU! I'M GLAD YOU'VE MADE IT. WE ARE UP TO EIGHTEEN.
EIGHTEEN *WHAT?* WHAT HAPPENED HERE?
THEY DIDN'T TELL YOU?
COME WITH ME... I'M AFRAID YOU REALLY MUST SEE THIS FOR YOURSELF.
MY GOD, SOME OF THESE MEN LOOK POSITIVELY *SHELL-SHOCKED!*
I'M AFRAID, DETECTIVE, I HAVE LITTLE WORDS TO DESCRIBE WHATEVER HAS HAPPENED HERE. ALL I CAN SAY IS...

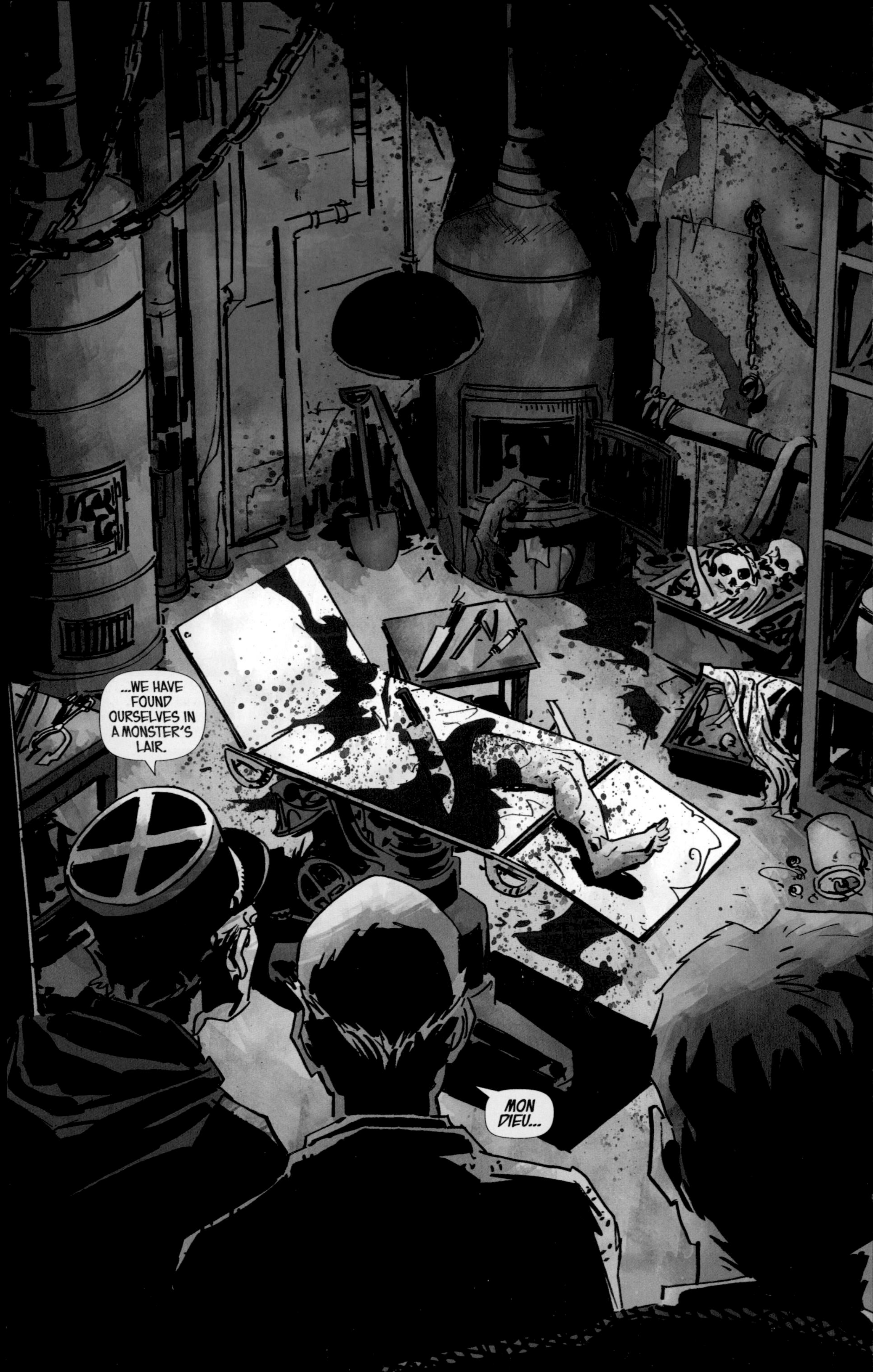
...WE HAVE FOUND OURSELVES IN A MONSTER'S LAIR.
MON DIEU...

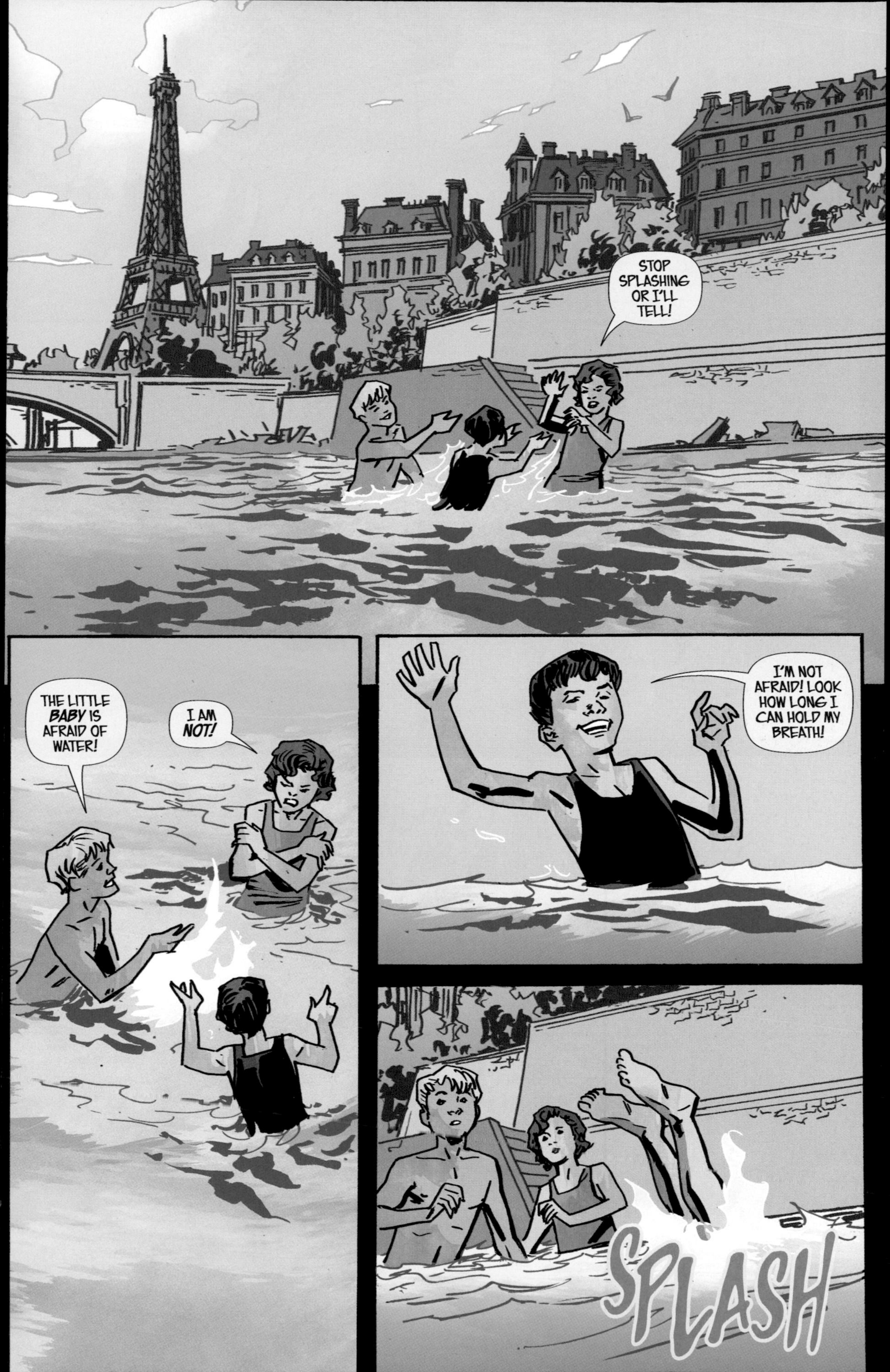
STOP SPLASHING OR I'LL TELL!
THE LITTLE *BABY* IS AFRAID OF WATER!
I AM *NOT!*
I'M NOT AFRAID! LOOK HOW LONG I CAN HOLD MY BREATH!
SPLASH

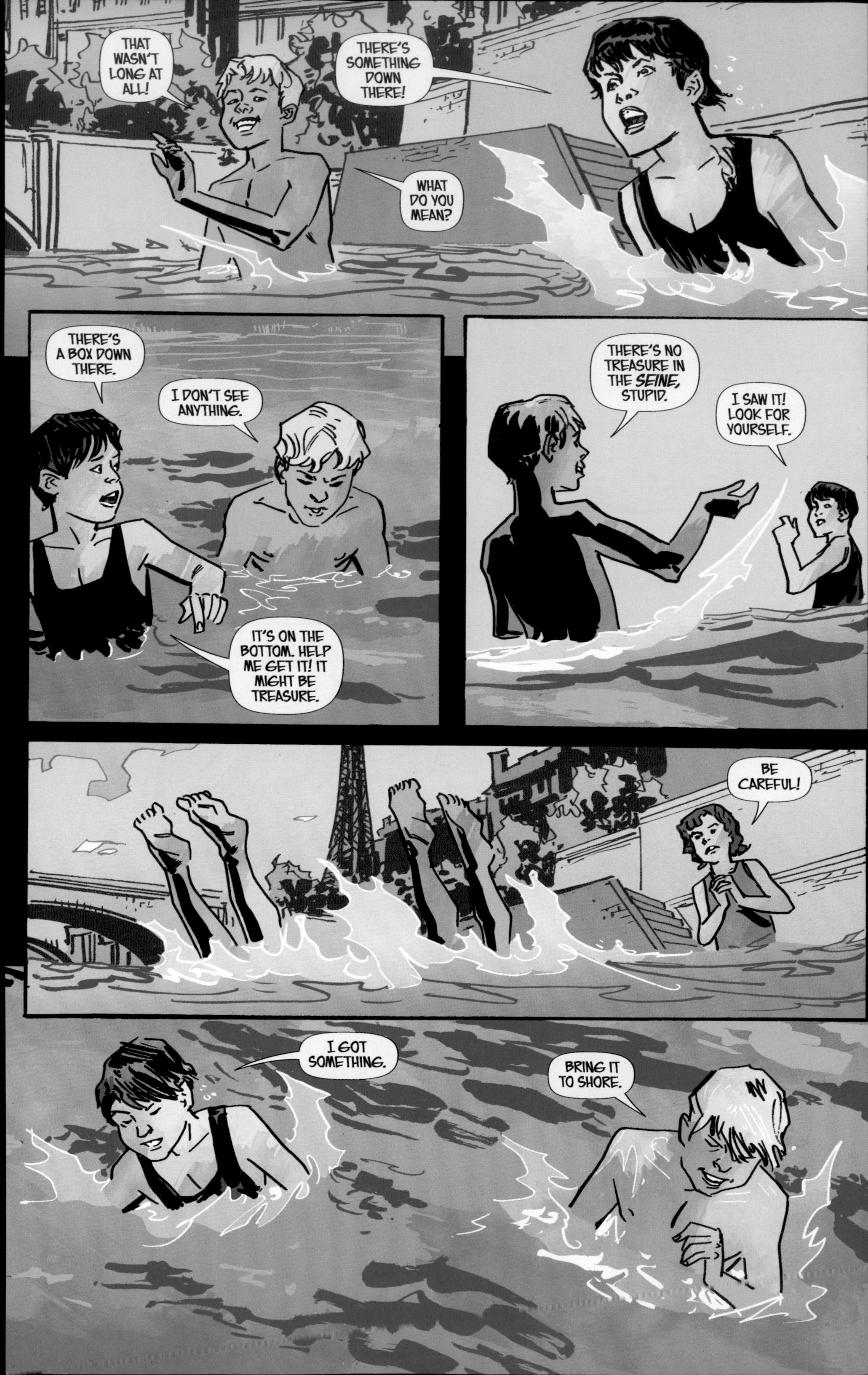
THAT WASN'T LONG AT ALL!
THERE'S SOMETHING DOWN THERE!
WHAT DO YOU MEAN?
THERE'S A BOX DOWN THERE.
I DON'T SEE ANYTHING.
IT'S ON THE BOTTOM. HELP ME GET IT! IT MIGHT BE TREASURE.
THERE'S NO TREASURE IN THE *SEINE,* STUPID.
I SAW IT! LOOK FOR YOURSELF.
BE CAREFUL!
I GOT SOMETHING.
BRING IT TO SHORE.

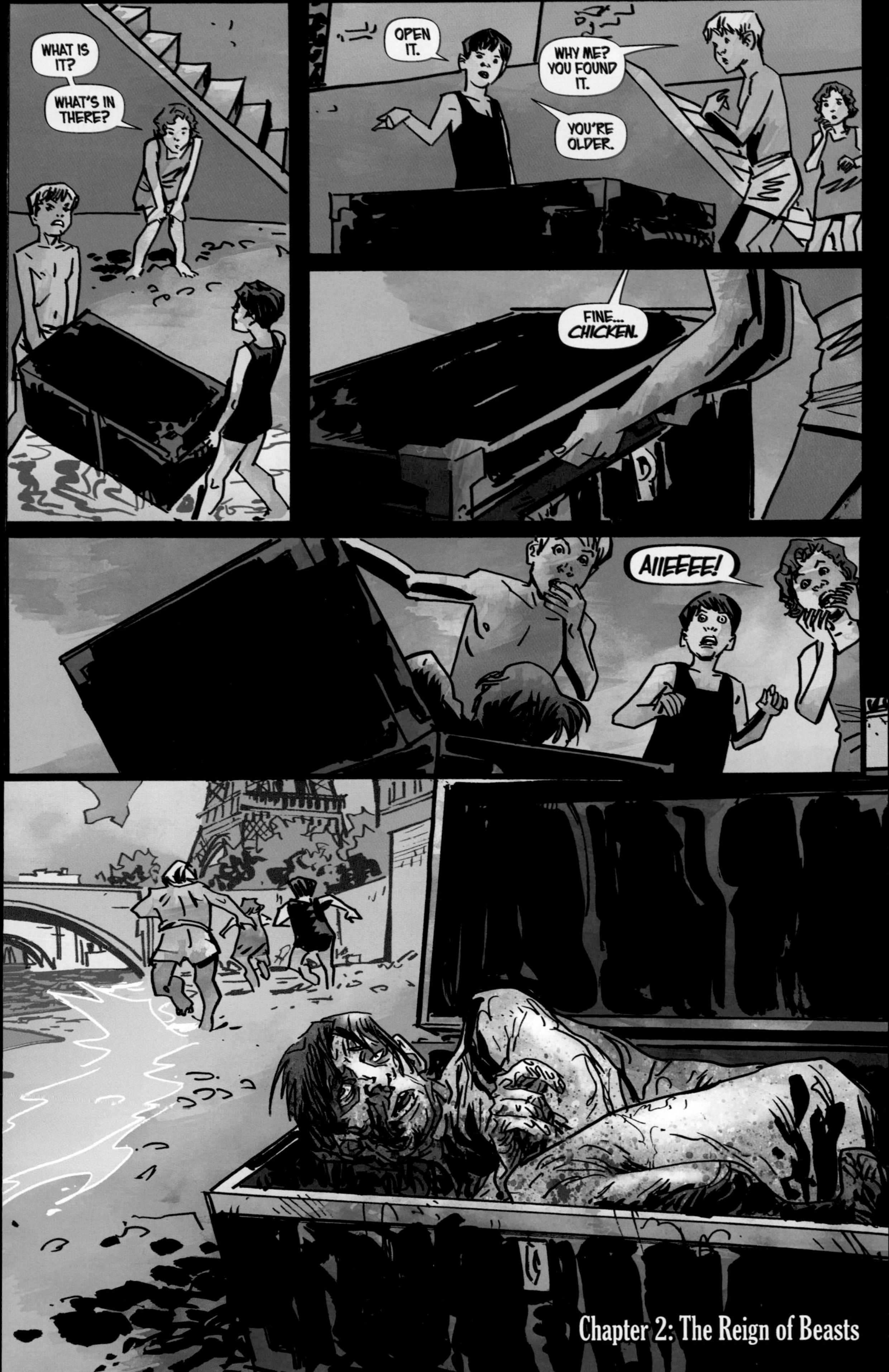
WHAT IS IT?
WHAT'S IN THERE?
OPEN IT.
WHY ME? YOU FOUND IT.
YOU'RE OLDER.
FINE... CHICKEN.
AIIEEEE!
Chapter 2: The Reign of Beasts

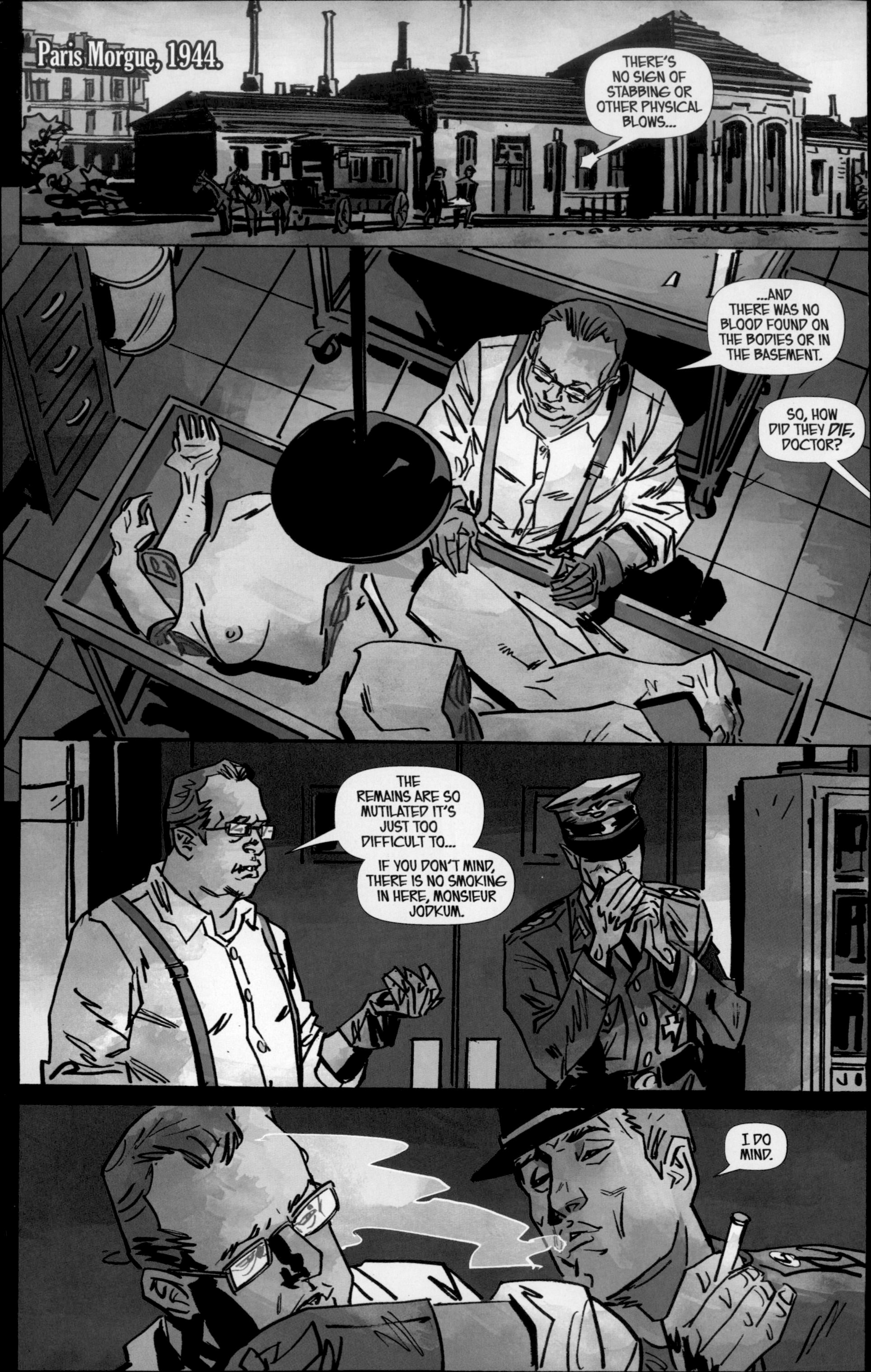
Paris Morgue, 1944.
THERE'S NO SIGN OF STABBING OR OTHER PHYSICAL BLOWS...
...AND THERE WAS NO BLOOD FOUND ON THE BODIES OR IN THE BASEMENT.
SO, HOW DID THEY *DIE*, DOCTOR?
THE REMAINS ARE SO MUTILATED IT'S JUST TOO DIFFICULT TO...
IF YOU DON'T MIND, THERE IS NO SMOKING IN HERE, MONSIEUR JODKUM.
I DO MIND.

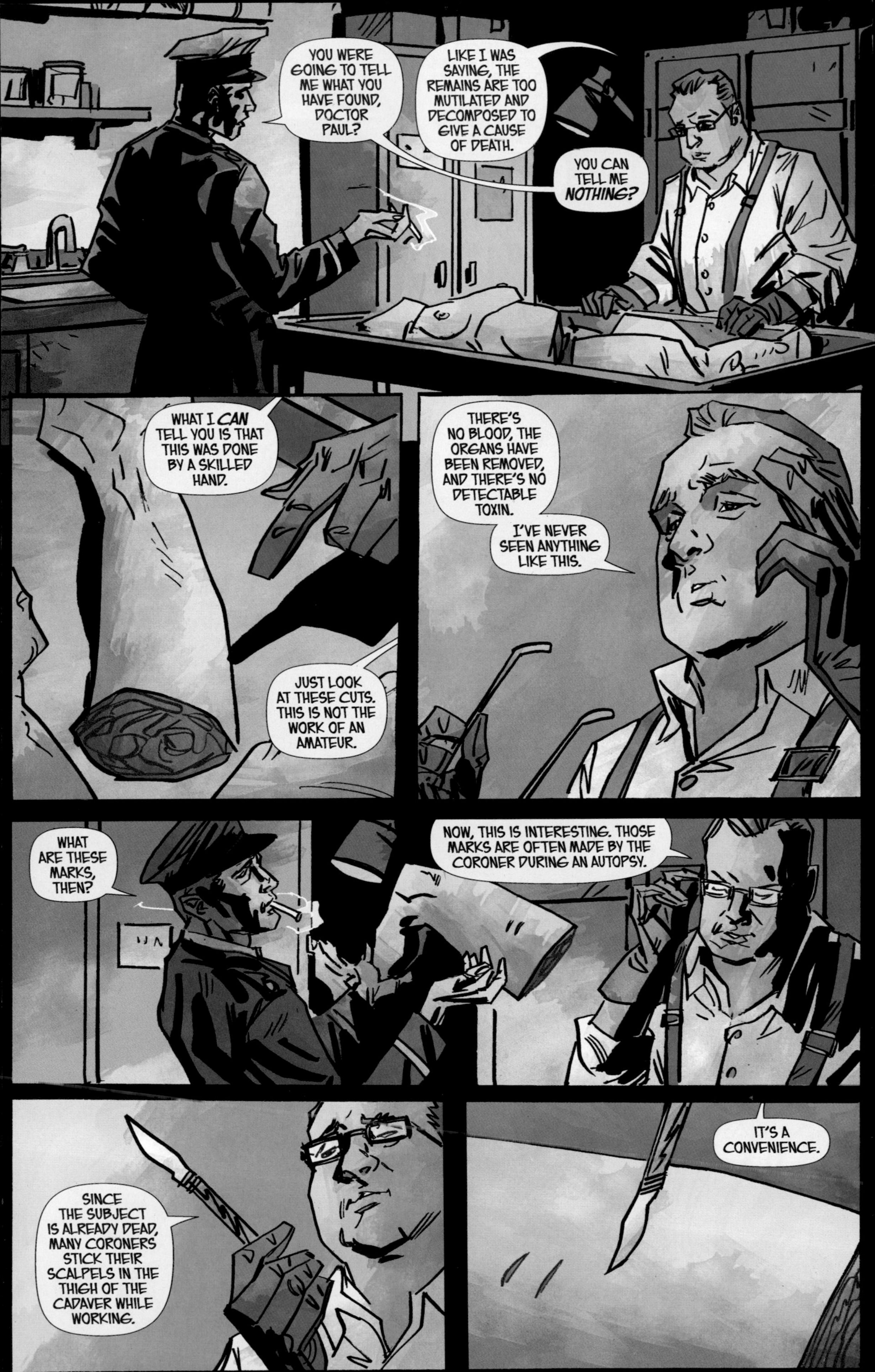
YOU WERE GOING TO TELL ME WHAT YOU HAVE FOUND, DOCTOR PAUL?
LIKE I WAS SAYING, THE REMAINS ARE TOO MUTILATED AND DECOMPOSED TO GIVE A CAUSE OF DEATH.
YOU CAN TELL ME NOTHING?
WHAT I CAN TELL YOU IS THAT THIS WAS DONE BY A SKILLED HAND.
JUST LOOK AT THESE CUTS. THIS IS NOT THE WORK OF AN AMATEUR.
THERE'S NO BLOOD, THE ORGANS HAVE BEEN REMOVED, AND THERE'S NO DETECTABLE TOXIN.
I'VE NEVER SEEN ANYTHING LIKE THIS.
WHAT ARE THESE MARKS, THEN?
NOW, THIS IS INTERESTING. THOSE MARKS ARE OFTEN MADE BY THE CORONER DURING AN AUTOPSY.
SINCE THE SUBJECT IS ALREADY DEAD, MANY CORONERS STICK THEIR SCALPELS IN THE THIGH OF THE CADAVER WHILE WORKING.
IT'S A CONVENIENCE.

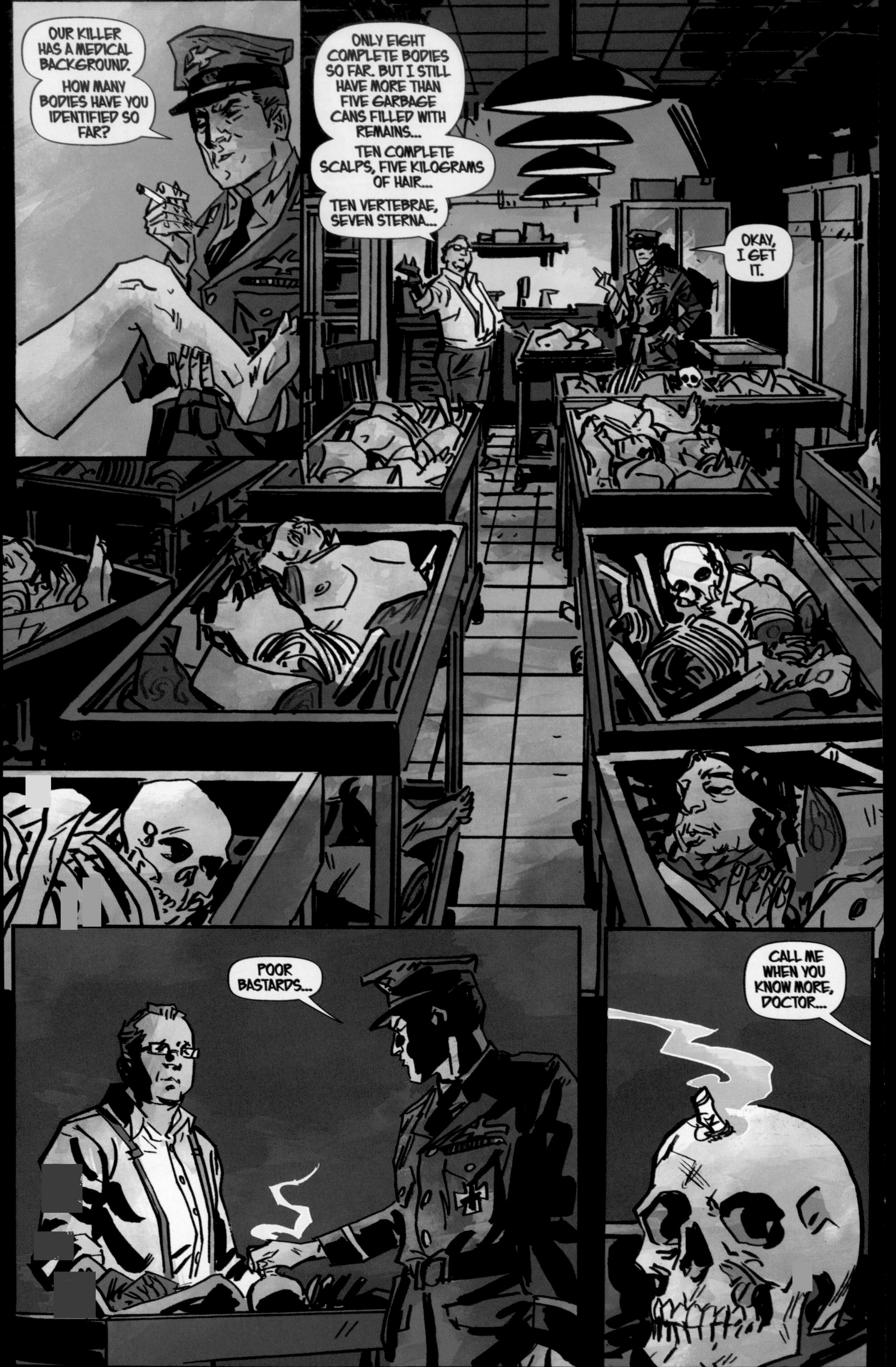
OUR KILLER HAS A MEDICAL BACKGROUND.
HOW MANY BODIES HAVE YOU IDENTIFIED SO FAR?
ONLY EIGHT COMPLETE BODIES SO FAR. BUT I STILL HAVE MORE THAN FIVE GARBAGE CANS FILLED WITH REMAINS...
TEN COMPLETE SCALPS, FIVE KILOGRAMS OF HAIR...
TEN VERTEBRAE, SEVEN STERNA...
OKAY, I GET IT.
POOR BASTARDS...
CALL ME WHEN YOU KNOW MORE, DOCTOR...

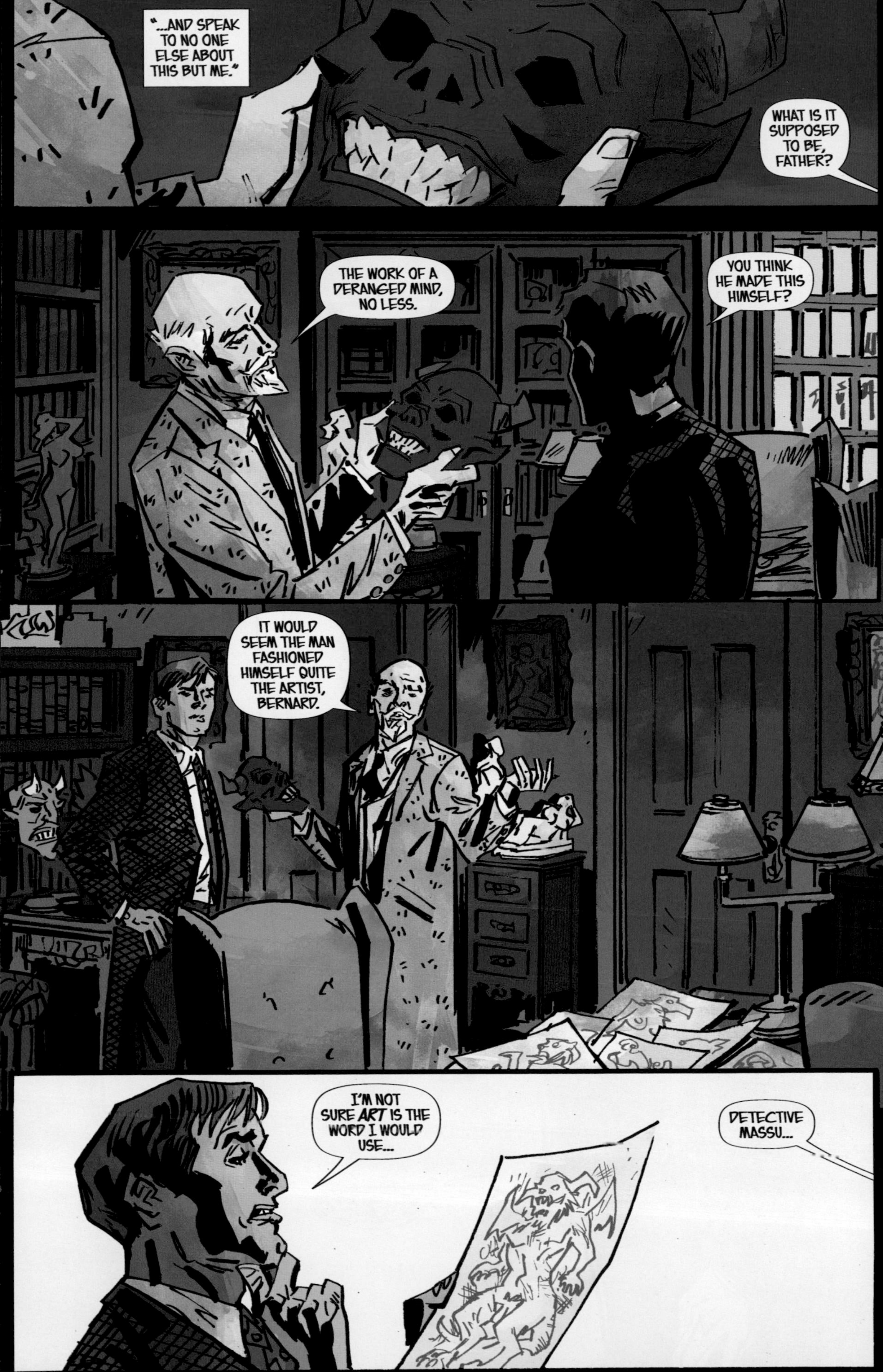
"...AND SPEAK TO NO ONE ELSE ABOUT THIS BUT ME."
WHAT IS IT SUPPOSED TO BE, FATHER?
THE WORK OF A DERANGED MIND, NO LESS.
YOU THINK HE MADE THIS HIMSELF?
IT WOULD SEEM THE MAN FASHIONED HIMSELF QUITE THE ARTIST, BERNARD.
I'M NOT SURE *ART* IS THE WORD I WOULD USE...
DETECTIVE MASSU...

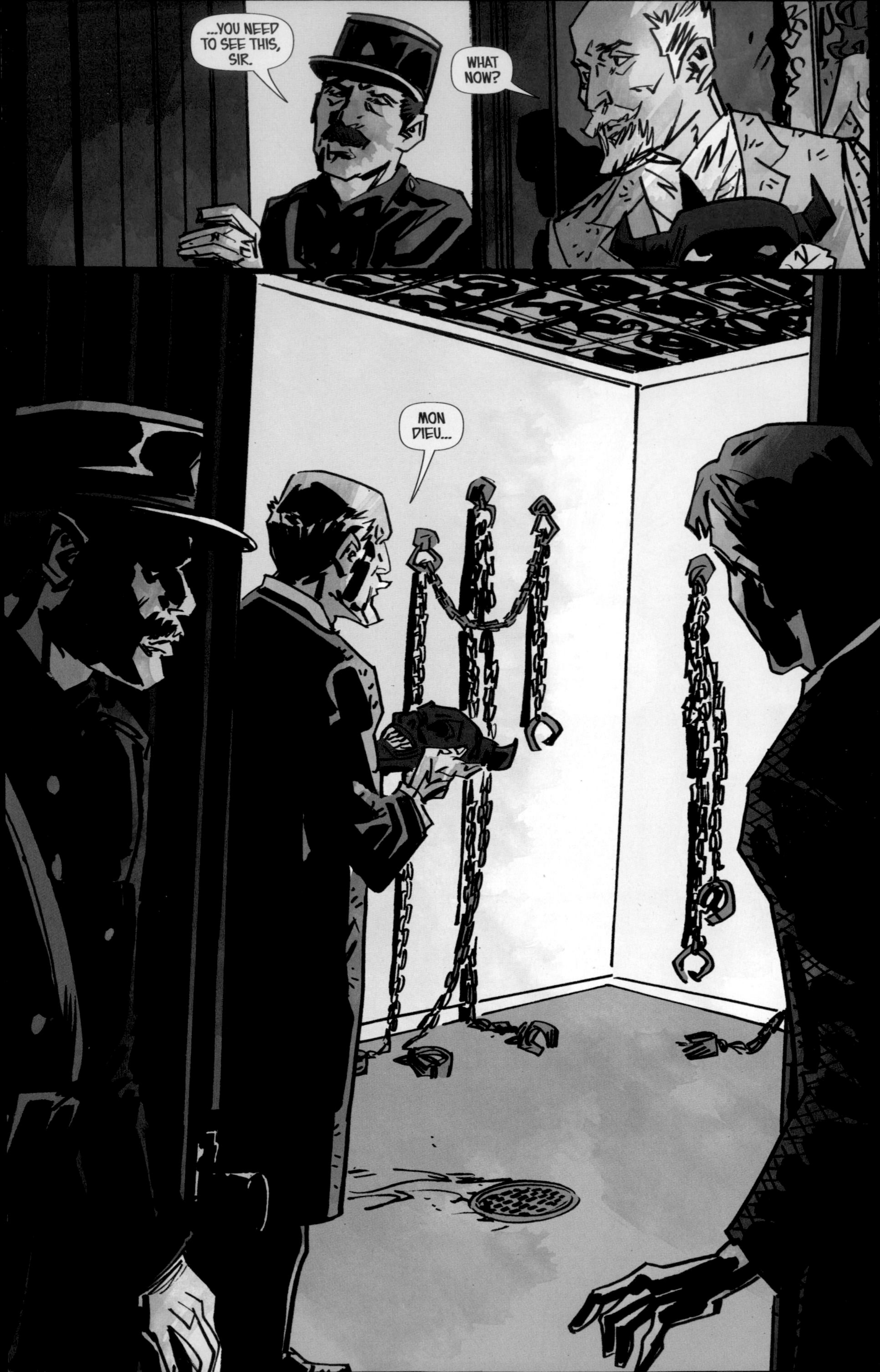
...YOU NEED TO SEE THIS, SIR.
WHAT NOW?
MON DIEU...

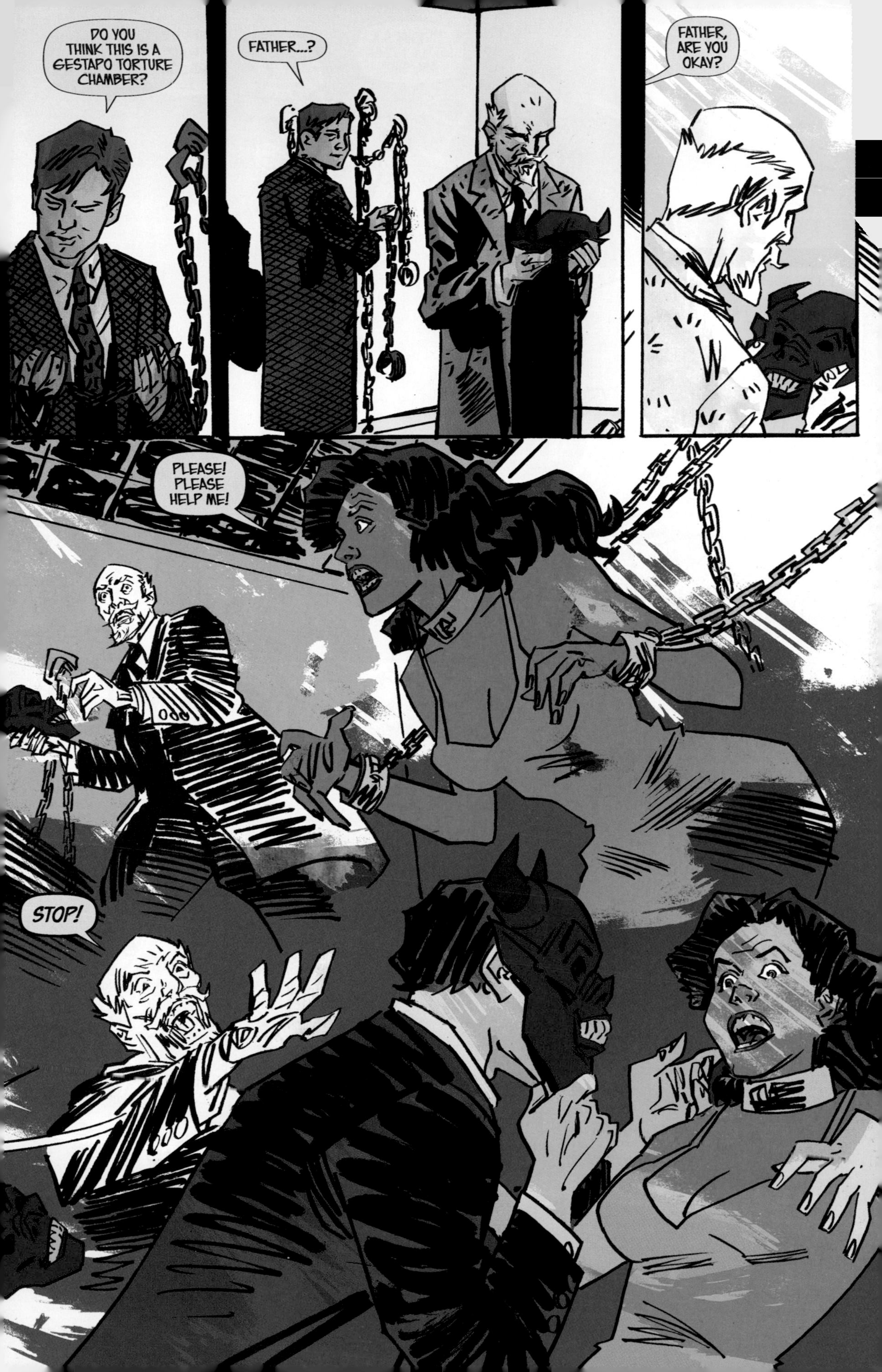
DO YOU THINK THIS IS A GESTAPO TORTURE CHAMBER?
FATHER...?
FATHER, ARE YOU OKAY?
PLEASE! PLEASE HELP ME!
STOP!

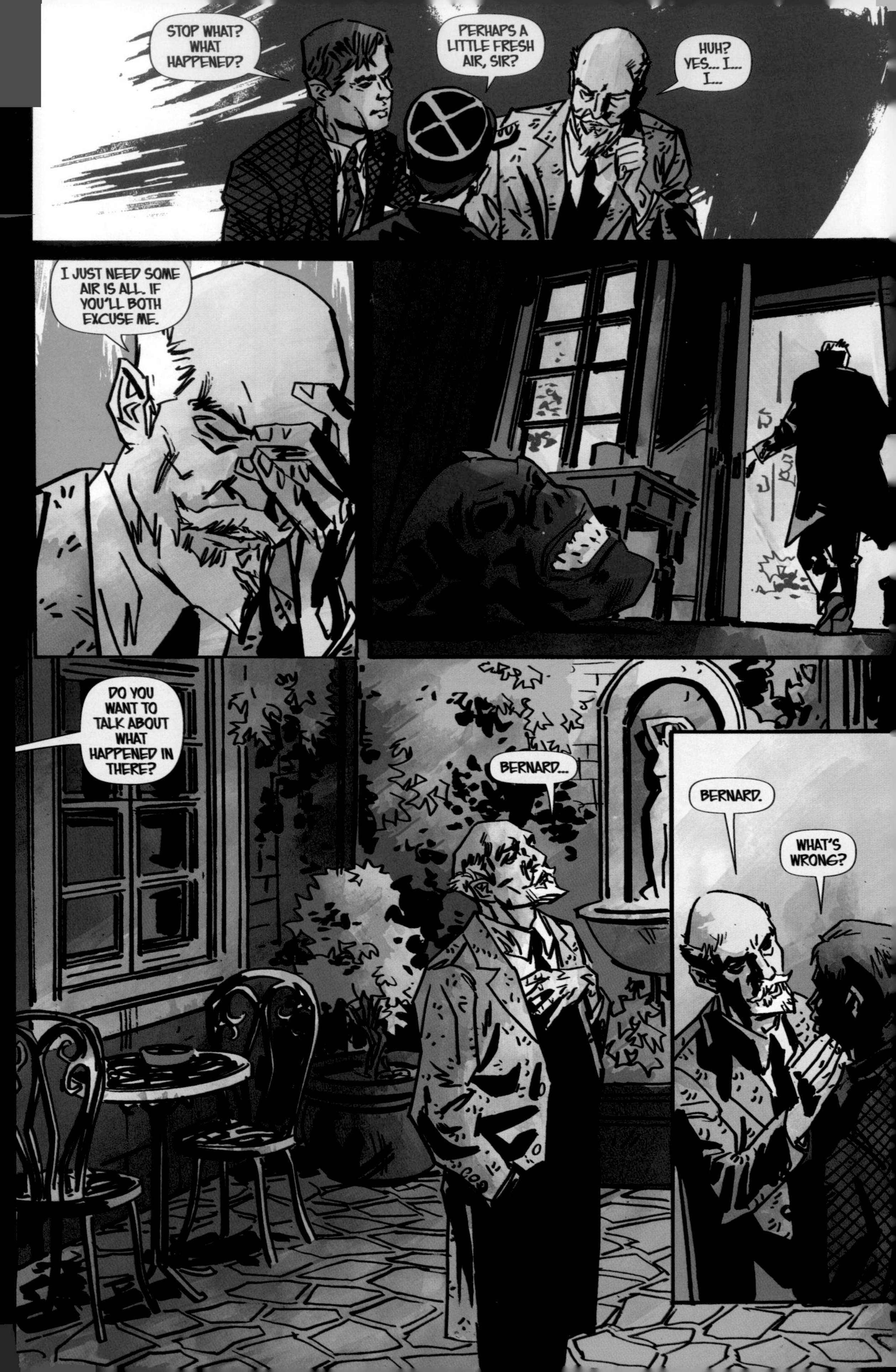
STOP WHAT? WHAT HAPPENED?
PERHAPS A LITTLE FRESH AIR, SIR?
HUH? YES... I... I...
I JUST NEED SOME AIR IS ALL. IF YOU'LL BOTH EXCUSE ME.
DO YOU WANT TO TALK ABOUT WHAT HAPPENED IN THERE?
BERNARD...
BERNARD.
WHAT'S WRONG?

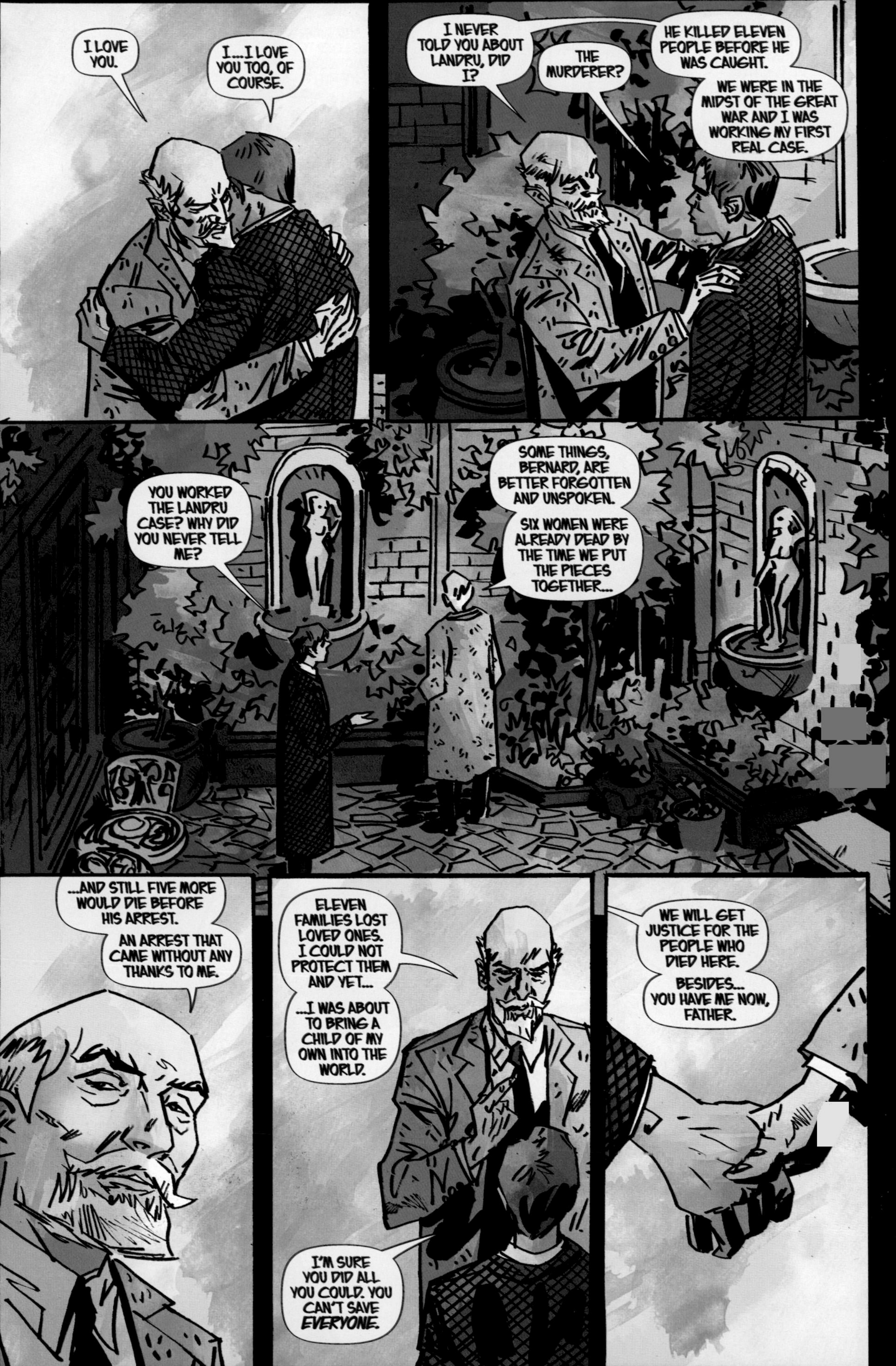
I LOVE YOU.
I...I LOVE YOU TOO, OF COURSE.
I NEVER TOLD YOU ABOUT LANDRU, DID I?
THE MURDERER?
HE KILLED ELEVEN PEOPLE BEFORE HE WAS CAUGHT.
WE WERE IN THE MIDST OF THE GREAT WAR AND I WAS WORKING MY FIRST REAL CASE.
YOU WORKED THE LANDRU CASE? WHY DID YOU NEVER TELL ME?
SOME THINGS, BERNARD, ARE BETTER FORGOTTEN AND UNSPOKEN.
SIX WOMEN WERE ALREADY DEAD BY THE TIME WE PUT THE PIECES TOGETHER...
...AND STILL FIVE MORE WOULD DIE BEFORE HIS ARREST.
AN ARREST THAT CAME WITHOUT ANY THANKS TO ME.
ELEVEN FAMILIES LOST LOVED ONES. I COULD NOT PROTECT THEM AND YET...
...I WAS ABOUT TO BRING A CHILD OF MY OWN INTO THE WORLD.
I'M SURE YOU DID ALL YOU COULD. YOU CAN'T SAVE *EVERYONE*.
WE WILL GET JUSTICE FOR THE PEOPLE WHO DIED HERE.
BESIDES... YOU HAVE ME NOW, FATHER.

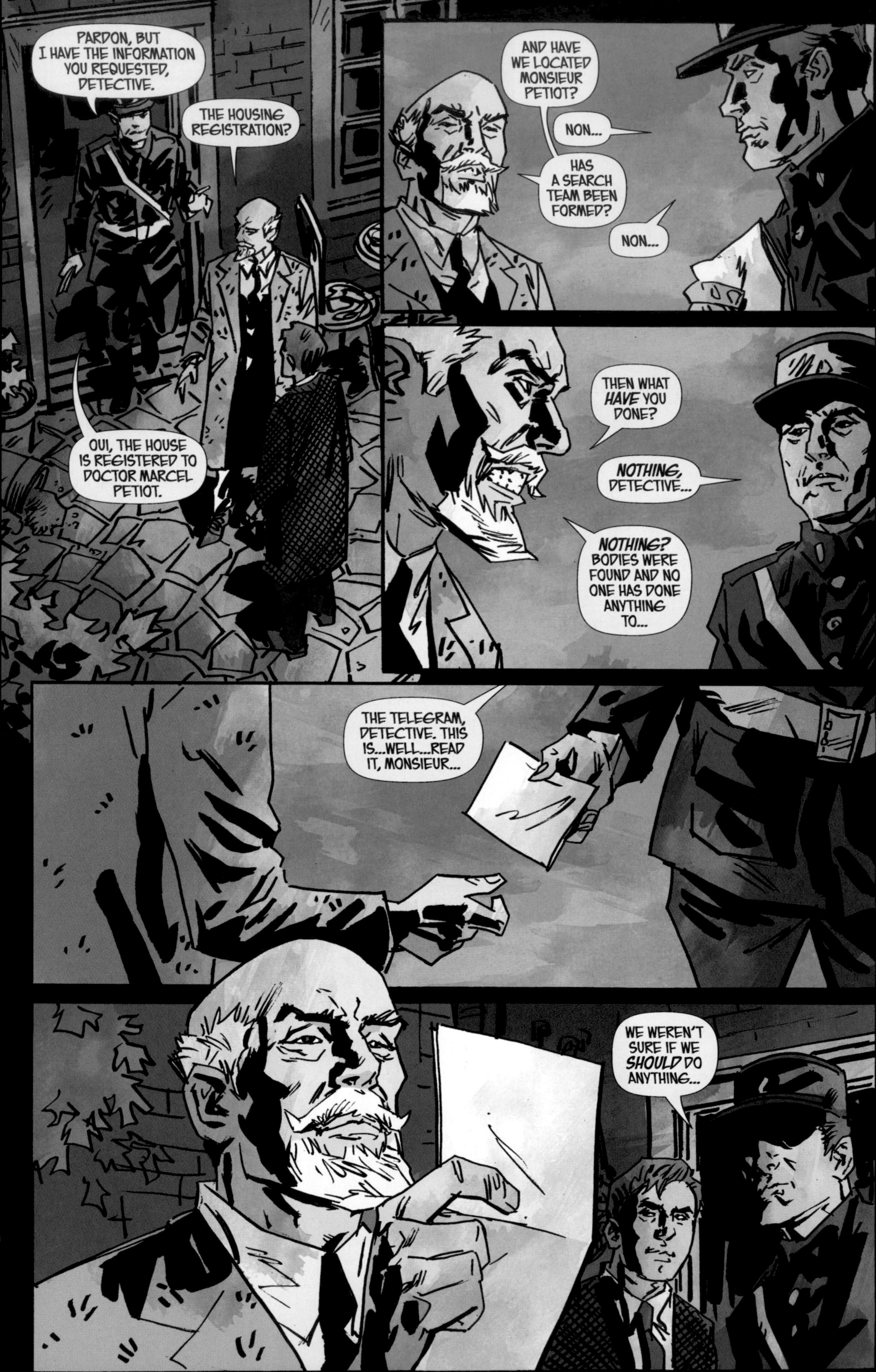
PARDON, BUT I HAVE THE INFORMATION YOU REQUESTED, DETECTIVE.
THE HOUSING REGISTRATION?
OUI, THE HOUSE IS REGISTERED TO DOCTOR MARCEL PETIOT.
AND HAVE WE LOCATED MONSIEUR PETIOT?
NON...
HAS A SEARCH TEAM BEEN FORMED?
NON...
THEN WHAT HAVE YOU DONE?
NOTHING, DETECTIVE...
NOTHING? BODIES WERE FOUND AND NO ONE HAS DONE ANYTHING TO...
THE TELEGRAM, DETECTIVE. THIS IS...WELL...READ IT, MONSIEUR...
WE WEREN'T SURE IF WE SHOULD DO ANYTHING...

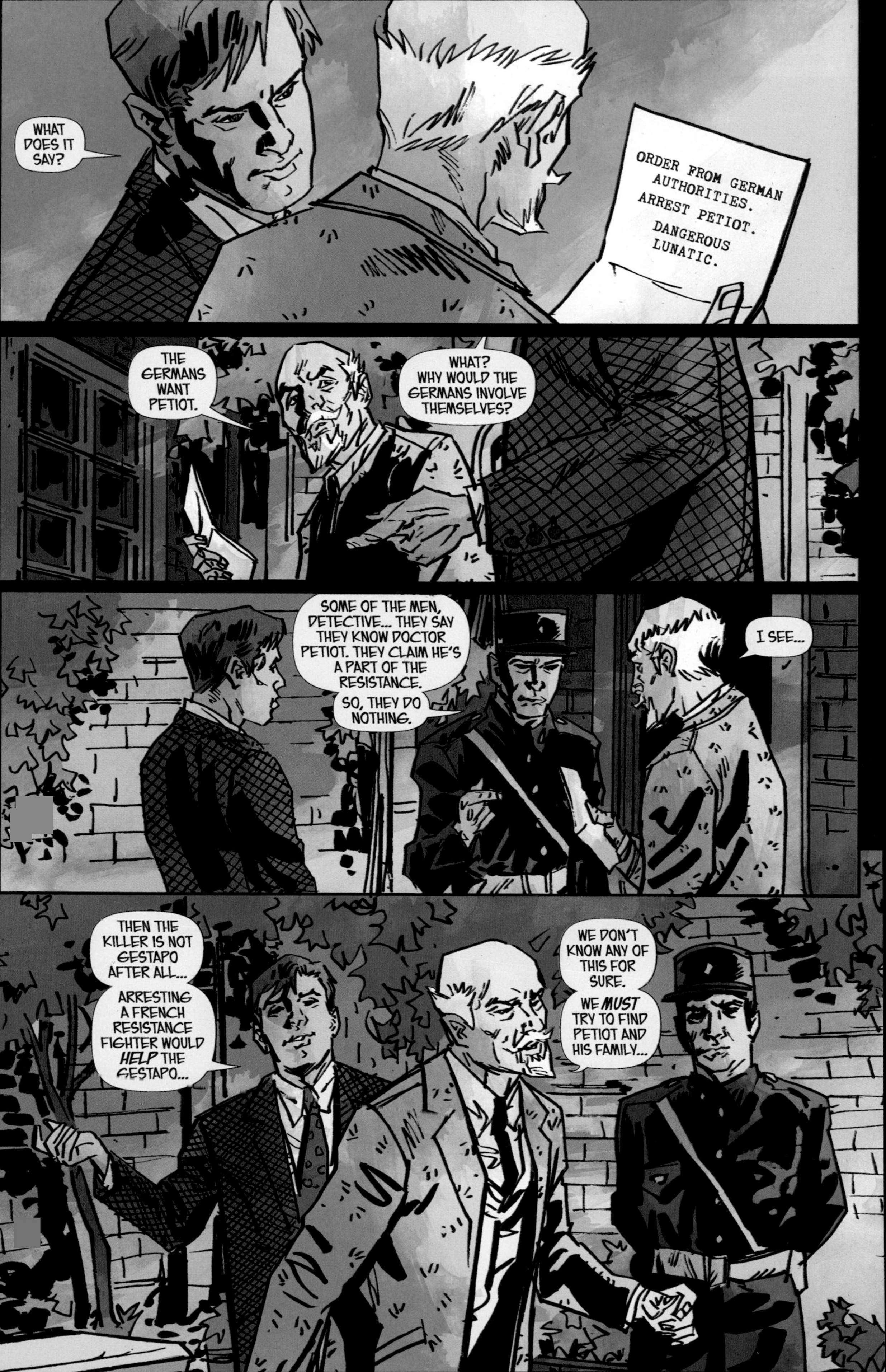
WHAT DOES IT SAY?
ORDER FROM GERMAN AUTHORITIES. ARREST PETIOT. DANGEROUS LUNATIC.
THE GERMANS WANT PETIOT.
WHAT? WHY WOULD THE GERMANS INVOLVE THEMSELVES?
SOME OF THE MEN, DETECTIVE... THEY SAY THEY KNOW DOCTOR PETIOT. THEY CLAIM HE'S A PART OF THE RESISTANCE.
SO, THEY DO NOTHING.
I SEE...
THEN THE KILLER IS NOT GESTAPO AFTER ALL...
ARRESTING A FRENCH RESISTANCE FIGHTER WOULD HELP THE GESTAPO...
WE DON'T KNOW ANY OF THIS FOR SURE.
WE MUST TRY TO FIND PETIOT AND HIS FAMILY...

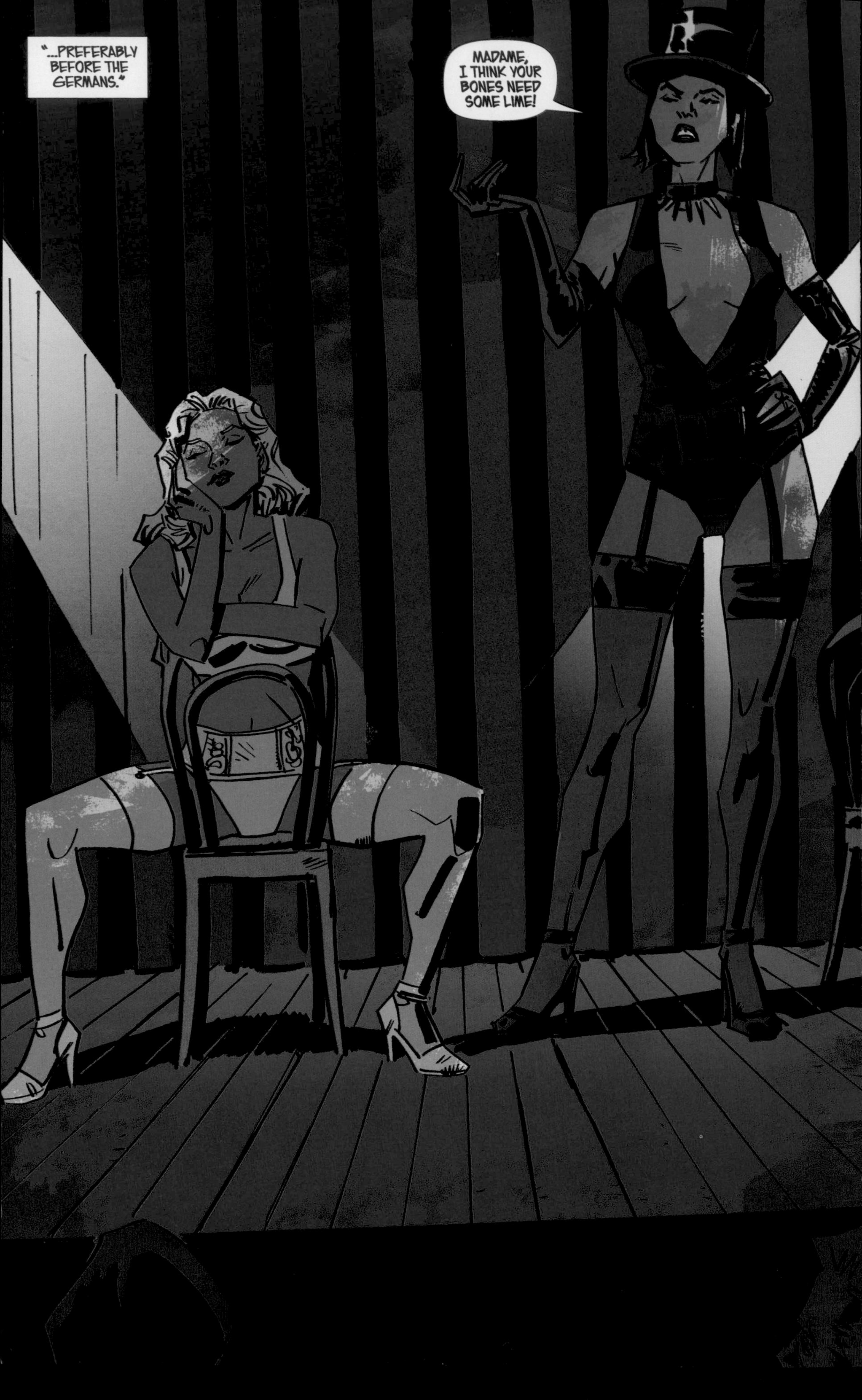
"...PREFERABLY BEFORE THE GERMANS."
MADAME, I THINK YOUR BONES NEED SOME LIME!

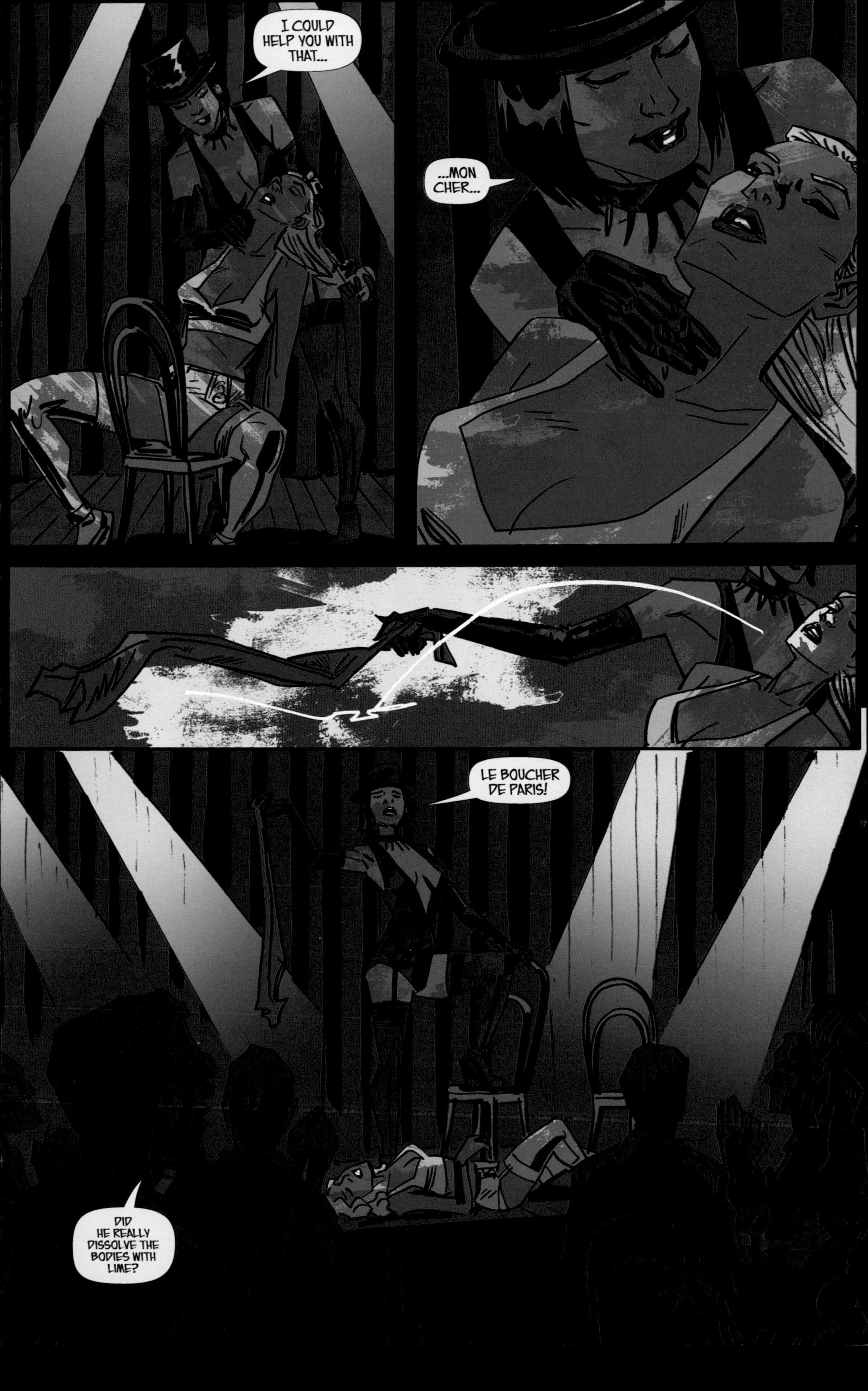
I COULD HELP YOU WITH THAT...
...MON CHER...
LE BOUCHER DE PARIS!
DID HE REALLY DISSOLVE THE BODIES WITH LIME?

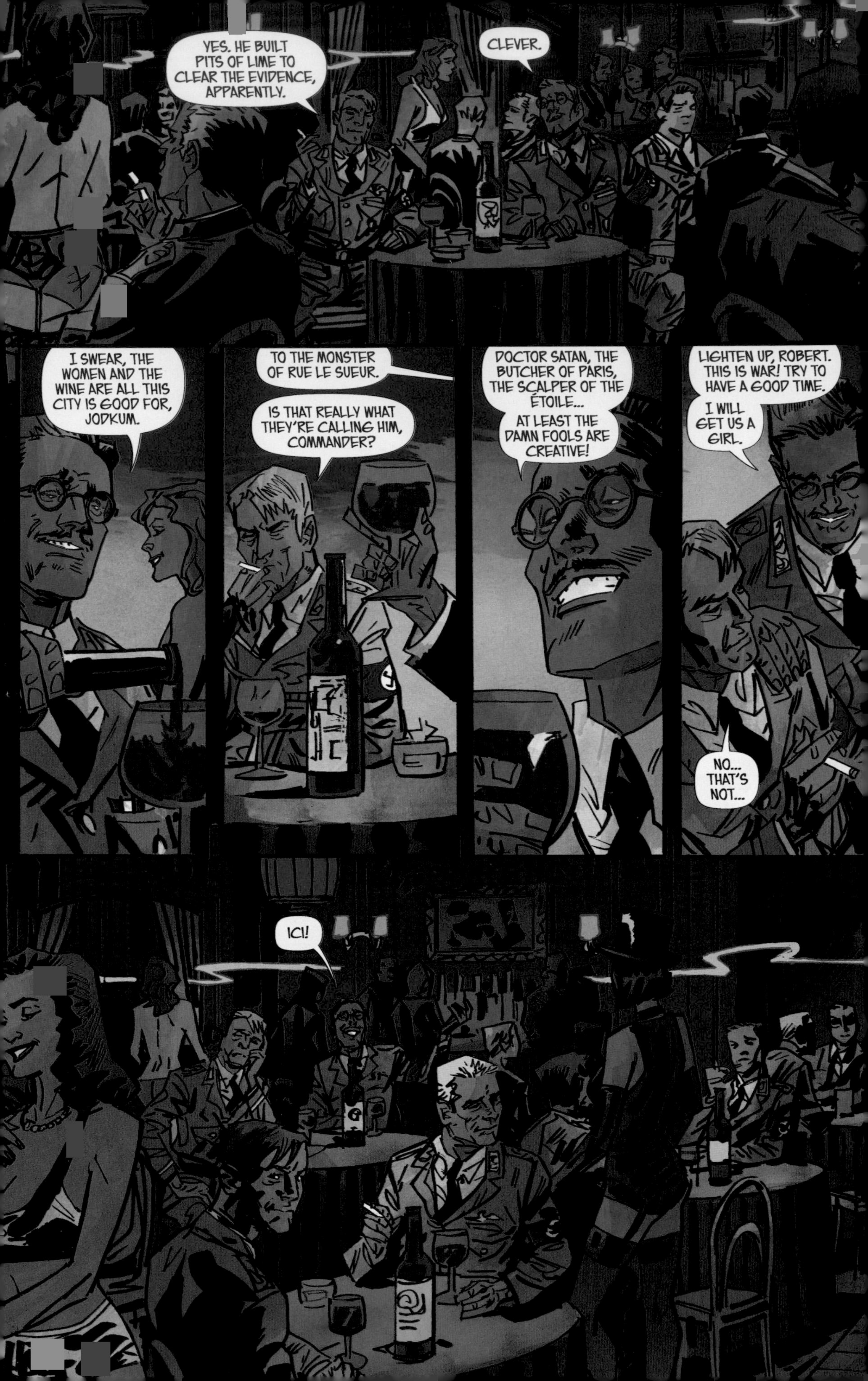
YES. HE BUILT PITS OF LIME TO CLEAR THE EVIDENCE, APPARENTLY.
CLEVER.
I SWEAR, THE WOMEN AND THE WINE ARE ALL THIS CITY IS GOOD FOR, JODKUM.
TO THE MONSTER OF RUE LE SUEUR.
IS THAT REALLY WHAT THEY'RE CALLING HIM, COMMANDER?
DOCTOR SATAN, THE BUTCHER OF PARIS, THE SCALPER OF THE ÉTOILE...
AT LEAST THE DAMN FOOLS ARE CREATIVE!
LIGHTEN UP, ROBERT. THIS IS WAR! TRY TO HAVE A GOOD TIME.
I WILL GET US A GIRL.
NO... THAT'S NOT...
ICI!

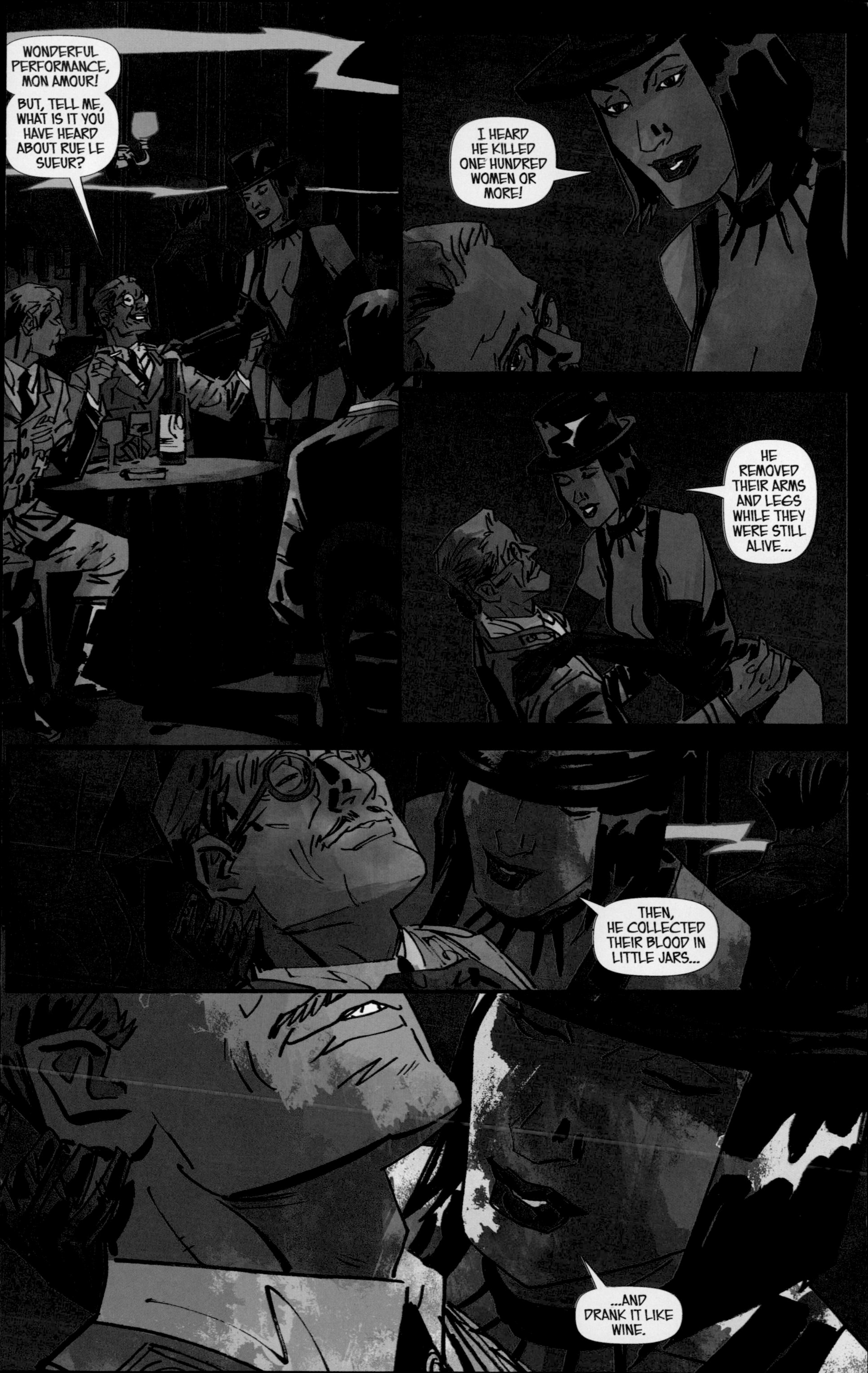
WONDERFUL PERFORMANCE, MON AMOUR!
BUT, TELL ME, WHAT IS IT YOU HAVE HEARD ABOUT RUE LE SUEUR?
I HEARD HE KILLED ONE HUNDRED WOMEN OR MORE!
HE REMOVED THEIR ARMS AND LEGS WHILE THEY WERE STILL ALIVE...
THEN, HE COLLECTED THEIR BLOOD IN LITTLE JARS...
...AND DRANK IT LIKE WINE.

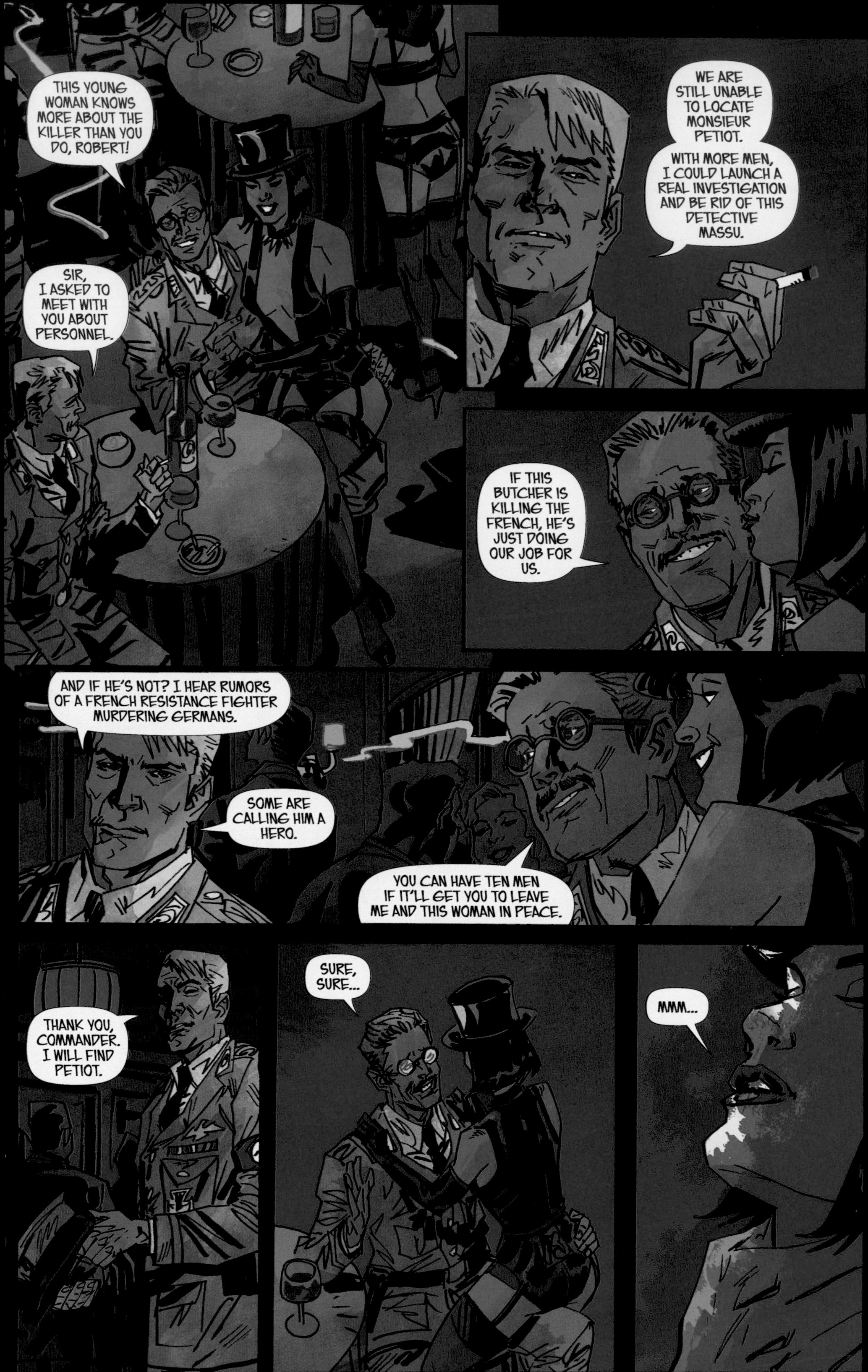
THIS YOUNG WOMAN KNOWS MORE ABOUT THE KILLER THAN YOU DO, ROBERT!
SIR, I ASKED TO MEET WITH YOU ABOUT PERSONNEL.
WE ARE STILL UNABLE TO LOCATE MONSIEUR PETIOT.
WITH MORE MEN, I COULD LAUNCH A REAL INVESTIGATION AND BE RID OF THIS DETECTIVE MASSU.
IF THIS BUTCHER IS KILLING THE FRENCH, HE'S JUST DOING OUR JOB FOR US.
AND IF HE'S NOT? I HEAR RUMORS OF A FRENCH RESISTANCE FIGHTER MURDERING GERMANS.
SOME ARE CALLING HIM A HERO.
YOU CAN HAVE TEN MEN IF IT'LL GET YOU TO LEAVE ME AND THIS WOMAN IN PEACE.
THANK YOU, COMMANDER. I WILL FIND PETIOT.
SURE, SURE...
MMM...

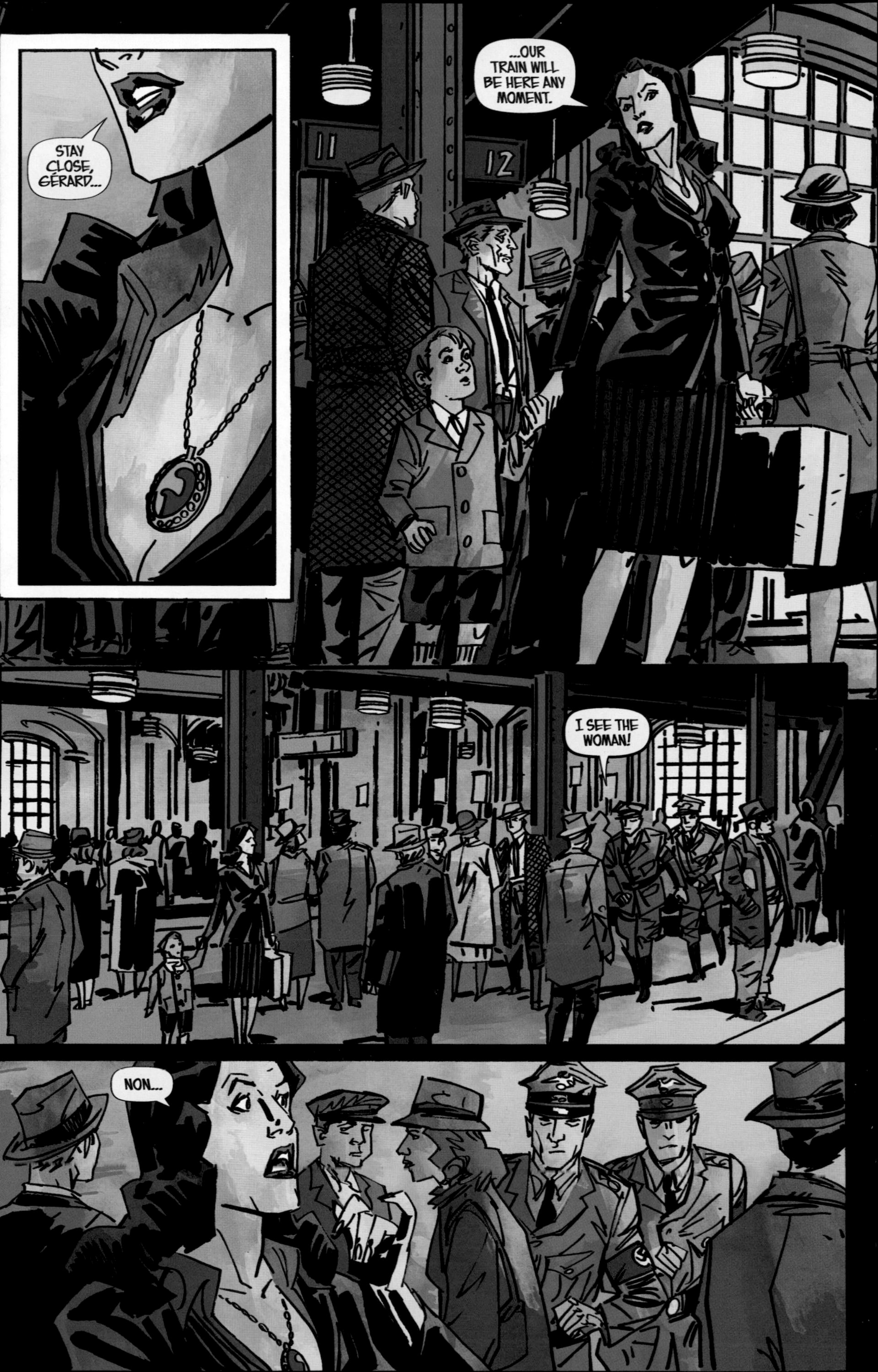
STAY CLOSE, GÉRARD...
...OUR TRAIN WILL BE HERE ANY MOMENT.
I SEE THE WOMAN!
NON...

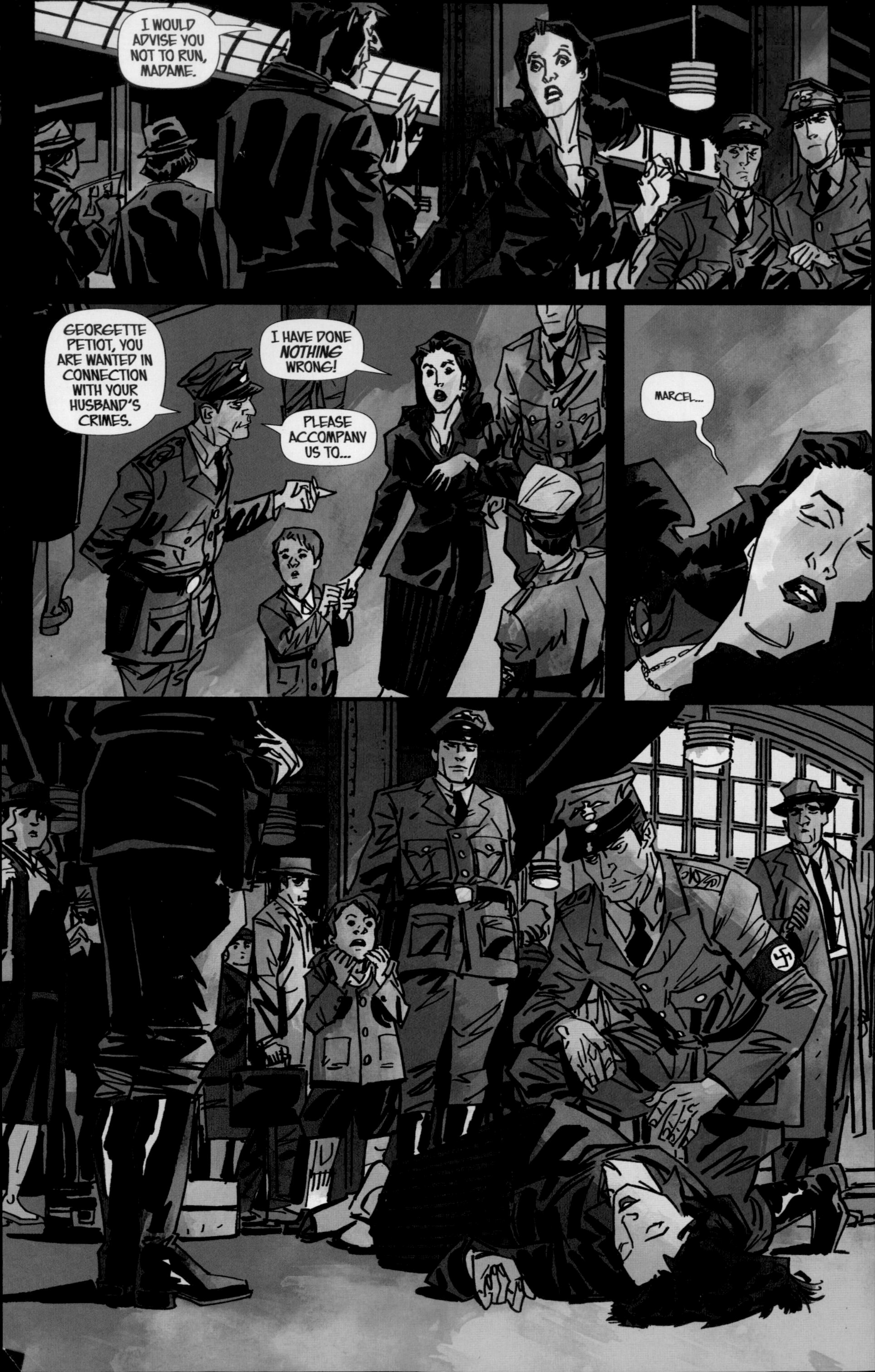
I WOULD ADVISE YOU NOT TO RUN, MADAME.
GEORGETTE PETIOT, YOU ARE WANTED IN CONNECTION WITH YOUR HUSBAND'S CRIMES.
I HAVE DONE *NOTHING* WRONG!
PLEASE ACCOMPANY US TO...
MARCEL...

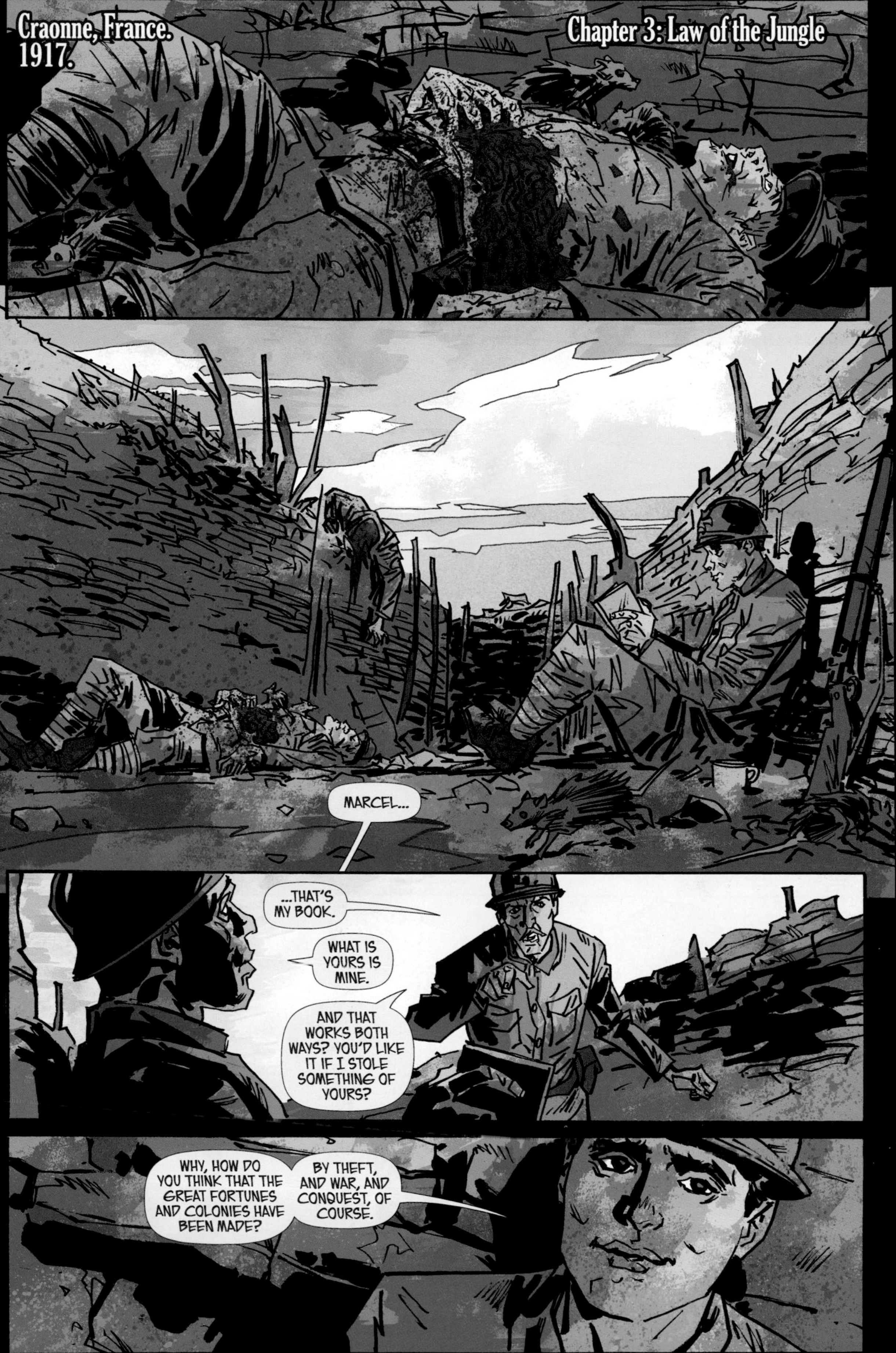

Craonne, France.
1917.
Chapter 3: Law of the Jungle
MARCEL...
...THAT'S MY BOOK.
WHAT IS YOURS IS MINE.
AND THAT WORKS BOTH WAYS? YOU'D LIKE IT IF I STOLE SOMETHING OF YOURS?
WHY, HOW DO YOU THINK THAT THE GREAT FORTUNES AND COLONIES HAVE BEEN MADE?
BY THEFT, AND WAR, AND CONQUEST, OF COURSE.

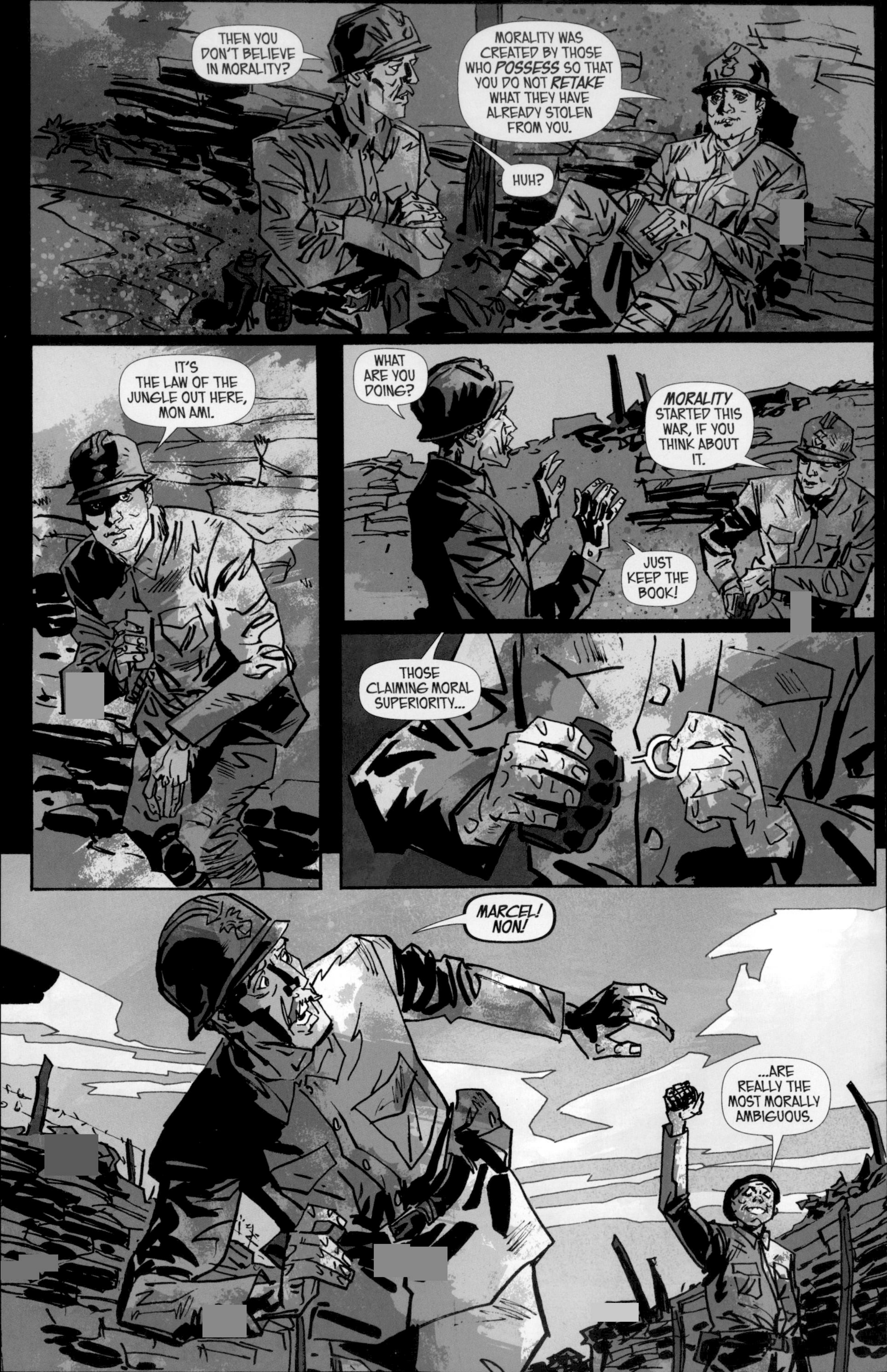
THEN YOU DON'T BELIEVE IN MORALITY?
MORALITY WAS CREATED BY THOSE WHO *POSSESS* SO THAT YOU DO NOT *RETAKE* WHAT THEY HAVE ALREADY STOLEN FROM YOU.
HUH?
IT'S THE LAW OF THE JUNGLE OUT HERE, MON AMI.
WHAT ARE YOU DOING?
MORALITY STARTED THIS WAR, IF YOU THINK ABOUT IT.
JUST KEEP THE BOOK!
THOSE CLAIMING MORAL SUPERIORITY...
MARCEL! NON!
...ARE REALLY THE MOST MORALLY AMBIGUOUS.

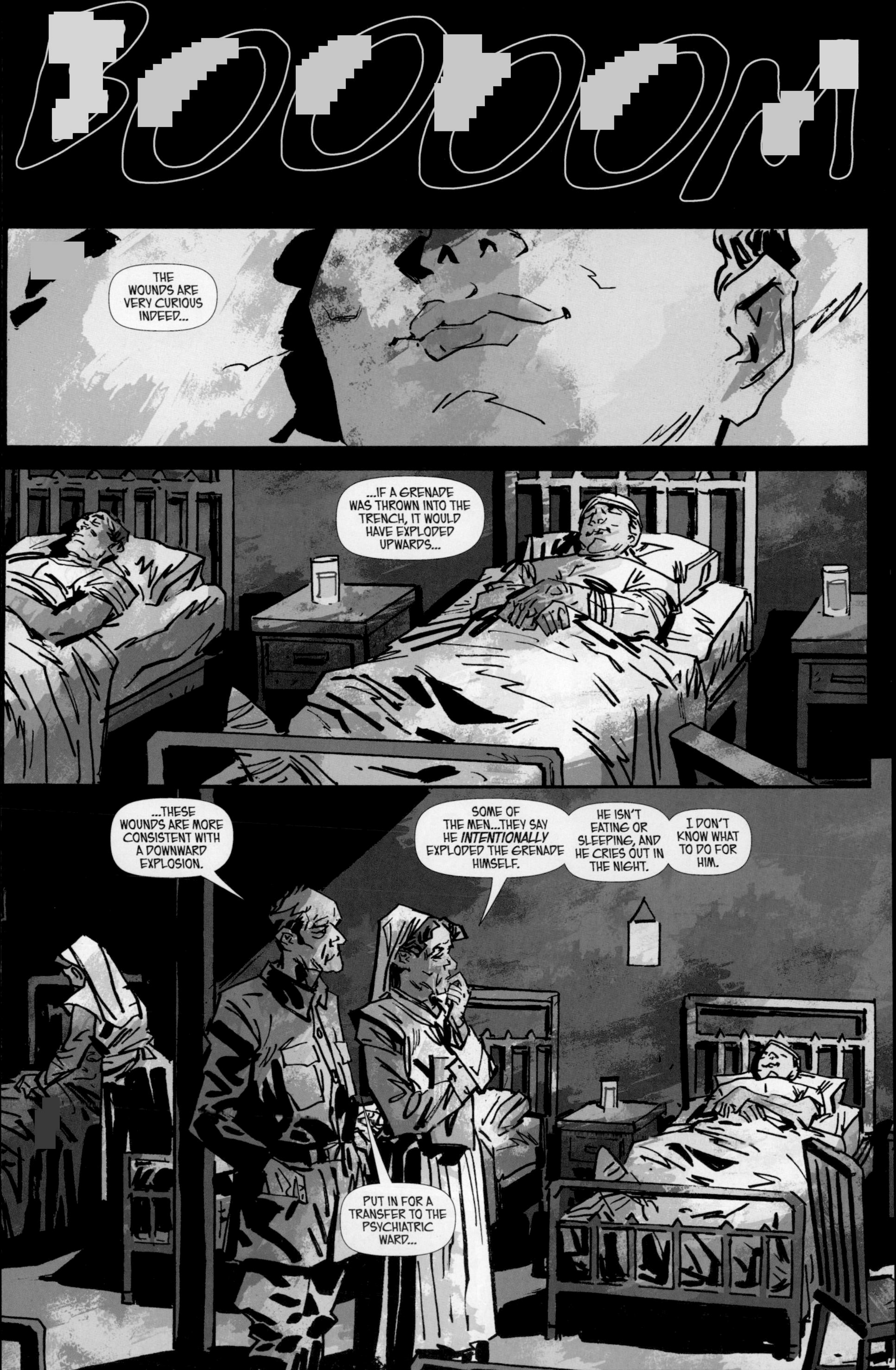
BOOOOM
THE WOUNDS ARE VERY CURIOUS INDEED...
...IF A GRENADE WAS THROWN INTO THE TRENCH, IT WOULD HAVE EXPLODED UPWARDS...
...THESE WOUNDS ARE MORE CONSISTENT WITH A DOWNWARD EXPLOSION.
SOME OF THE MEN...THEY SAY HE INTENTIONALLY EXPLODED THE GRENADE HIMSELF.
HE ISN'T EATING OR SLEEPING, AND HE CRIES OUT IN THE NIGHT.
I DON'T KNOW WHAT TO DO FOR HIM.
PUT IN FOR A TRANSFER TO THE PSYCHIATRIC WARD...

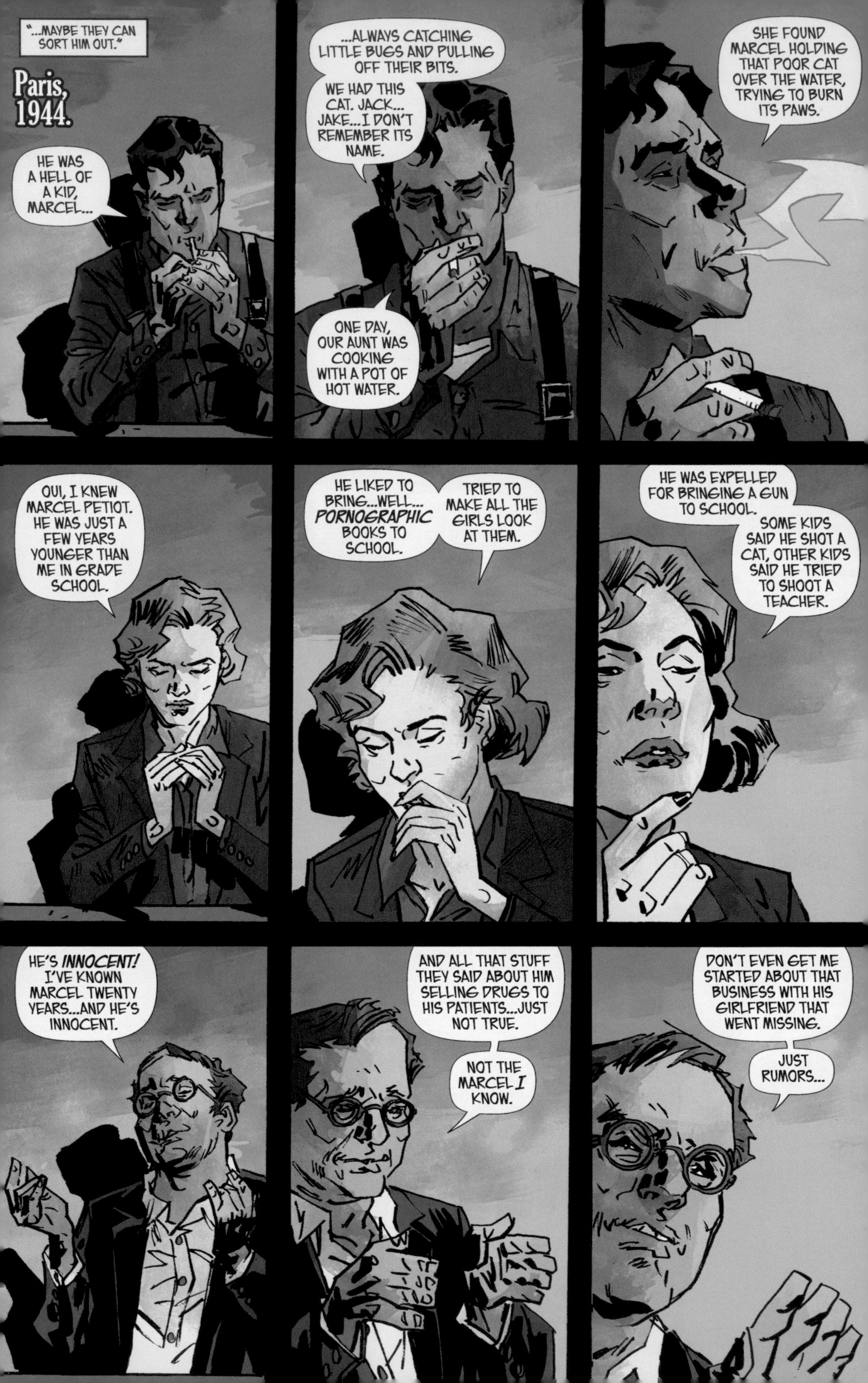
"...MAYBE THEY CAN SORT HIM OUT."
Paris, 1944.
HE WAS A HELL OF A KID, MARCEL...
...ALWAYS CATCHING LITTLE BUGS AND PULLING OFF THEIR BITS.
WE HAD THIS CAT. JACK... JAKE...I DON'T REMEMBER ITS NAME.
ONE DAY, OUR AUNT WAS COOKING WITH A POT OF HOT WATER.
SHE FOUND MARCEL HOLDING THAT POOR CAT OVER THE WATER, TRYING TO BURN ITS PAWS.
OUI, I KNEW MARCEL PETIOT. HE WAS JUST A FEW YEARS YOUNGER THAN ME IN GRADE SCHOOL.
HE LIKED TO BRING...WELL... *PORNOGRAPHIC* BOOKS TO SCHOOL.
TRIED TO MAKE ALL THE GIRLS LOOK AT THEM.
HE WAS EXPELLED FOR BRINGING A GUN TO SCHOOL.
SOME KIDS SAID HE SHOT A CAT, OTHER KIDS SAID HE TRIED TO SHOOT A TEACHER.
HE'S *INNOCENT!* I'VE KNOWN MARCEL TWENTY YEARS...AND HE'S INNOCENT.
AND ALL THAT STUFF THEY SAID ABOUT HIM SELLING DRUGS TO HIS PATIENTS...JUST NOT TRUE.
NOT THE MARCEL *I* KNOW.
DON'T EVEN GET ME STARTED ABOUT THAT BUSINESS WITH HIS GIRLFRIEND THAT WENT MISSING.
JUST RUMORS...

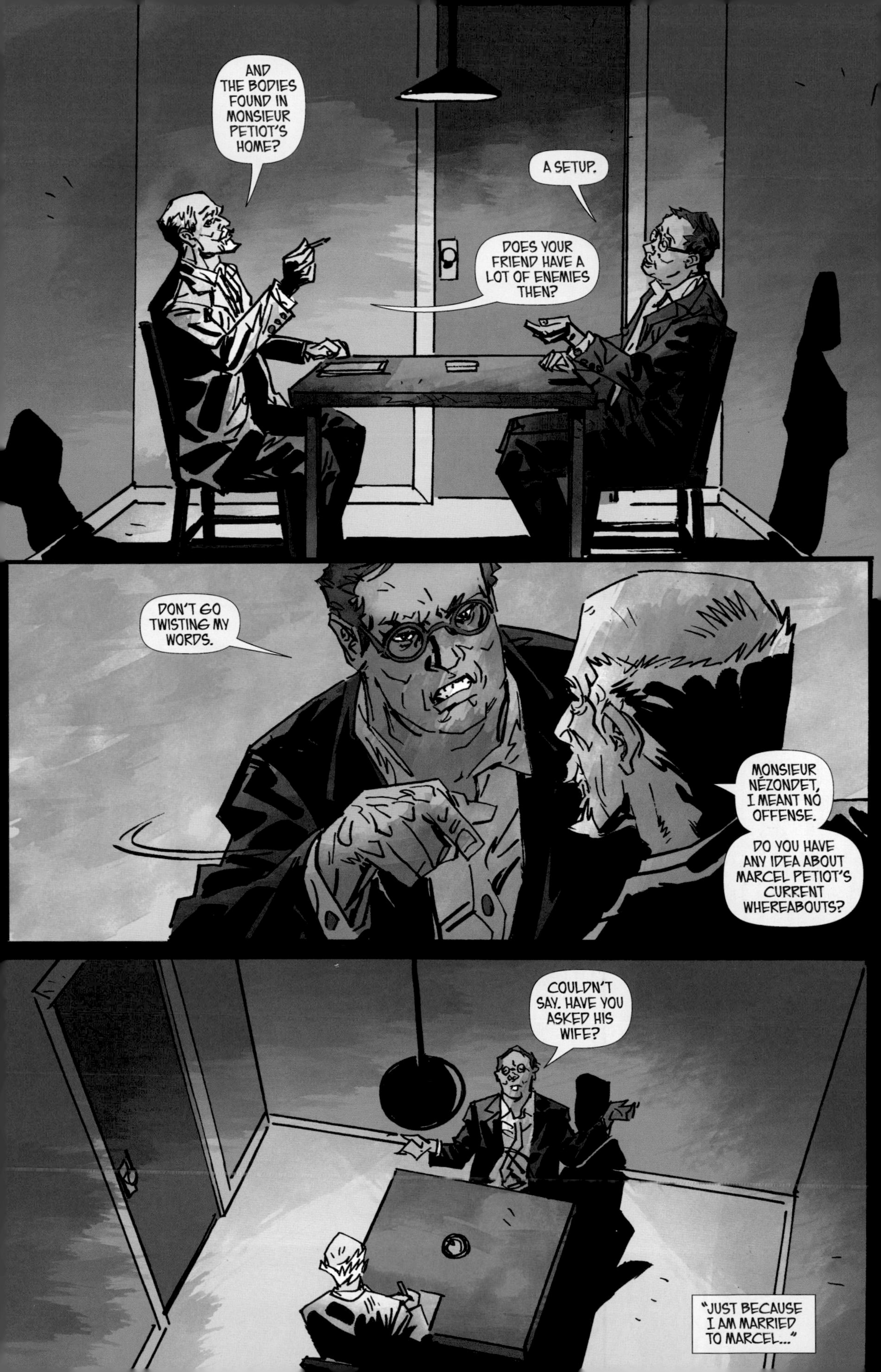
AND THE BODIES FOUND IN MONSIEUR PETIOT'S HOME?
A SETUP.
DOES YOUR FRIEND HAVE A LOT OF ENEMIES THEN?
DON'T GO TWISTING MY WORDS.
MONSIEUR NÉZONDET, I MEANT NO OFFENSE.
DO YOU HAVE ANY IDEA ABOUT MARCEL PETIOT'S CURRENT WHEREABOUTS?
COULDN'T SAY. HAVE YOU ASKED HIS WIFE?
"JUST BECAUSE I AM MARRIED TO MARCEL..."

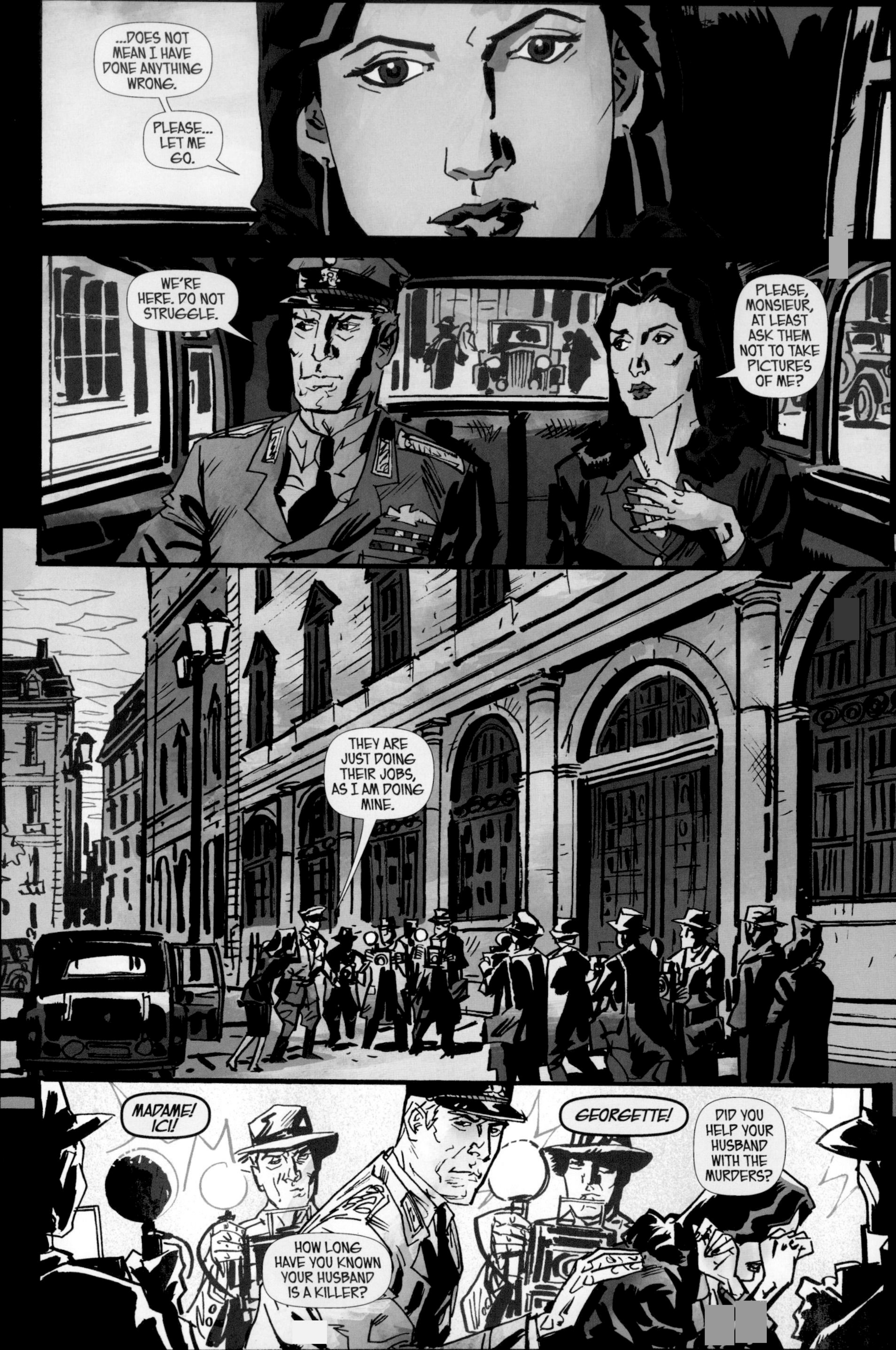
...DOES NOT MEAN I HAVE DONE ANYTHING WRONG.
PLEASE... LET ME GO.
WE'RE HERE. DO NOT STRUGGLE.
PLEASE, MONSIEUR, AT LEAST ASK THEM NOT TO TAKE PICTURES OF ME?
THEY ARE JUST DOING THEIR JOBS, AS I AM DOING MINE.
MADAME! ICI!
HOW LONG HAVE YOU KNOWN YOUR HUSBAND IS A KILLER?
GEORGETTE!
DID YOU HELP YOUR HUSBAND WITH THE MURDERS?

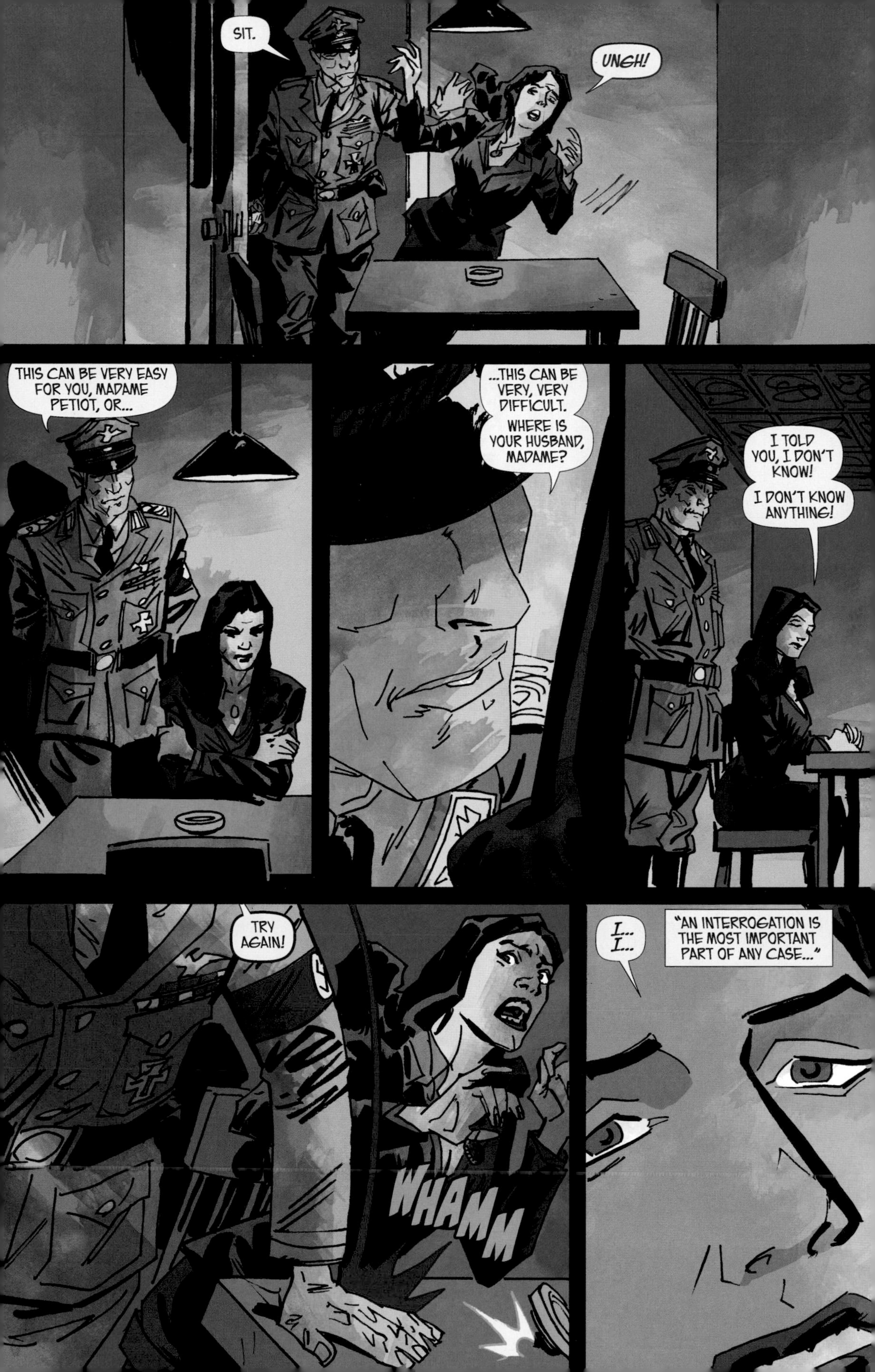
SIT.
UNGH!
THIS CAN BE VERY EASY FOR YOU, MADAME PETIOT, OR...
...THIS CAN BE VERY, VERY DIFFICULT.
WHERE IS YOUR HUSBAND, MADAME?
I TOLD YOU, I DON'T KNOW!
I DON'T KNOW ANYTHING!
TRY AGAIN!
WHAMM
I... I...
"AN INTERROGATION IS THE MOST IMPORTANT PART OF ANY CASE..."

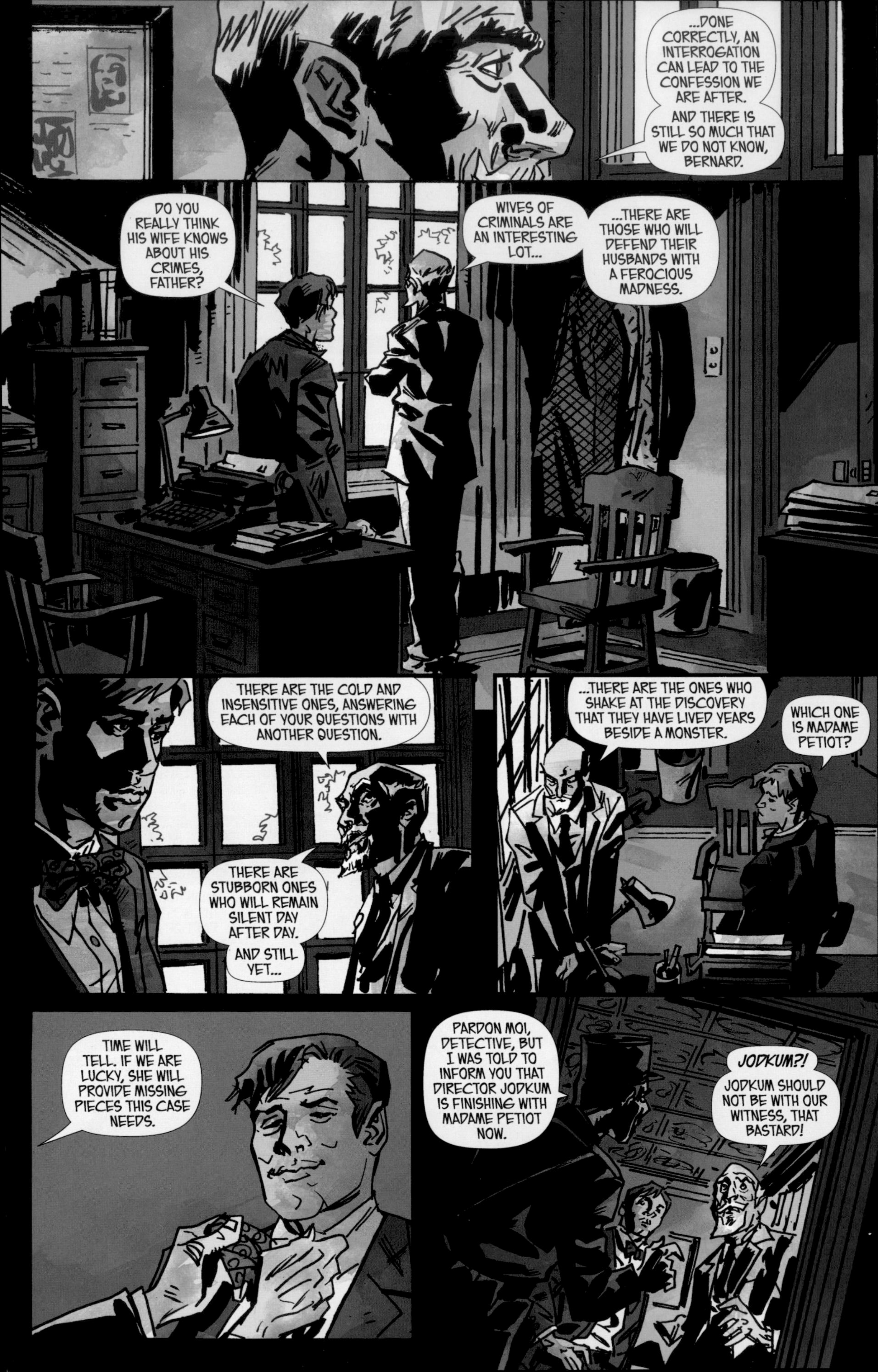
...DONE CORRECTLY, AN INTERROGATION CAN LEAD TO THE CONFESSION WE ARE AFTER.
AND THERE IS STILL SO MUCH THAT WE DO NOT KNOW, BERNARD.
DO YOU REALLY THINK HIS WIFE KNOWS ABOUT HIS CRIMES, FATHER?
WIVES OF CRIMINALS ARE AN INTERESTING LOT...
...THERE ARE THOSE WHO WILL DEFEND THEIR HUSBANDS WITH A FEROCIOUS MADNESS.
THERE ARE THE COLD AND INSENSITIVE ONES, ANSWERING EACH OF YOUR QUESTIONS WITH ANOTHER QUESTION.
THERE ARE STUBBORN ONES WHO WILL REMAIN SILENT DAY AFTER DAY.
AND STILL YET...
...THERE ARE THE ONES WHO SHAKE AT THE DISCOVERY THAT THEY HAVE LIVED YEARS BESIDE A MONSTER.
WHICH ONE IS MADAME PETIOT?
TIME WILL TELL. IF WE ARE LUCKY, SHE WILL PROVIDE MISSING PIECES THIS CASE NEEDS.
PARDON MOI, DETECTIVE, BUT I WAS TOLD TO INFORM YOU THAT DIRECTOR JODKUM IS FINISHING WITH MADAME PETIOT NOW.
JODKUM?!
JODKUM SHOULD NOT BE WITH OUR WITNESS, THAT BASTARD!

JODKUM! WHAT IS THE MEANING OF THIS?!

ONCE AGAIN, YOU OVERESTIMATE YOUR IMPORTANCE TO THIS DEPARTMENT, DETECTIVE.

MY WITNESS...

MY WITNESS WAS FOUND BY MY OFFICERS AND QUESTIONED BY MY INTERROGATORS.

THE WOMAN'S USELESS, ANYWAYS.

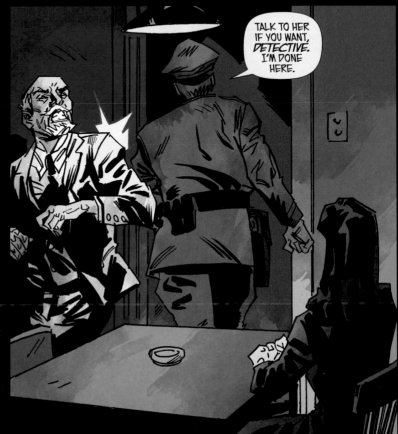

TALK TO HER IF YOU WANT, DETECTIVE. I'M DONE HERE.

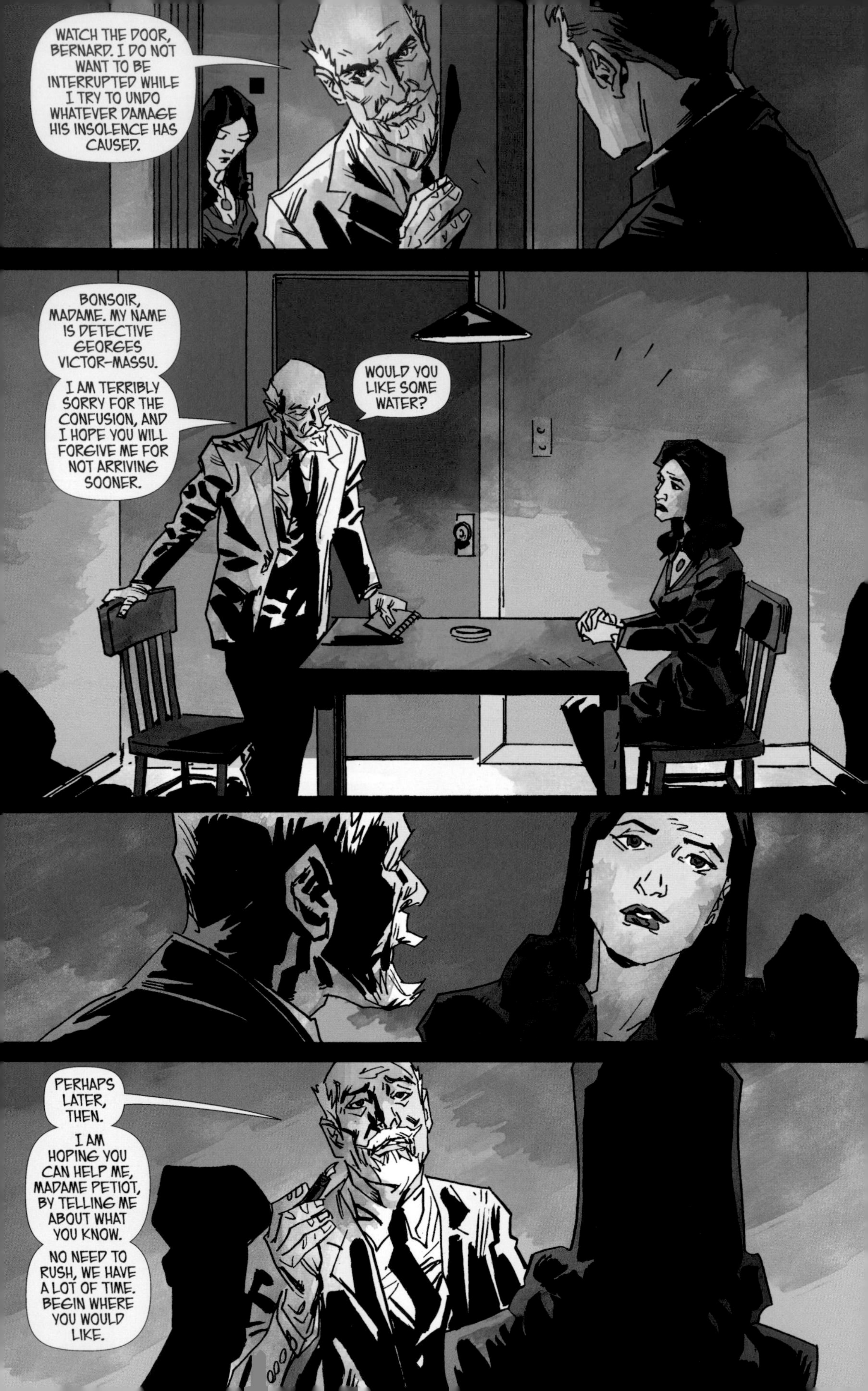
WATCH THE DOOR, BERNARD. I DO NOT WANT TO BE INTERRUPTED WHILE I TRY TO UNDO WHATEVER DAMAGE HIS INSOLENCE HAS CAUSED.
BONSOIR, MADAME. MY NAME IS DETECTIVE GEORGES VICTOR-MASSU.
I AM TERRIBLY SORRY FOR THE CONFUSION, AND I HOPE YOU WILL FORGIVE ME FOR NOT ARRIVING SOONER.
WOULD YOU LIKE SOME WATER?
PERHAPS LATER, THEN.
I AM HOPING YOU CAN HELP ME, MADAME PETIOT, BY TELLING ME ABOUT WHAT YOU KNOW.
NO NEED TO RUSH, WE HAVE A LOT OF TIME. BEGIN WHERE YOU WOULD LIKE.

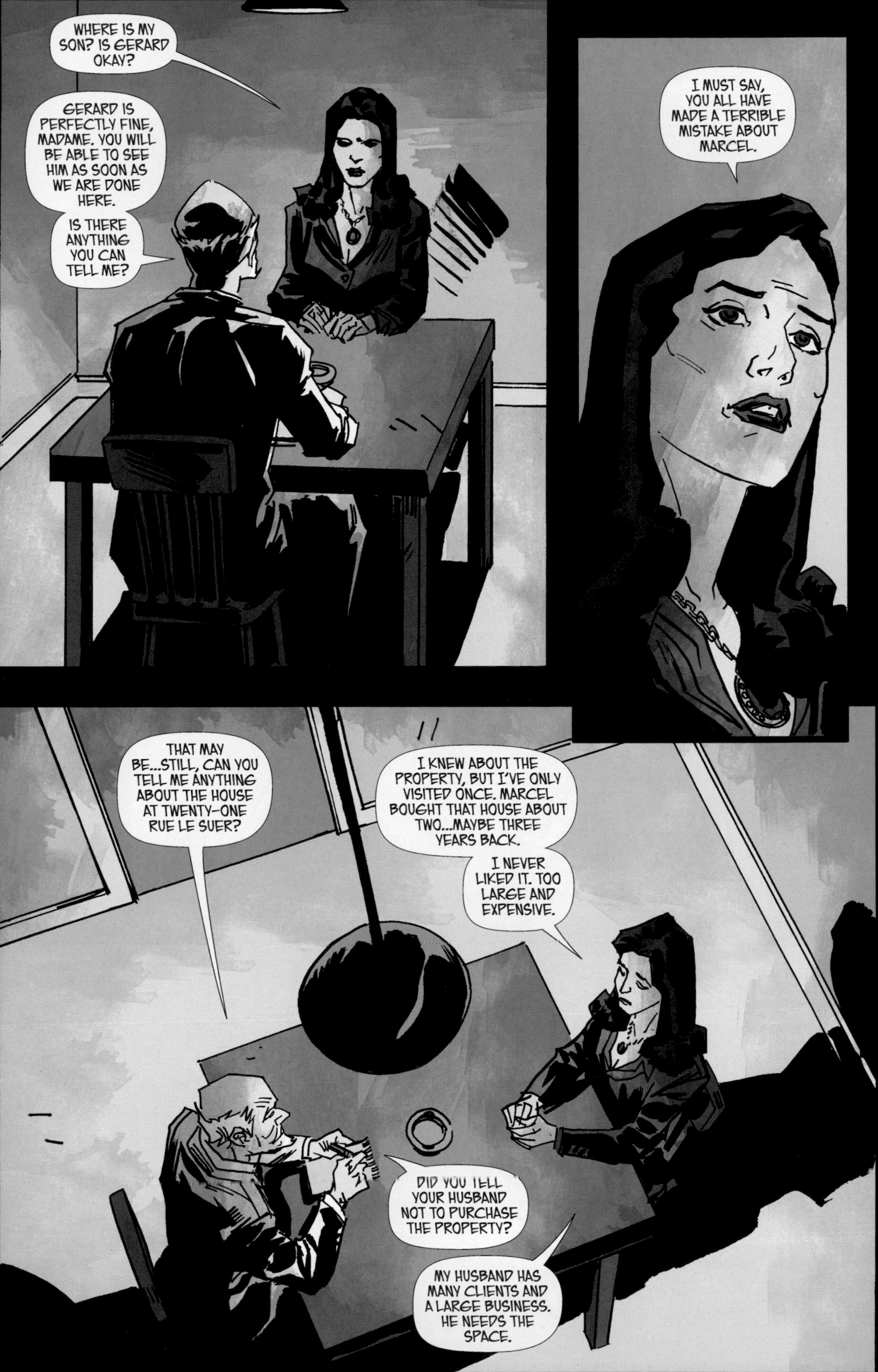
WHERE IS MY SON? IS GERARD OKAY?
GERARD IS PERFECTLY FINE, MADAME. YOU WILL BE ABLE TO SEE HIM AS SOON AS WE ARE DONE HERE.
IS THERE ANYTHING YOU CAN TELL ME?
I MUST SAY, YOU ALL HAVE MADE A TERRIBLE MISTAKE ABOUT MARCEL.
THAT MAY BE...STILL, CAN YOU TELL ME ANYTHING ABOUT THE HOUSE AT TWENTY-ONE RUE LE SUER?
I KNEW ABOUT THE PROPERTY, BUT I'VE ONLY VISITED ONCE. MARCEL BOUGHT THAT HOUSE ABOUT TWO...MAYBE THREE YEARS BACK.
I NEVER LIKED IT. TOO LARGE AND EXPENSIVE.
DID YOU TELL YOUR HUSBAND NOT TO PURCHASE THE PROPERTY?
MY HUSBAND HAS MANY CLIENTS AND A LARGE BUSINESS. HE NEEDS THE SPACE.

PLEASE, MADAME, HAVE MY HANDKERCHIEF.

HAS YOUR HUSBAND EVER ENCOUNTERED ANY PROBLEMS WITH THE LAW PREVIOUSLY?

NO...THOUGH, THERE WAS THAT ONE ISSUE WITH THE MEDICINES. YOU MAY HAVE HEARD ABOUT IT.

DO EXPLAIN.

IT WAS ALL A MISUNDERSTANDING, OF COURSE. *SOME* OF MY HUSBAND'S PATIENTS CLAIMED HE WAS COMMITTING BILLING FRAUD.

THEN CAME THE CLAIMS ABOUT INCORRECT PRESCRIPTIONS AND NARCOTIC SALES.

BUT THAT WAS ALL FALSE.

YOU SEE, MARCEL IS *LOVED* BY HIS PATIENTS. REVERED, EVEN. THAT'S HOW HE WAS ELECTED MAYOR WHEN WE LIVED IN YONNE.

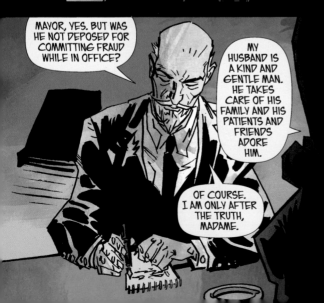

MAYOR, YES. BUT WAS HE NOT DEPOSED FOR COMMITTING FRAUD WHILE IN OFFICE?

MY HUSBAND IS A KIND AND GENTLE MAN. HE TAKES CARE OF HIS FAMILY AND HIS PATIENTS AND FRIENDS ADORE HIM.

OF COURSE. I AM ONLY AFTER THE TRUTH, MADAME.

THE TRUTH? THE TRUTH IS...

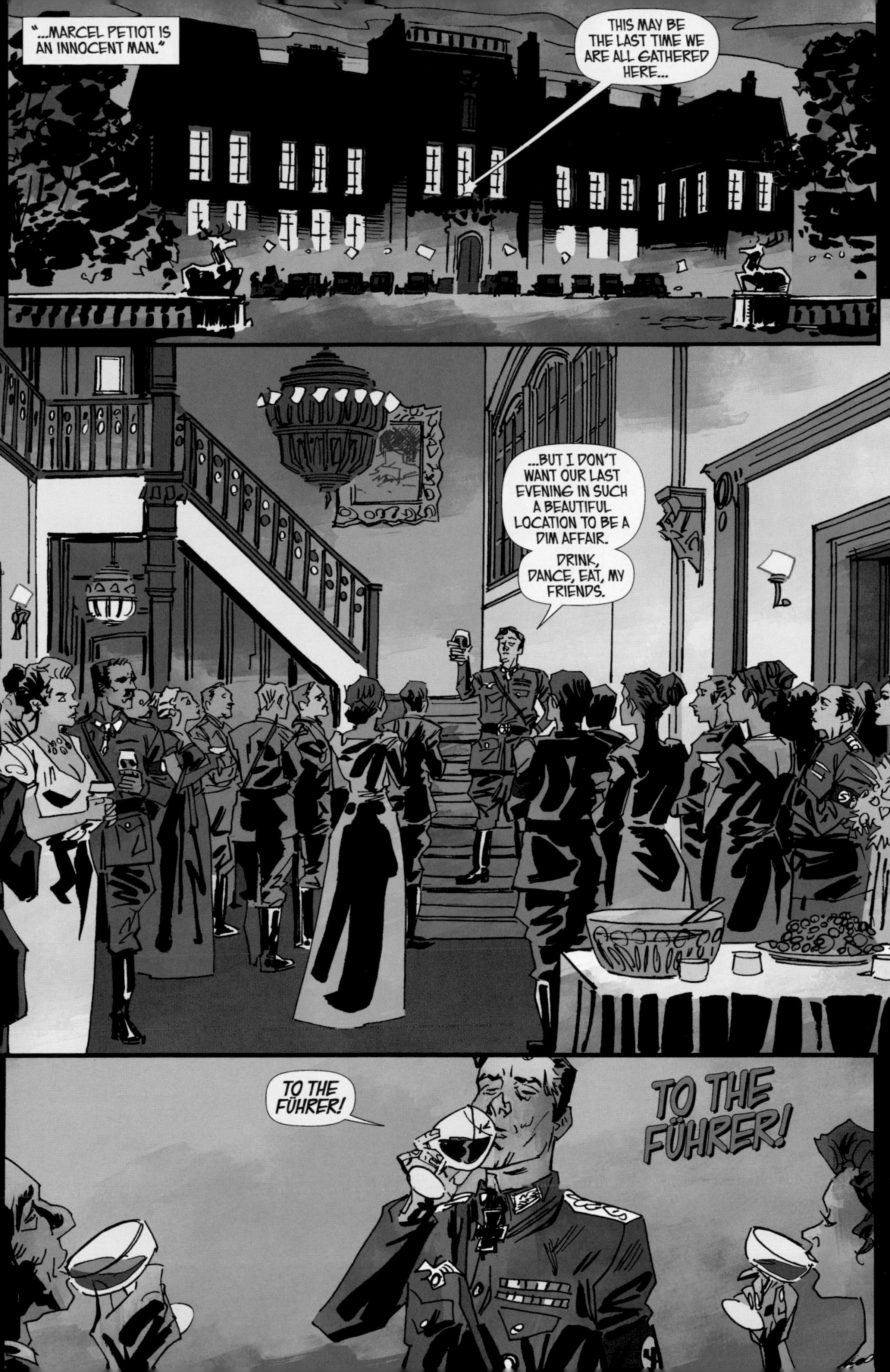
"...MARCEL PETIOT IS AN INNOCENT MAN."
THIS MAY BE THE LAST TIME WE ARE ALL GATHERED HERE...
...BUT I DON'T WANT OUR LAST EVENING IN SUCH A BEAUTIFUL LOCATION TO BE A DIM AFFAIR.
DRINK, DANCE, EAT, MY FRIENDS.
TO THE FÜHRER!
TO THE FÜHRER!

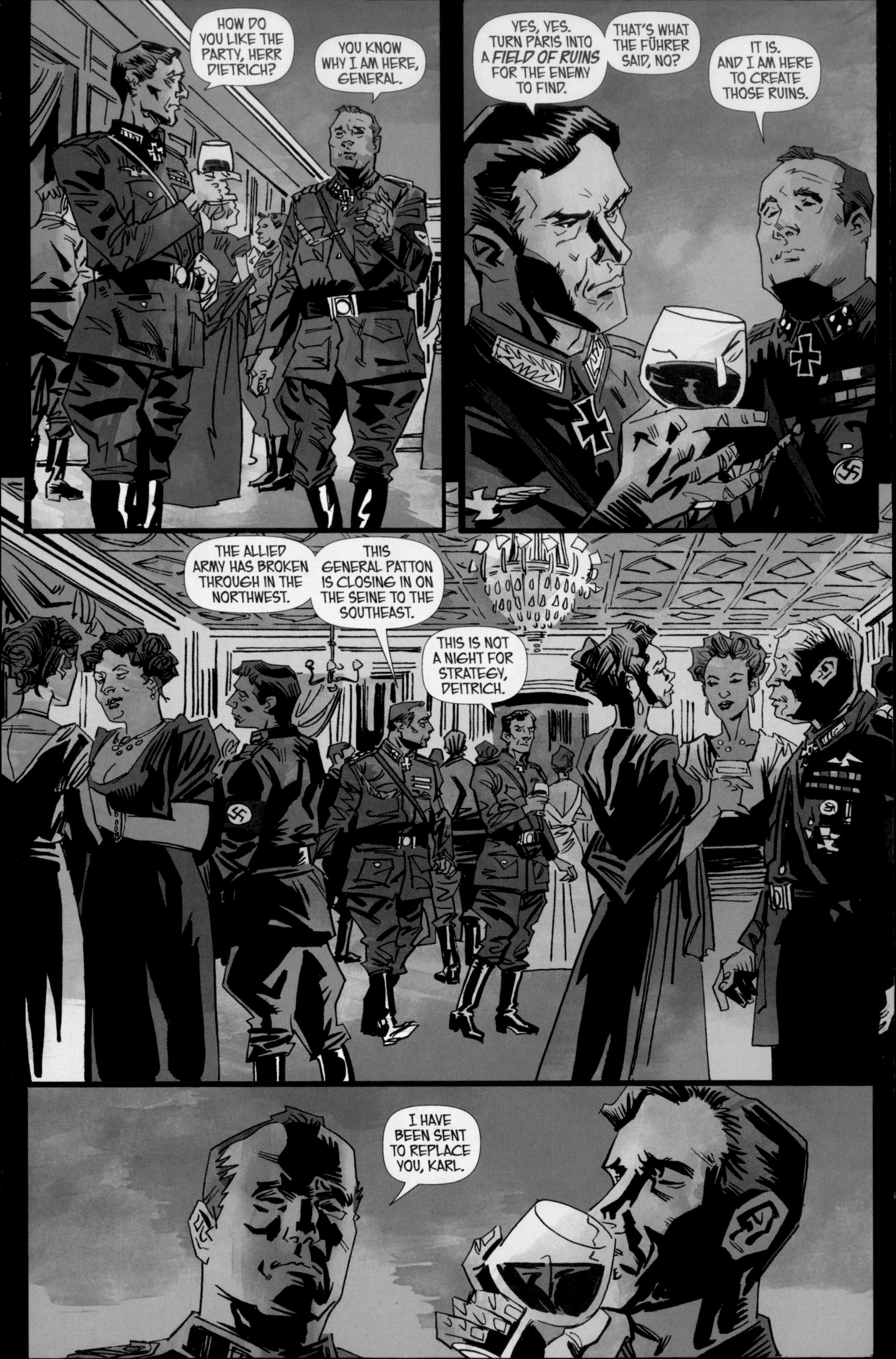
HOW DO YOU LIKE THE PARTY, HERR DIETRICH?
YOU KNOW WHY I AM HERE, GENERAL.
YES, YES. TURN PARIS INTO A ***FIELD OF RUINS*** FOR THE ENEMY TO FIND.
THAT'S WHAT THE FÜHRER SAID, NO?
IT IS. AND I AM HERE TO CREATE THOSE RUINS.
THE ALLIED ARMY HAS BROKEN THROUGH IN THE NORTHWEST.
THIS GENERAL PATTON IS CLOSING IN ON THE SEINE TO THE SOUTHEAST.
THIS IS NOT A NIGHT FOR STRATEGY, DEITRICH.
I HAVE BEEN SENT TO REPLACE YOU, KARL.

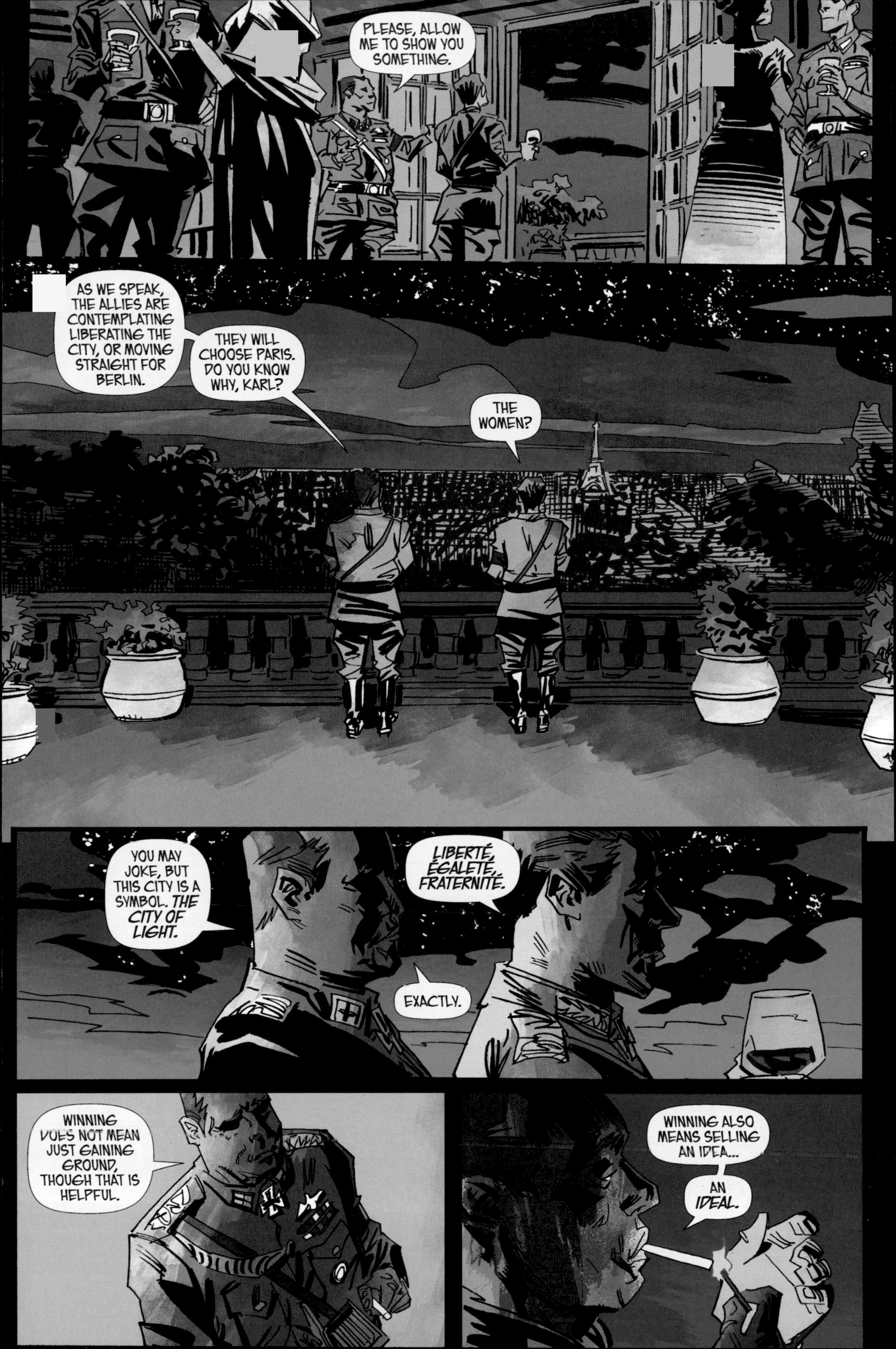
PLEASE, ALLOW ME TO SHOW YOU SOMETHING.
AS WE SPEAK, THE ALLIES ARE CONTEMPLATING LIBERATING THE CITY, OR MOVING STRAIGHT FOR BERLIN.
THEY WILL CHOOSE PARIS. DO YOU KNOW WHY, KARL?
THE WOMEN?
YOU MAY JOKE, BUT THIS CITY IS A SYMBOL. *THE CITY OF LIGHT.*
LIBERTÉ, ÉGALETÉ, FRATERNITÉ.
EXACTLY.
WINNING DOES NOT MEAN JUST GAINING GROUND, THOUGH THAT IS HELPFUL.
WINNING ALSO MEANS SELLING AN IDEA...
AN *IDEAL.*

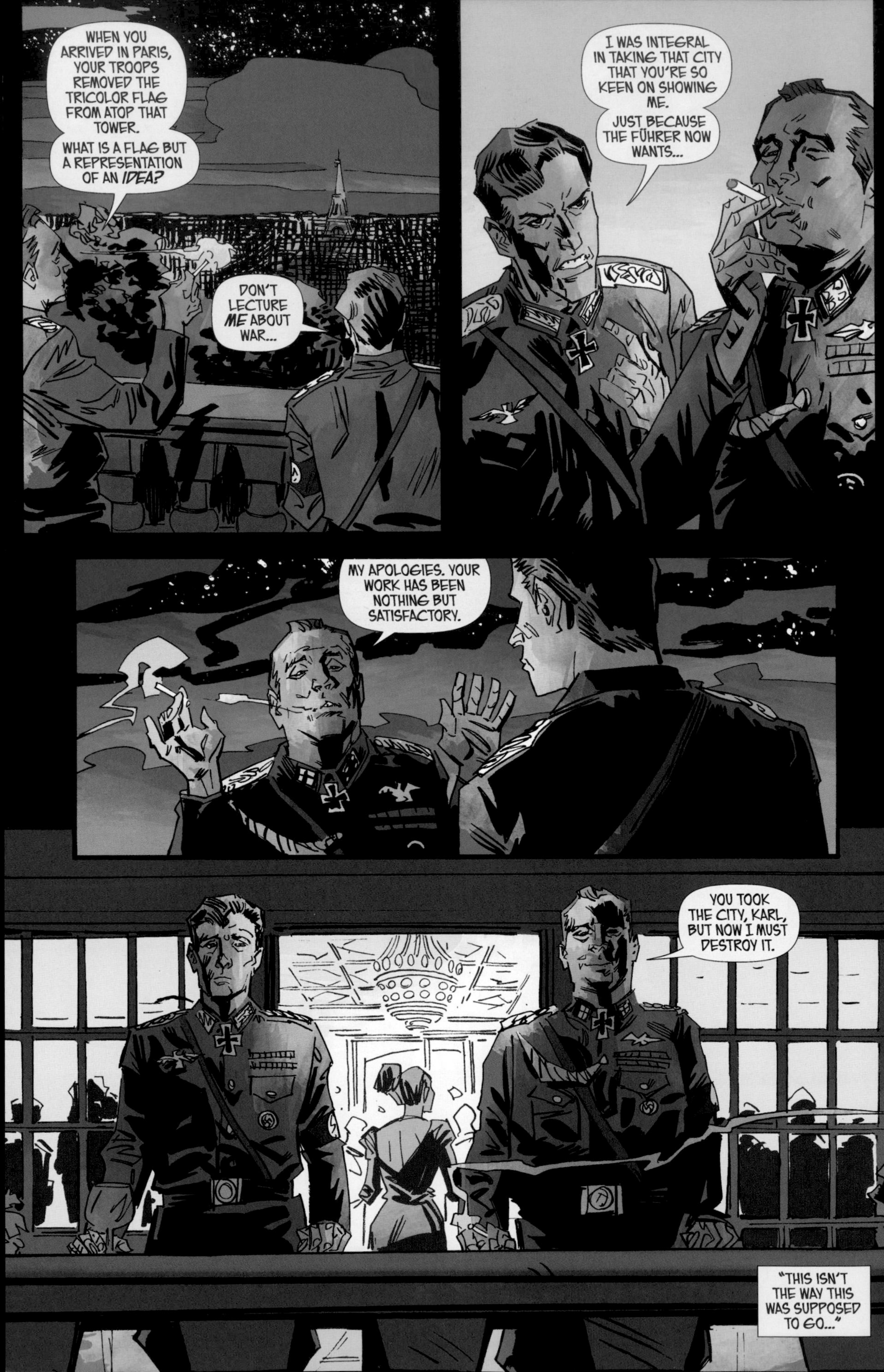
WHEN YOU ARRIVED IN PARIS, YOUR TROOPS REMOVED THE TRICOLOR FLAG FROM ATOP THAT TOWER.
WHAT IS A FLAG BUT A REPRESENTATION OF AN *IDEA?*
DON'T LECTURE *ME* ABOUT WAR...
I WAS INTEGRAL IN TAKING THAT CITY THAT YOU'RE SO KEEN ON SHOWING ME.
JUST BECAUSE THE FÜHRER NOW WANTS...
MY APOLOGIES. YOUR WORK HAS BEEN NOTHING BUT SATISFACTORY.
YOU TOOK THE CITY, KARL, BUT NOW I MUST DESTROY IT.
"THIS ISN'T THE WAY THIS WAS SUPPOSED TO GO..."

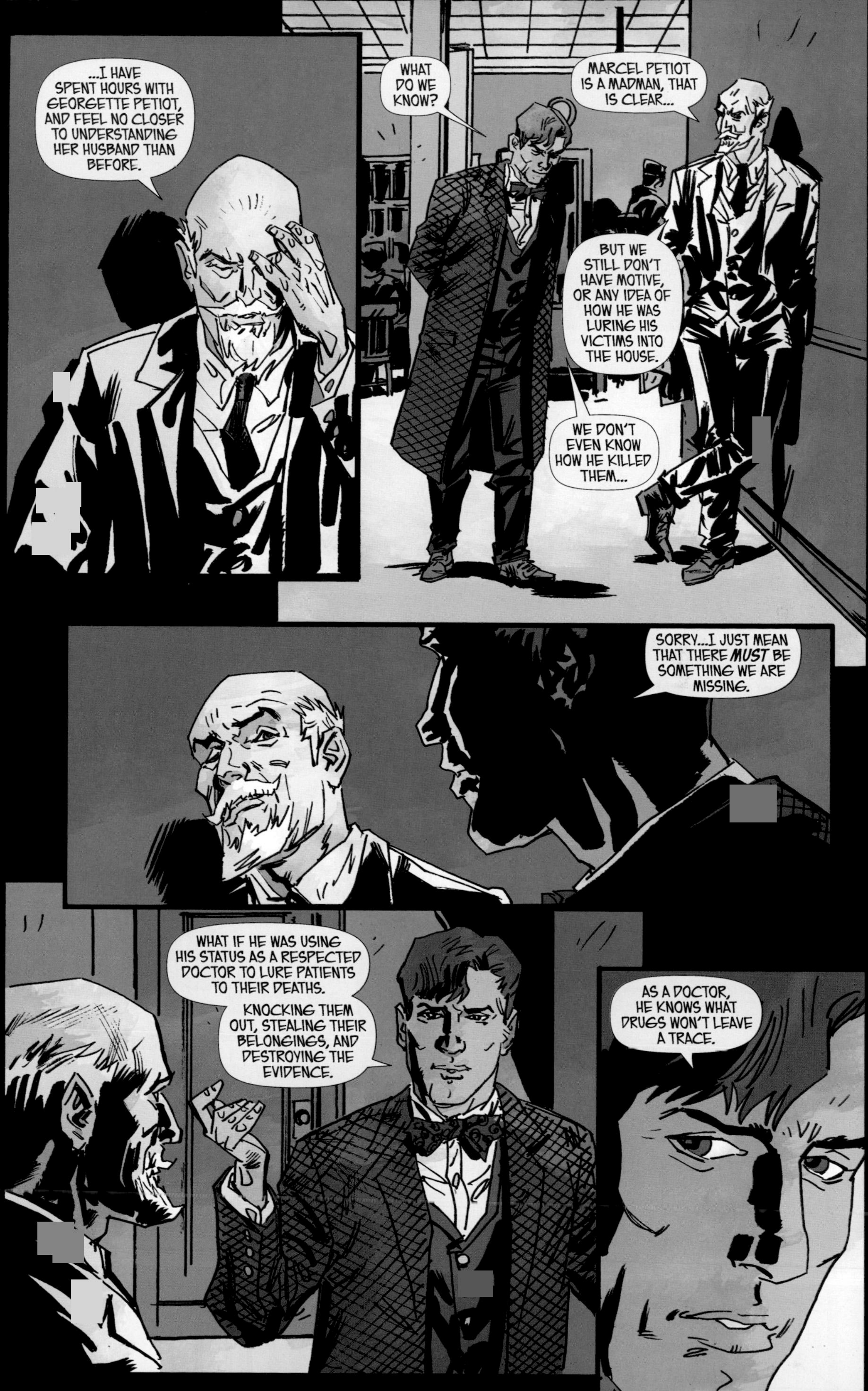
...I HAVE SPENT HOURS WITH GEORGETTE PETIOT, AND FEEL NO CLOSER TO UNDERSTANDING HER HUSBAND THAN BEFORE.
WHAT DO WE KNOW?
MARCEL PETIOT IS A MADMAN, THAT IS CLEAR...
BUT WE STILL DON'T HAVE MOTIVE, OR ANY IDEA OF HOW HE WAS LURING HIS VICTIMS INTO THE HOUSE.
WE DON'T EVEN KNOW HOW HE KILLED THEM...
SORRY...I JUST MEAN THAT THERE *MUST* BE SOMETHING WE ARE MISSING.
WHAT IF HE WAS USING HIS STATUS AS A RESPECTED DOCTOR TO LURE PATIENTS TO THEIR DEATHS.
KNOCKING THEM OUT, STEALING THEIR BELONGINGS, AND DESTROYING THE EVIDENCE.
AS A DOCTOR, HE KNOWS WHAT DRUGS WON'T LEAVE A TRACE.

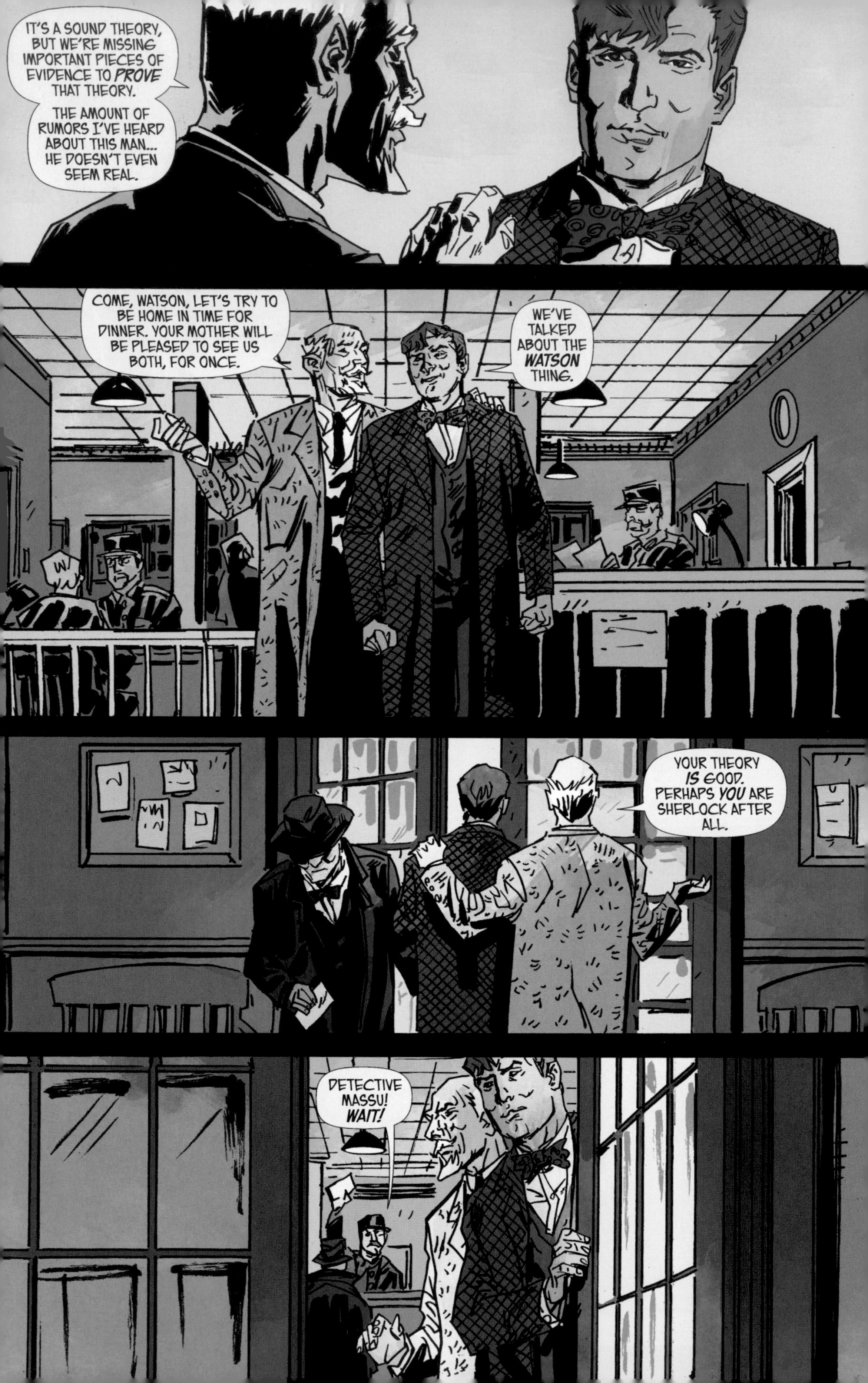
IT'S A SOUND THEORY, BUT WE'RE MISSING IMPORTANT PIECES OF EVIDENCE TO PROVE THAT THEORY.
THE AMOUNT OF RUMORS I'VE HEARD ABOUT THIS MAN... HE DOESN'T EVEN SEEM REAL.
COME, WATSON, LET'S TRY TO BE HOME IN TIME FOR DINNER. YOUR MOTHER WILL BE PLEASED TO SEE US BOTH, FOR ONCE.
WE'VE TALKED ABOUT THE WATSON THING.
YOUR THEORY IS GOOD. PERHAPS YOU ARE SHERLOCK AFTER ALL.
DETECTIVE MASSU! WAIT!

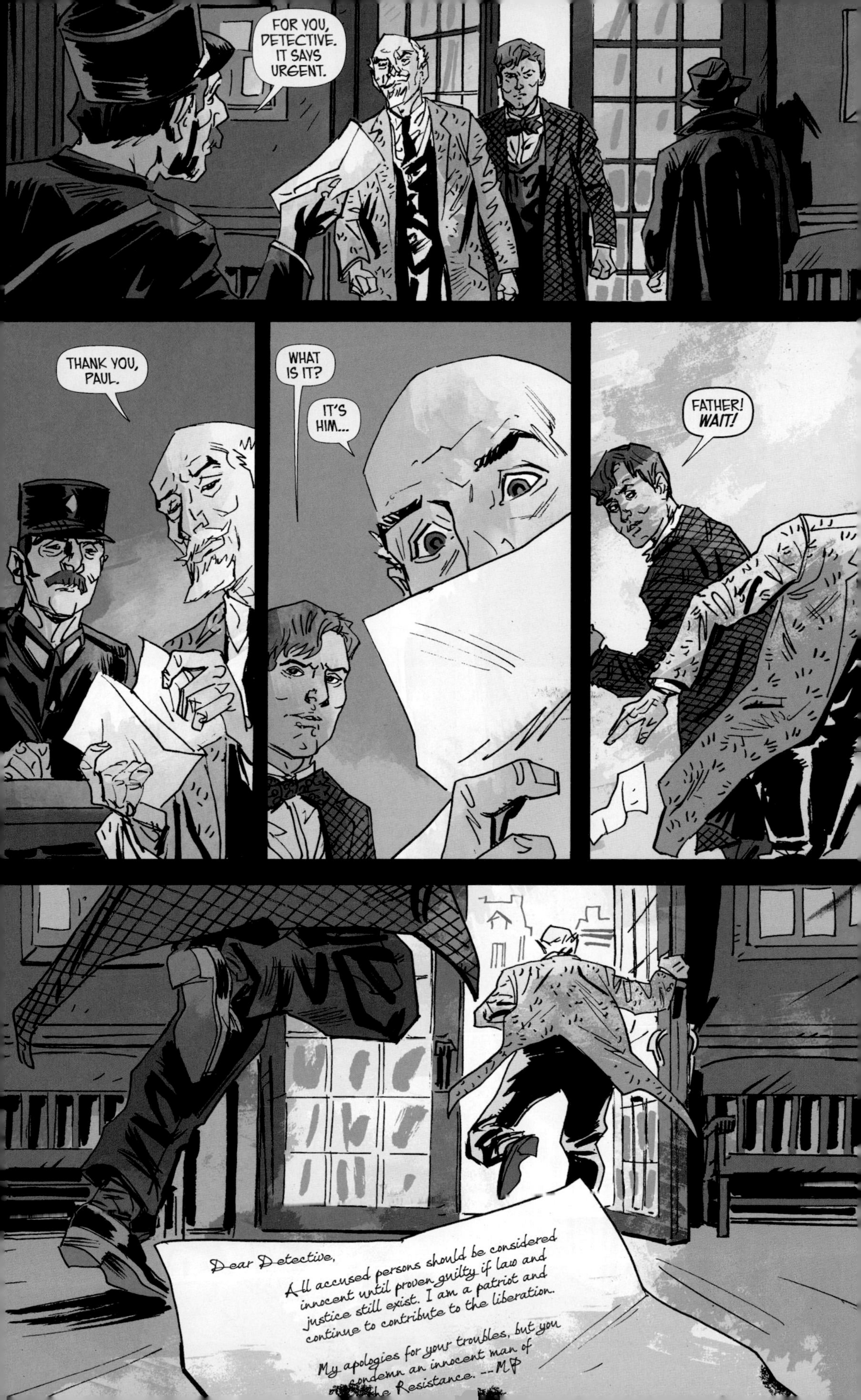
FOR YOU, DETECTIVE. IT SAYS URGENT.
THANK YOU, PAUL.
WHAT IS IT?
IT'S HIM...
FATHER! WAIT!
Dear Detective,
All accused persons should be considered innocent until proven guilty if law and justice still exist. I am a patriot and continue to contribute to the liberation.
My apologies for your troubles, but you condemn an innocent man of ...he Resistance. --MP

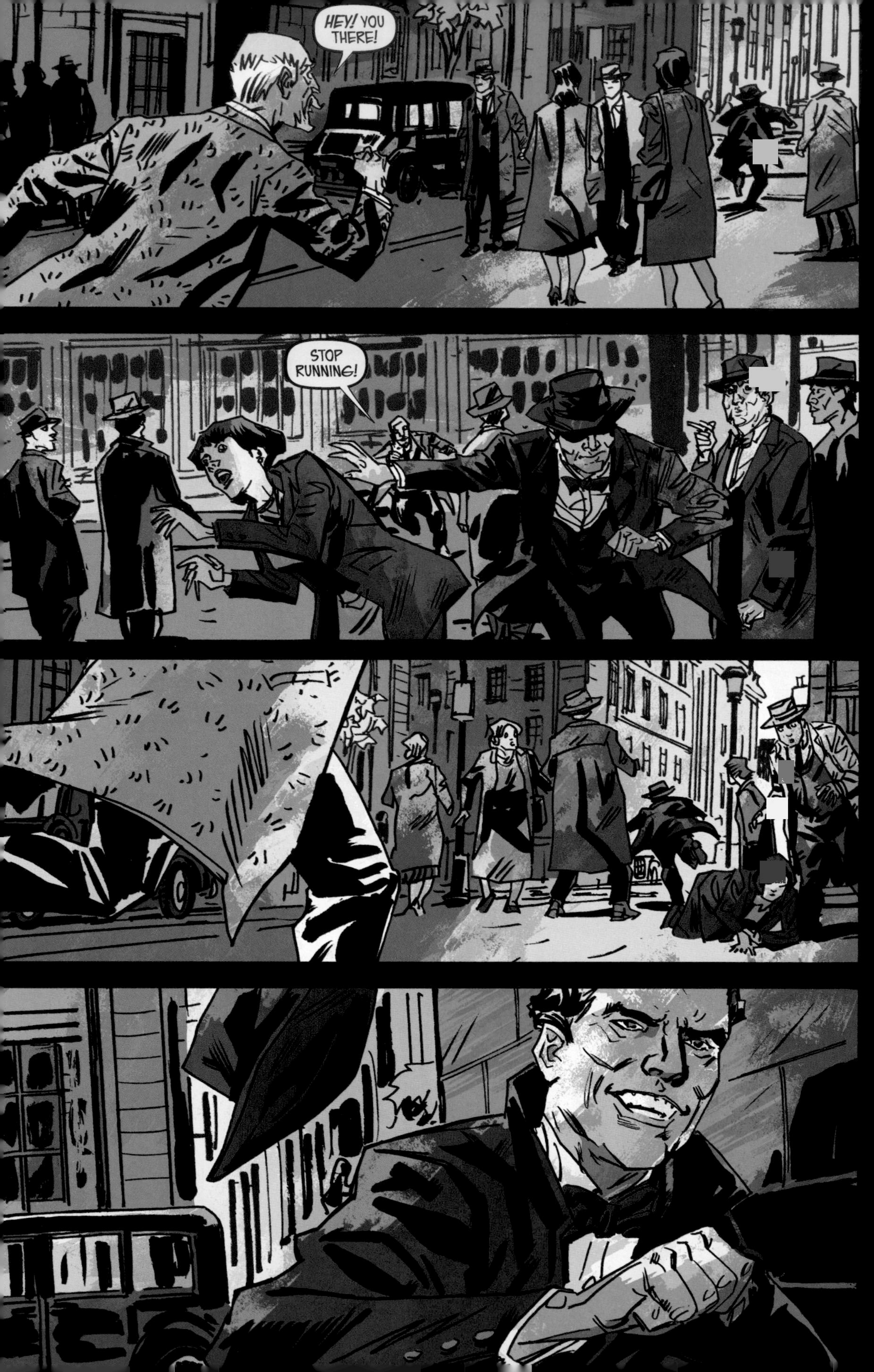
HEY! YOU THERE!
STOP RUNNING!

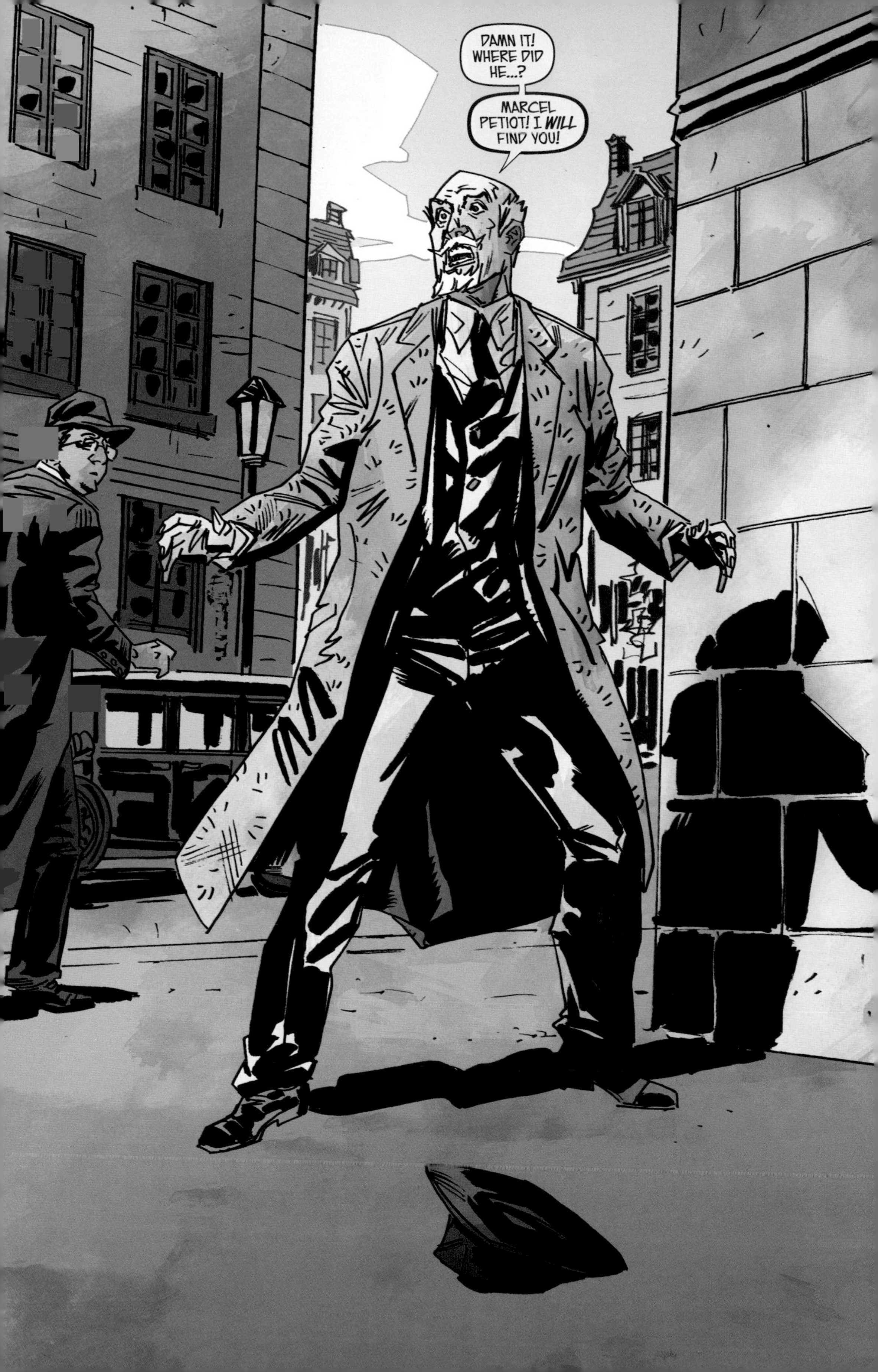
DAMN IT! WHERE DID HE...?
MARCEL PETIOT! I WILL FIND YOU!

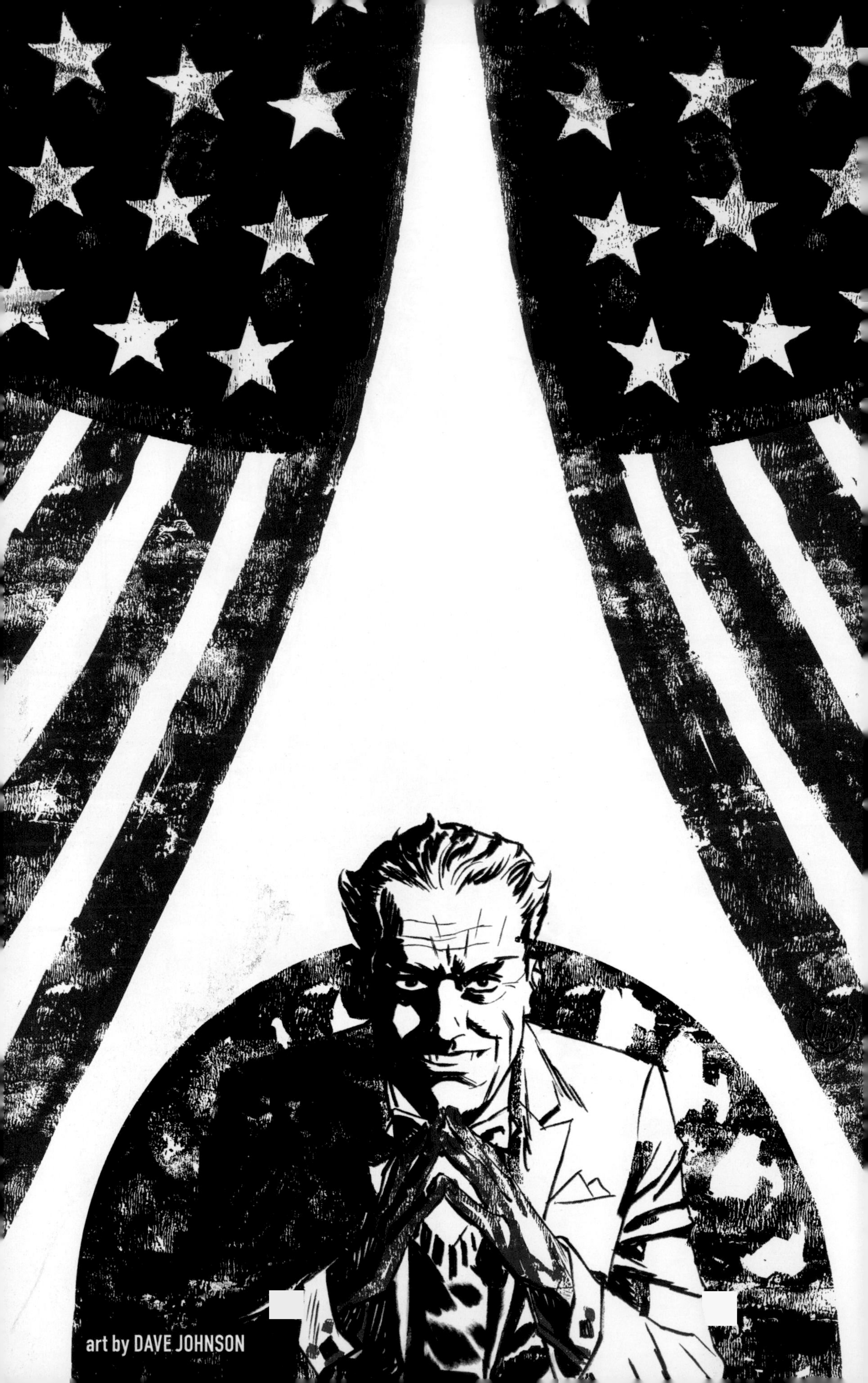

art by DAVE JOHNSON

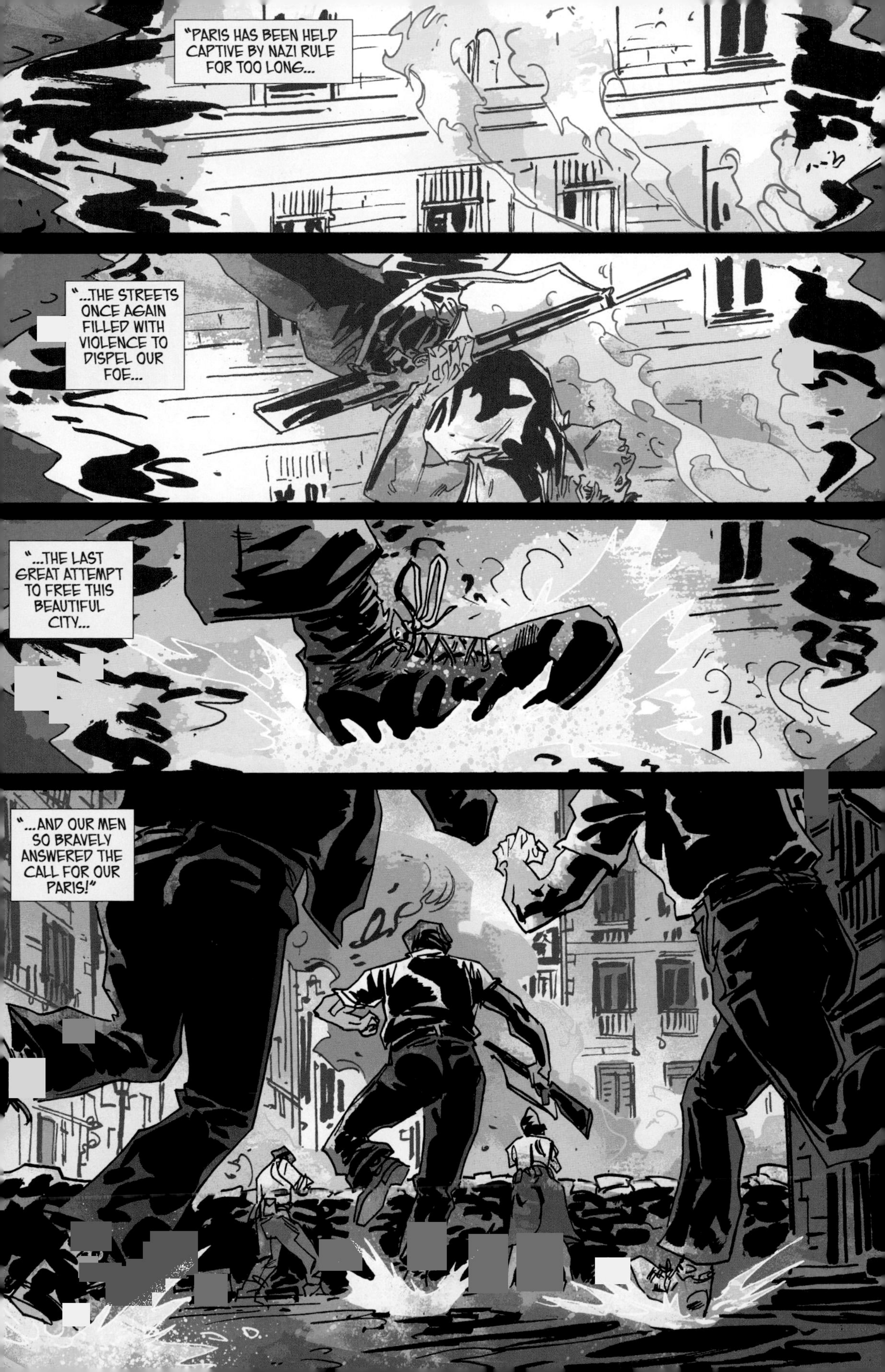
"PARIS HAS BEEN HELD CAPTIVE BY NAZI RULE FOR TOO LONG...
"...THE STREETS ONCE AGAIN FILLED WITH VIOLENCE TO DISPEL OUR FOE...
"...THE LAST GREAT ATTEMPT TO FREE THIS BEAUTIFUL CITY...
"...AND OUR MEN SO BRAVELY ANSWERED THE CALL FOR OUR PARIS!"

Chapter 4: Liberté

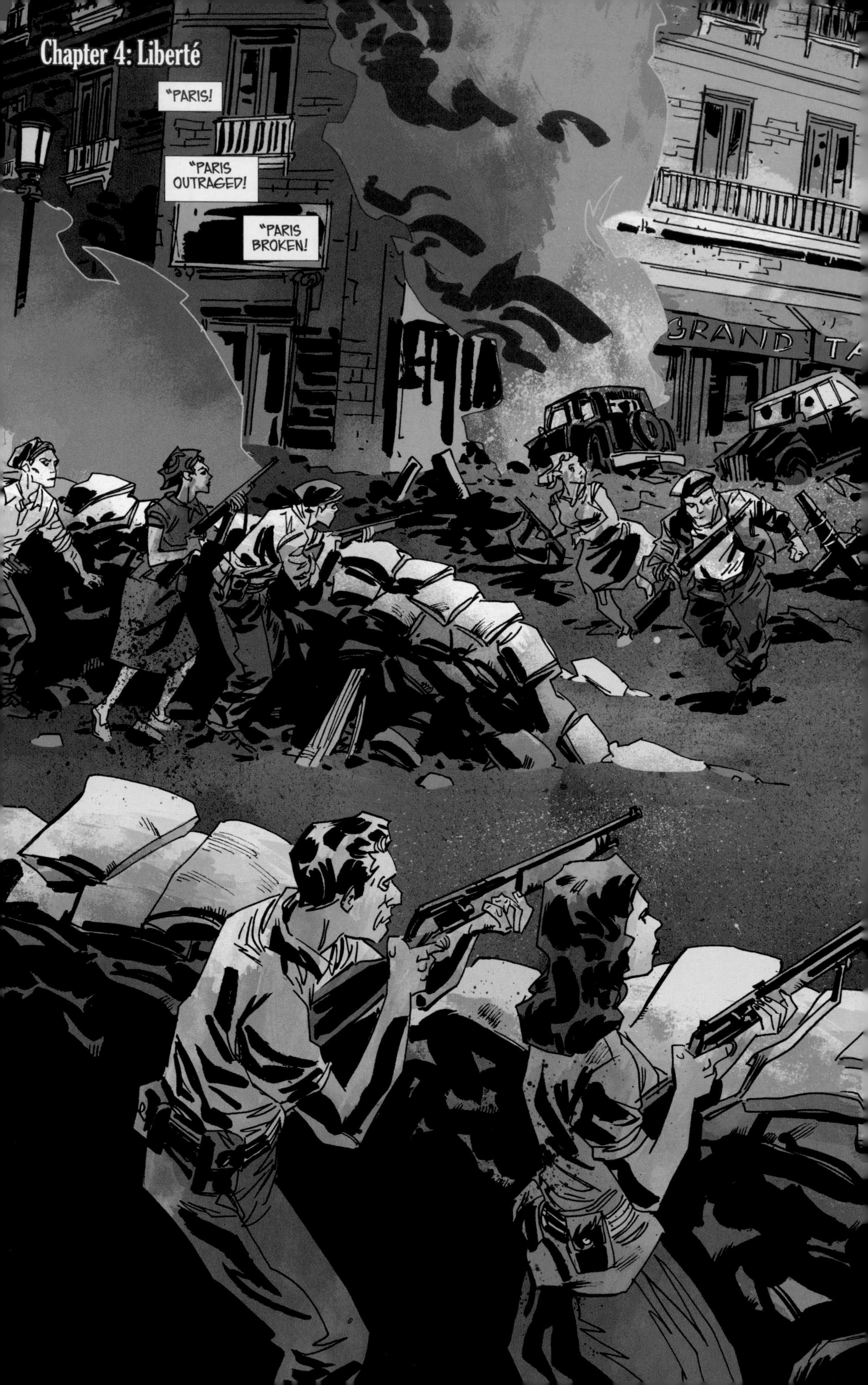
"PARIS!
"PARIS OUTRAGED!
"PARIS BROKEN!
GRAND

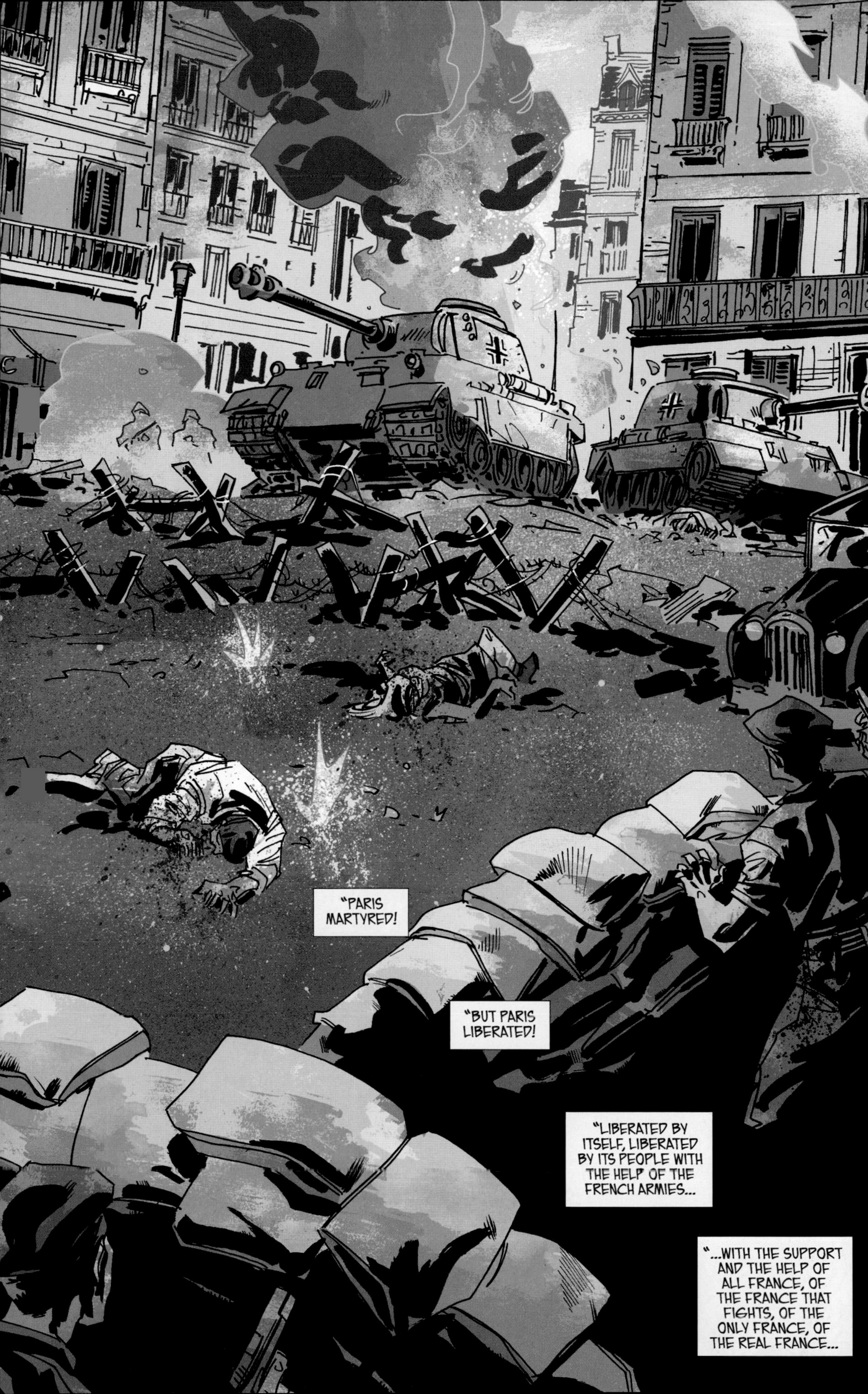
"PARIS MARTYRED!
"BUT PARIS LIBERATED!
"LIBERATED BY ITSELF, LIBERATED BY ITS PEOPLE WITH THE HELP OF THE FRENCH ARMIES...
"...WITH THE SUPPORT AND THE HELP OF ALL FRANCE, OF THE FRANCE THAT FIGHTS, OF THE ONLY FRANCE, OF THE REAL FRANCE...

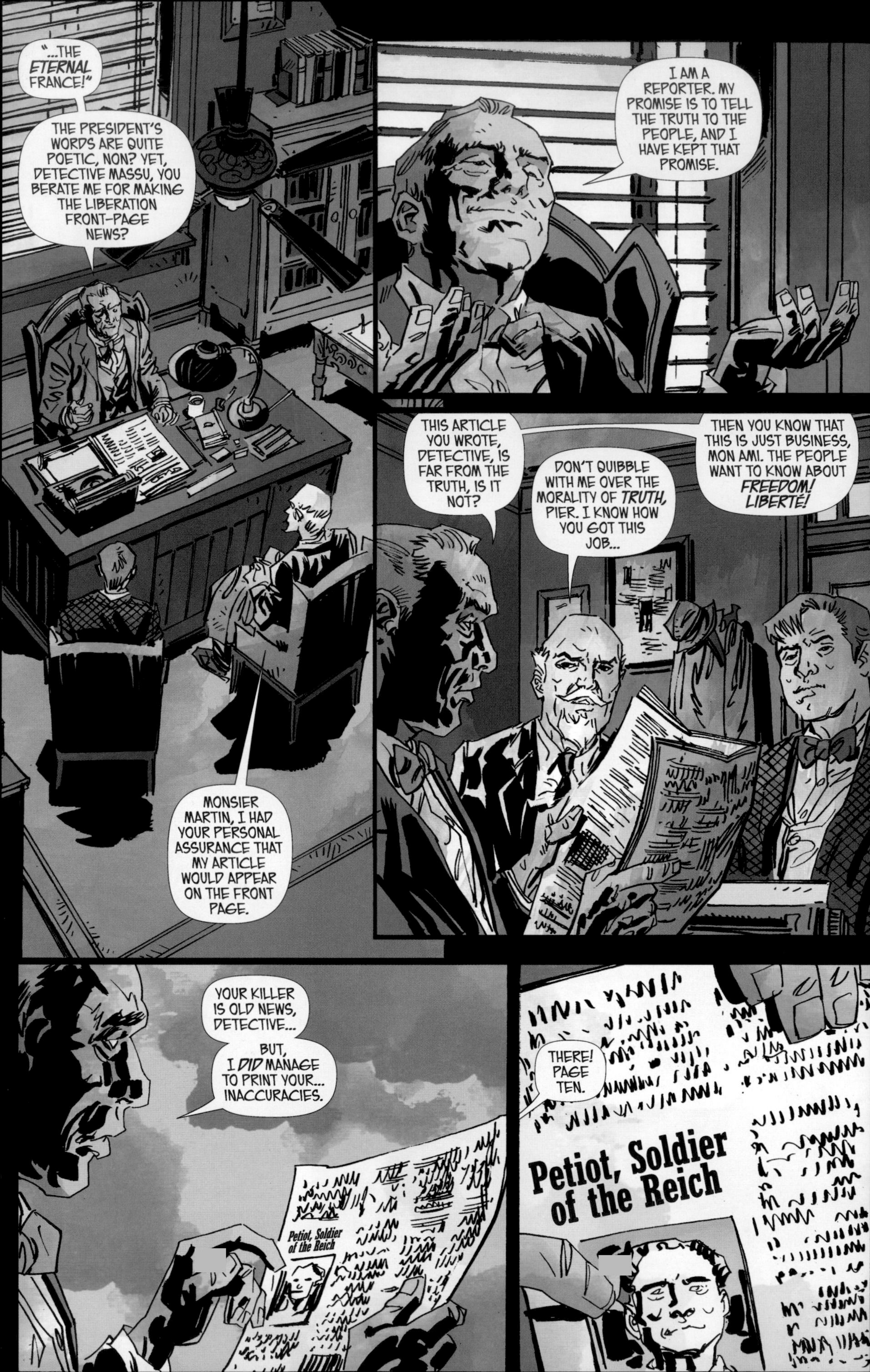
"...THE ETERNAL FRANCE!"
THE PRESIDENT'S WORDS ARE QUITE POETIC, NON? YET, DETECTIVE MASSU, YOU BERATE ME FOR MAKING THE LIBERATION FRONT-PAGE NEWS?
I AM A REPORTER. MY PROMISE IS TO TELL THE TRUTH TO THE PEOPLE, AND I HAVE KEPT THAT PROMISE.
MONSIER MARTIN, I HAD YOUR PERSONAL ASSURANCE THAT MY ARTICLE WOULD APPEAR ON THE FRONT PAGE.
THIS ARTICLE YOU WROTE, DETECTIVE, IS FAR FROM THE TRUTH, IS IT NOT?
DON'T QUIBBLE WITH ME OVER THE MORALITY OF TRUTH, PIER. I KNOW HOW YOU GOT THIS JOB...
THEN YOU KNOW THAT THIS IS JUST BUSINESS, MON AMI. THE PEOPLE WANT TO KNOW ABOUT FREEDOM! LIBERTÉ!
YOUR KILLER IS OLD NEWS, DETECTIVE...
BUT, I DID MANAGE TO PRINT YOUR... INACCURACIES.
Petiot, Soldier of the Reich
THERE! PAGE TEN.
Petiot, Soldier of the Reich

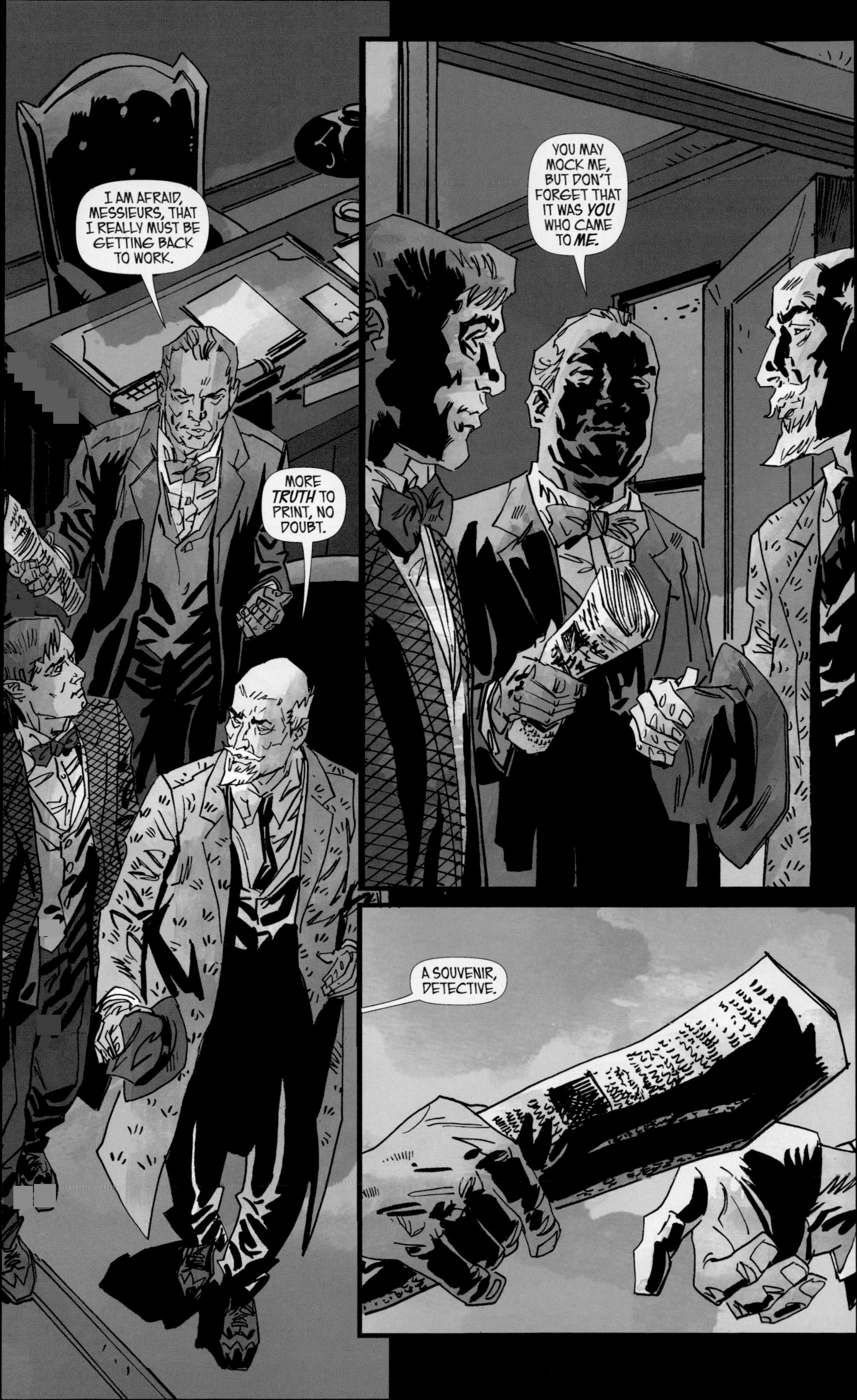
I AM AFRAID, MESSIEURS, THAT I REALLY MUST BE GETTING BACK TO WORK.
MORE TRUTH TO PRINT, NO DOUBT.
YOU MAY MOCK ME, BUT DON'T FORGET THAT IT WAS YOU WHO CAME TO ME.
A SOUVENIR, DETECTIVE.

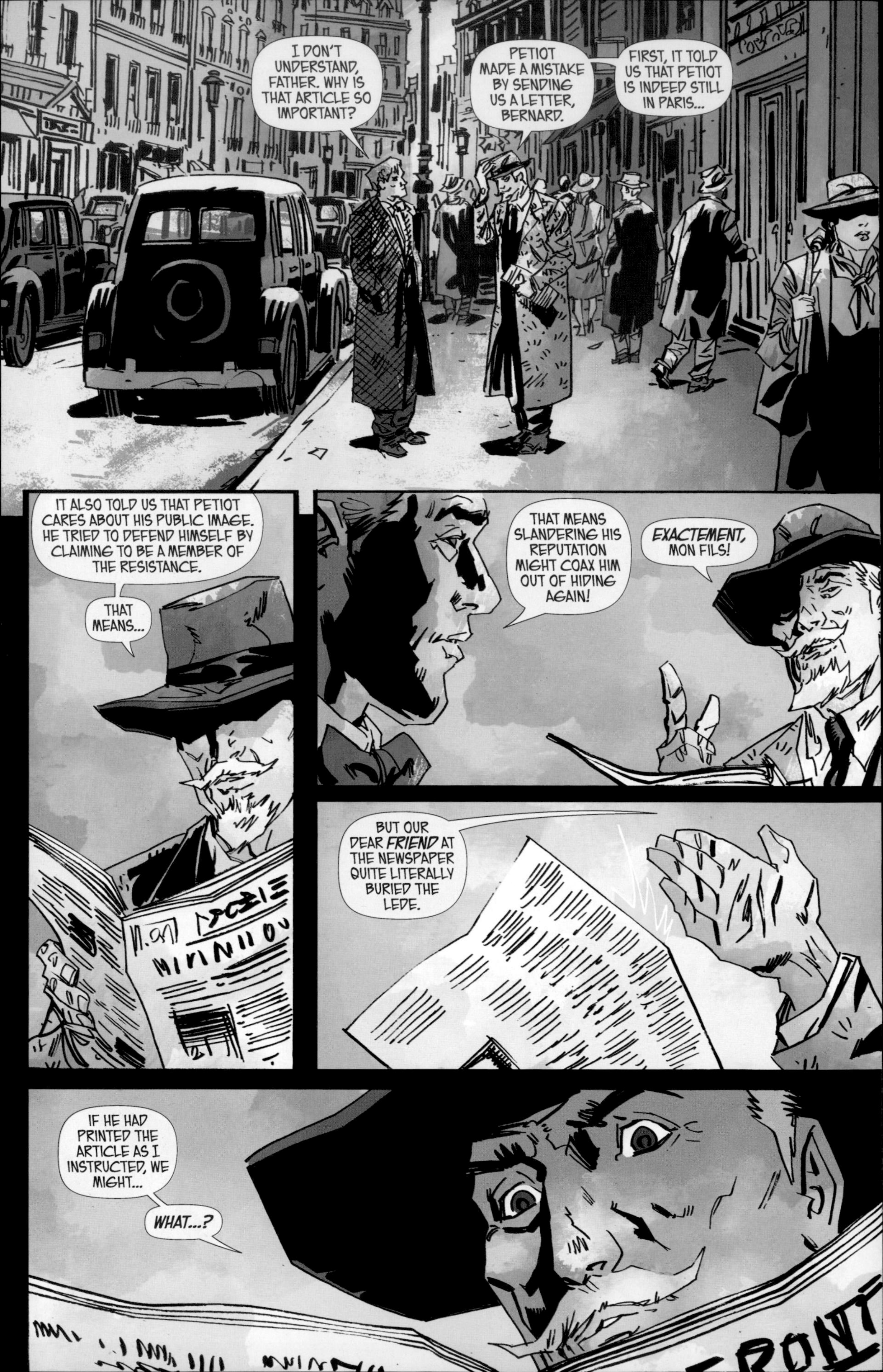
I DON'T UNDERSTAND, FATHER. WHY IS THAT ARTICLE SO IMPORTANT?
PETIOT MADE A MISTAKE BY SENDING US A LETTER, BERNARD.
FIRST, IT TOLD US THAT PETIOT IS INDEED STILL IN PARIS...
IT ALSO TOLD US THAT PETIOT CARES ABOUT HIS PUBLIC IMAGE. HE TRIED TO DEFEND HIMSELF BY CLAIMING TO BE A MEMBER OF THE RESISTANCE.
THAT MEANS...
THAT MEANS SLANDERING HIS REPUTATION MIGHT COAX HIM OUT OF HIDING AGAIN!
EXACTEMENT, MON FILS!
BUT OUR DEAR *FRIEND* AT THE NEWSPAPER QUITE LITERALLY BURIED THE LEDE.
IF HE HAD PRINTED THE ARTICLE AS I INSTRUCTED, WE MIGHT...
WHAT...?

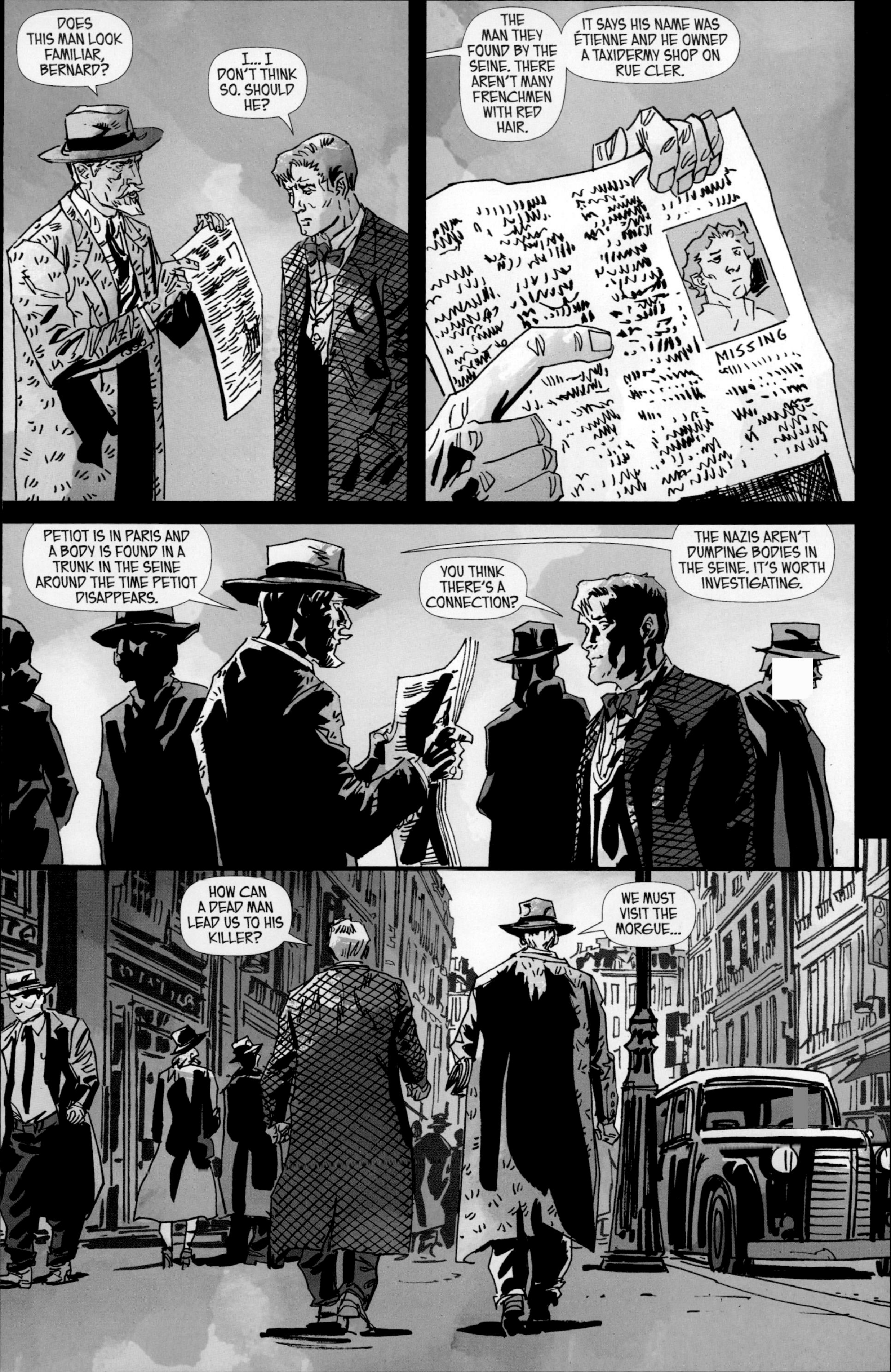
DOES THIS MAN LOOK FAMILIAR, BERNARD?
I... I DON'T THINK SO. SHOULD HE?
THE MAN THEY FOUND BY THE SEINE. THERE AREN'T MANY FRENCHMEN WITH RED HAIR.
IT SAYS HIS NAME WAS ÉTIENNE AND HE OWNED A TAXIDERMY SHOP ON RUE CLER.
MISSING
PETIOT IS IN PARIS AND A BODY IS FOUND IN A TRUNK IN THE SEINE AROUND THE TIME PETIOT DISAPPEARS.
YOU THINK THERE'S A CONNECTION?
THE NAZIS AREN'T DUMPING BODIES IN THE SEINE. IT'S WORTH INVESTIGATING.
HOW CAN A DEAD MAN LEAD US TO HIS KILLER?
WE MUST VISIT THE MORGUE...

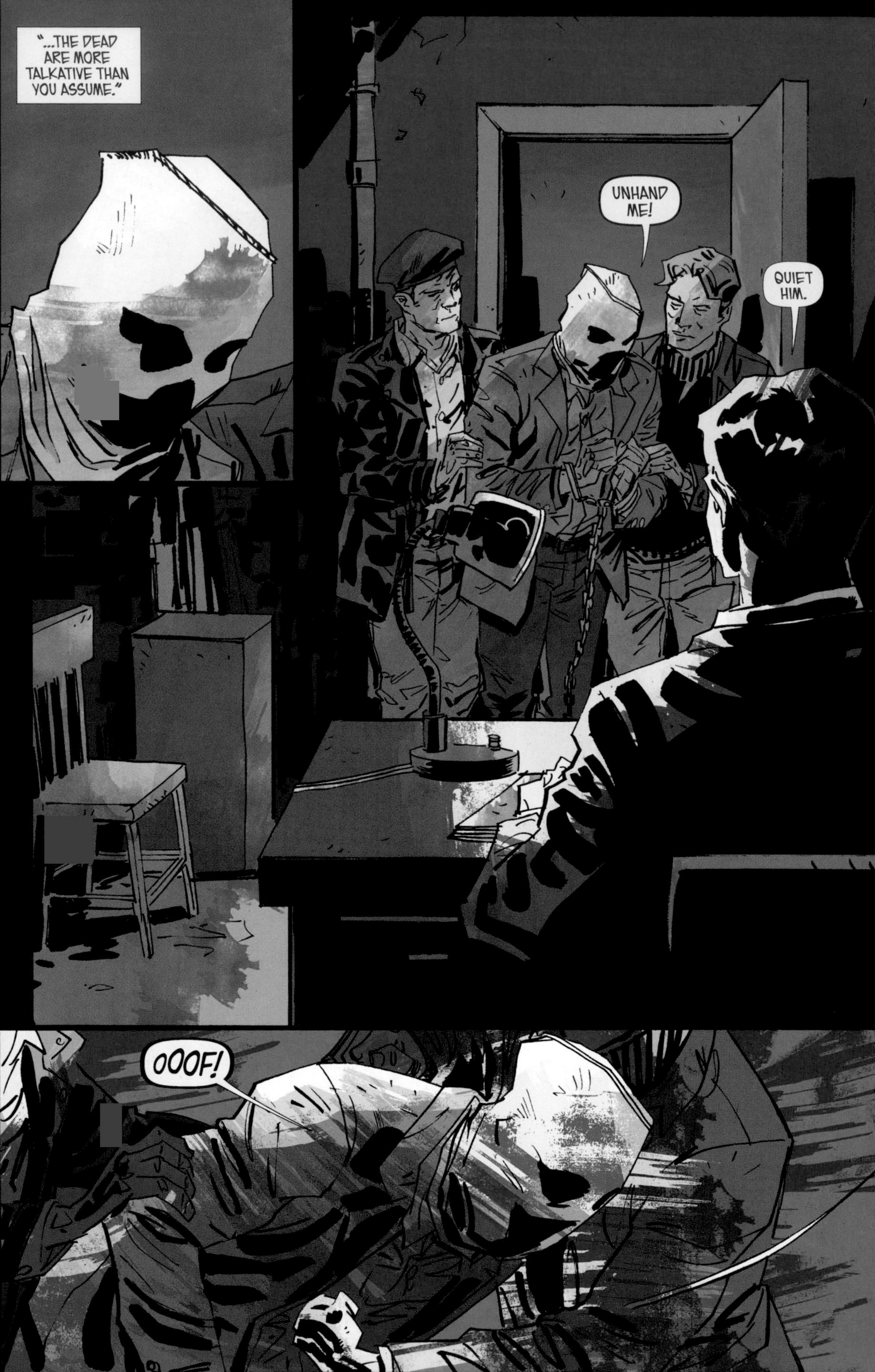
"...THE DEAD ARE MORE TALKATIVE THAN YOU ASSUME."
UNHAND ME!
QUIET HIM.
OOOF!

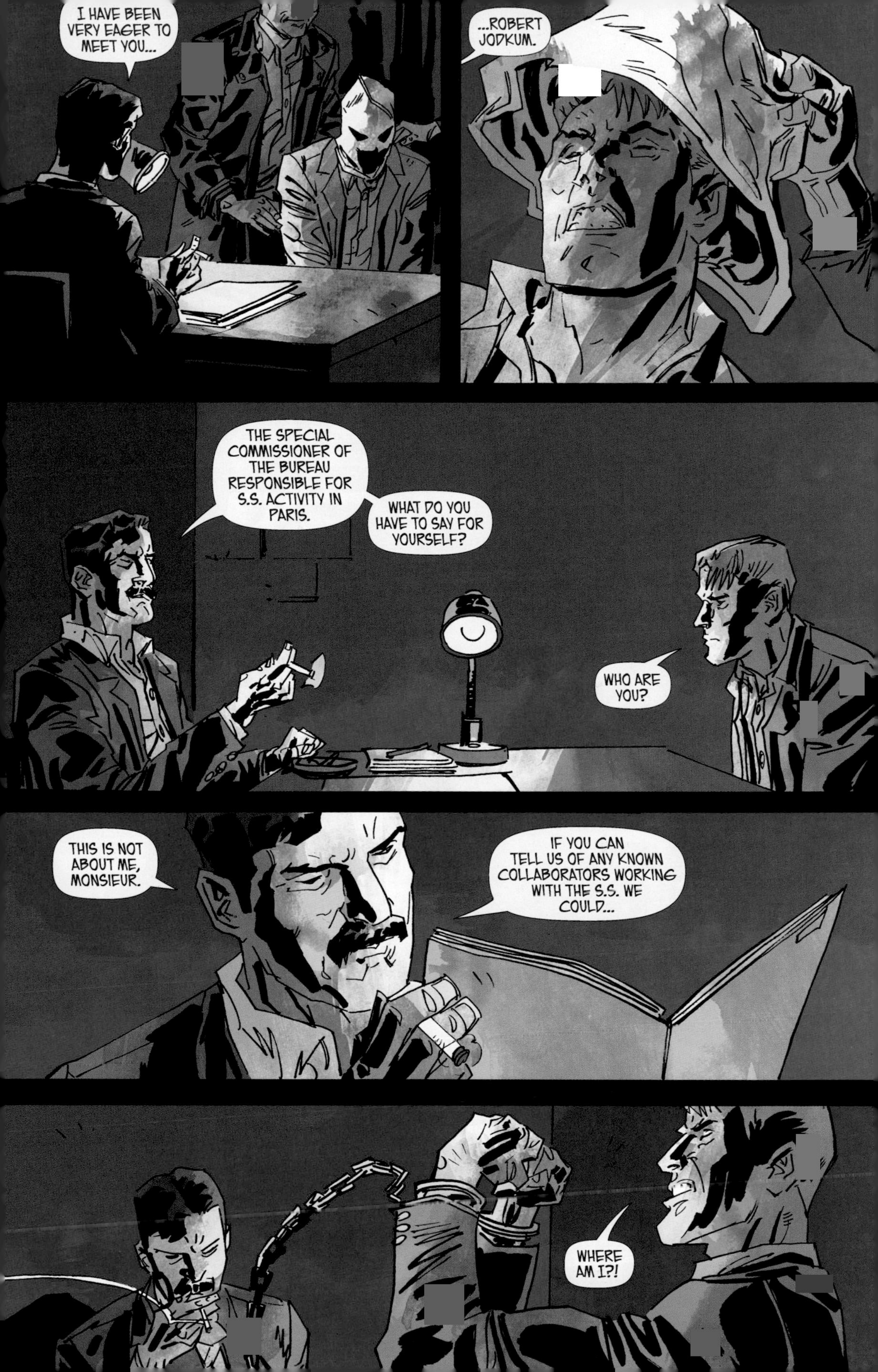
I HAVE BEEN VERY EAGER TO MEET YOU...
...ROBERT JODKUM.
THE SPECIAL COMMISSIONER OF THE BUREAU RESPONSIBLE FOR S.S. ACTIVITY IN PARIS.
WHAT DO YOU HAVE TO SAY FOR YOURSELF?
WHO ARE YOU?
THIS IS NOT ABOUT ME, MONSIEUR.
IF YOU CAN TELL US OF ANY KNOWN COLLABORATORS WORKING WITH THE S.S. WE COULD...
WHERE AM I?!

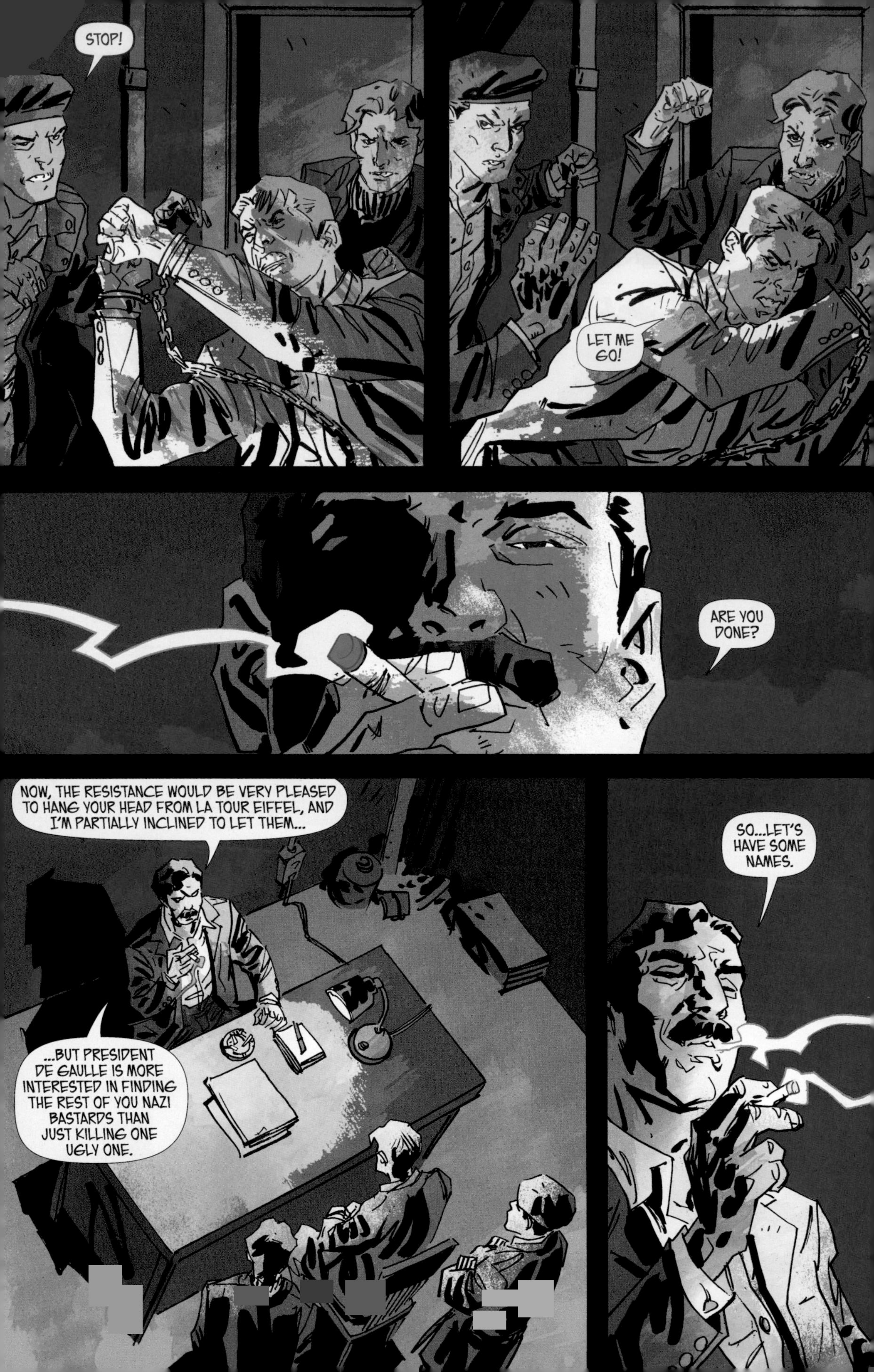
STOP!
LET ME GO!
ARE YOU DONE?
NOW, THE RESISTANCE WOULD BE VERY PLEASED TO HANG YOUR HEAD FROM LA TOUR EIFFEL, AND I'M PARTIALLY INCLINED TO LET THEM...
...BUT PRESIDENT DE GAULLE IS MORE INTERESTED IN FINDING THE REST OF YOU NAZI BASTARDS THAN JUST KILLING ONE UGLY ONE.
SO...LET'S HAVE SOME NAMES.

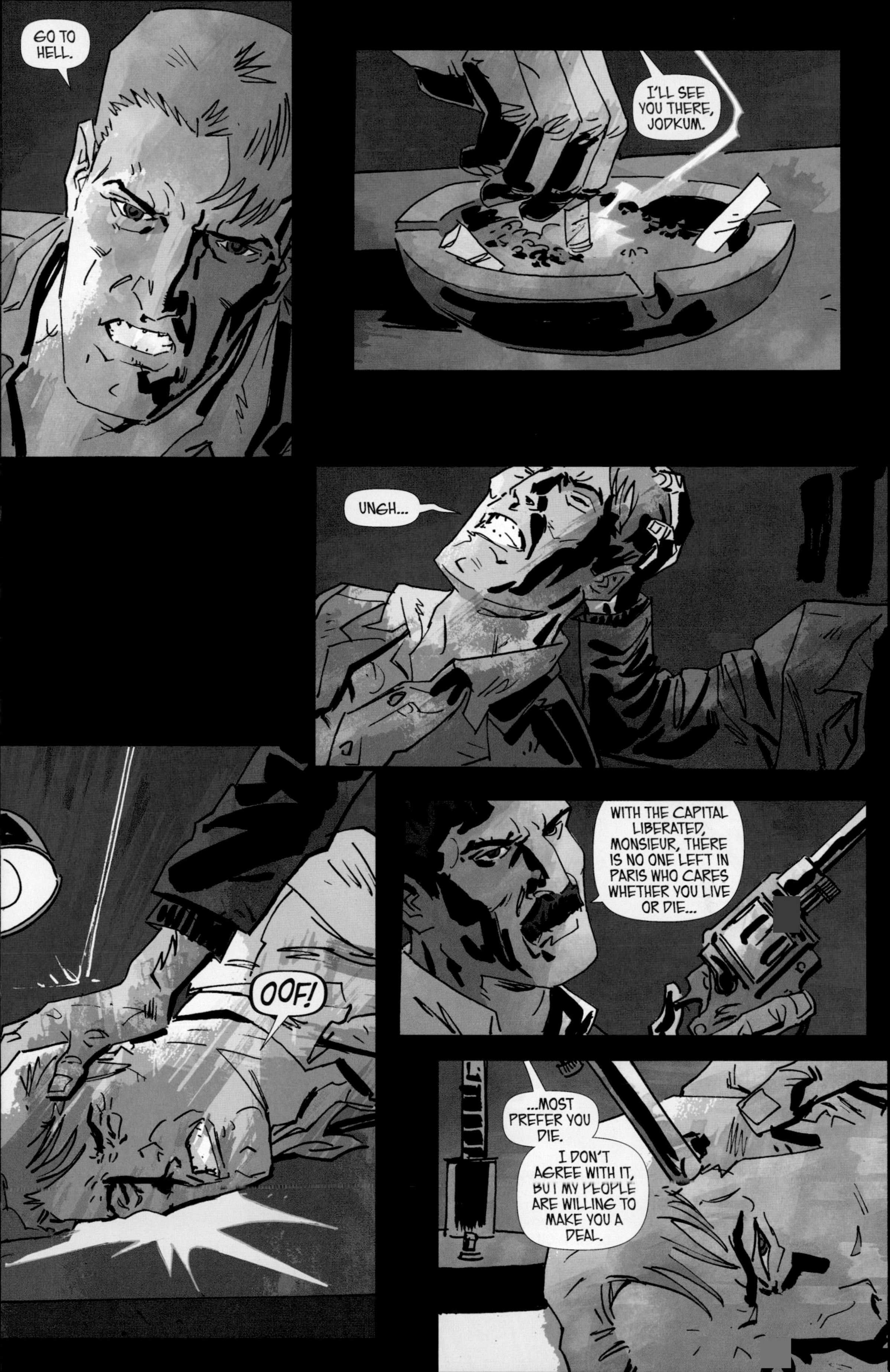
GO TO HELL.
I'LL SEE YOU THERE, JODKUM.
UNGH...
OOF!
WITH THE CAPITAL LIBERATED, MONSIEUR, THERE IS NO ONE LEFT IN PARIS WHO CARES WHETHER YOU LIVE OR DIE...
...MOST PREFER YOU DIE.
I DON'T AGREE WITH IT, BUT MY PEOPLE ARE WILLING TO MAKE YOU A DEAL.

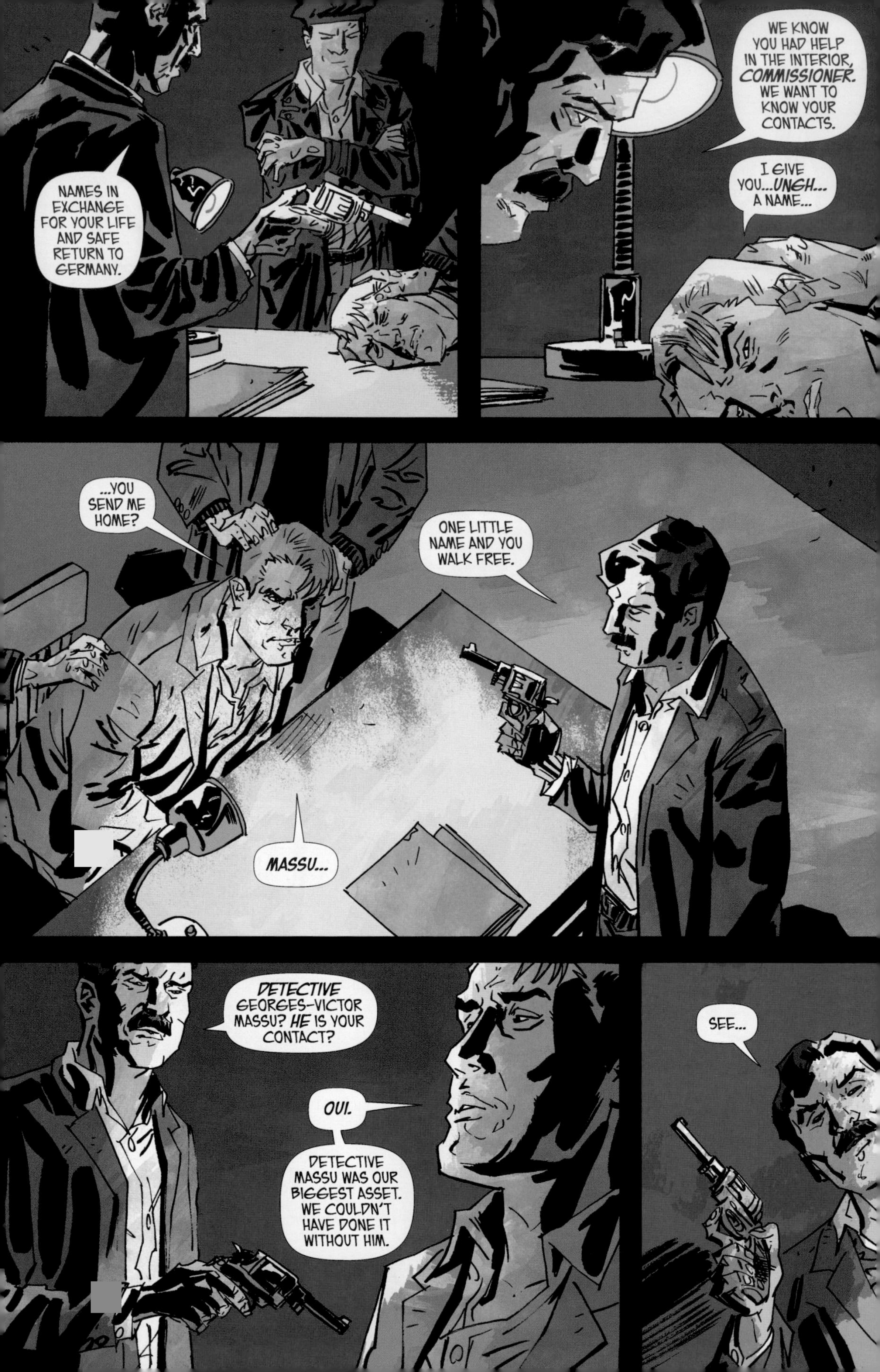
NAMES IN EXCHANGE FOR YOUR LIFE AND SAFE RETURN TO GERMANY.
WE KNOW YOU HAD HELP IN THE INTERIOR, COMMISSIONER. WE WANT TO KNOW YOUR CONTACTS.
I GIVE YOU...UNGH... A NAME...
...YOU SEND ME HOME?
ONE LITTLE NAME AND YOU WALK FREE.
MASSU...
DETECTIVE GEORGES-VICTOR MASSU? HE IS YOUR CONTACT?
OUI.
DETECTIVE MASSU WAS OUR BIGGEST ASSET. WE COULDN'T HAVE DONE IT WITHOUT HIM.
SEE...

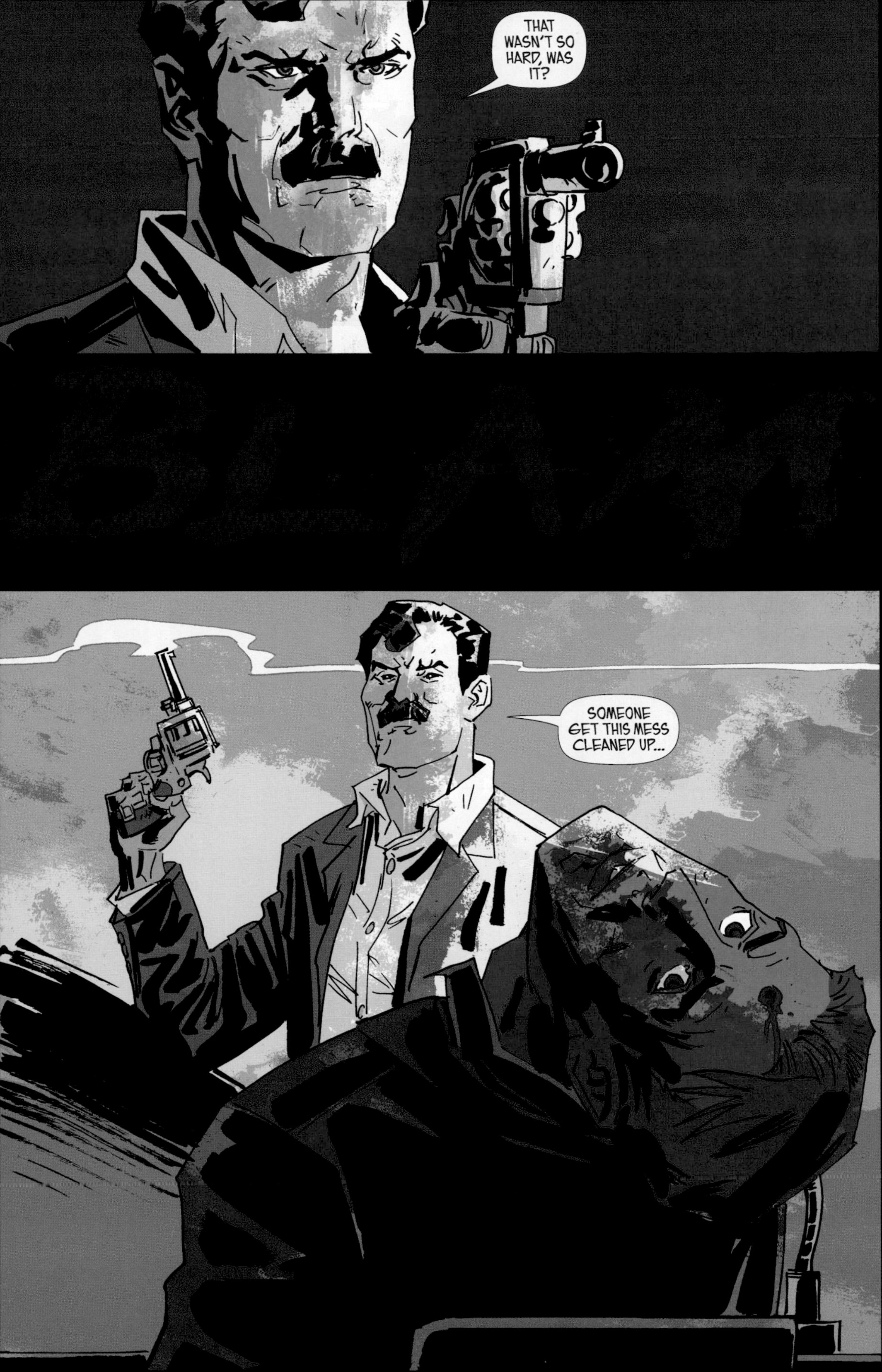
THAT WASN'T SO HARD, WAS IT?
BLAM!
SOMEONE GET THIS MESS CLEANED UP...

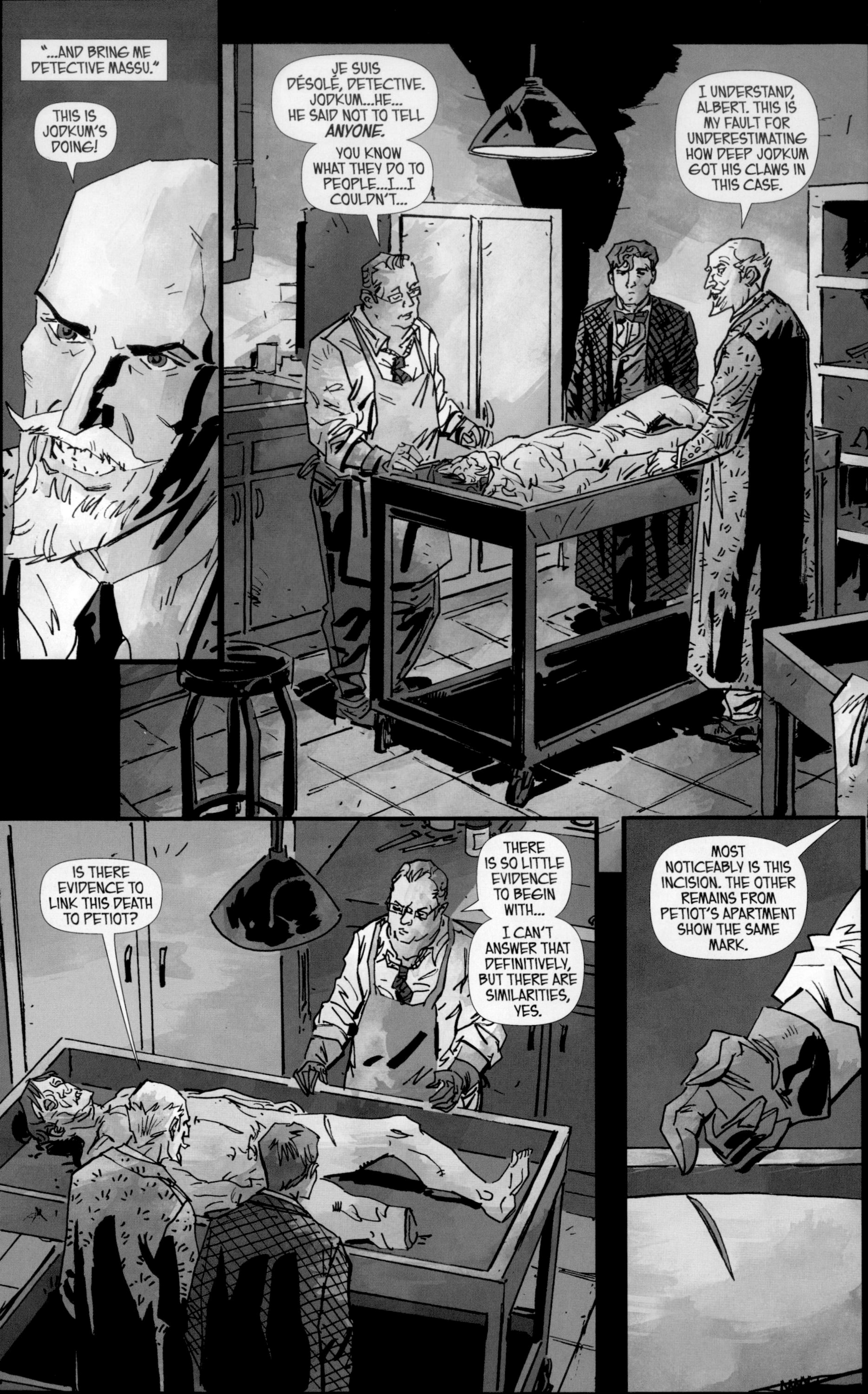

"...AND BRING ME DETECTIVE MASSU."
THIS IS JODKUM'S DOING!
JE SUIS DÉSOLÉ, DETECTIVE. JODKUM...HE... HE SAID NOT TO TELL *ANYONE.*
YOU KNOW WHAT THEY DO TO PEOPLE...I...I COULDN'T...
I UNDERSTAND, ALBERT. THIS IS MY FAULT FOR UNDERESTIMATING HOW DEEP JODKUM GOT HIS CLAWS IN THIS CASE.
IS THERE EVIDENCE TO LINK THIS DEATH TO PETIOT?
THERE IS SO LITTLE EVIDENCE TO BEGIN WITH...
I CAN'T ANSWER THAT DEFINITIVELY, BUT THERE ARE SIMILARITIES, YES.
MOST NOTICEABLY IS THIS INCISION. THE OTHER REMAINS FROM PETIOT'S APARTMENT SHOW THE SAME MARK.

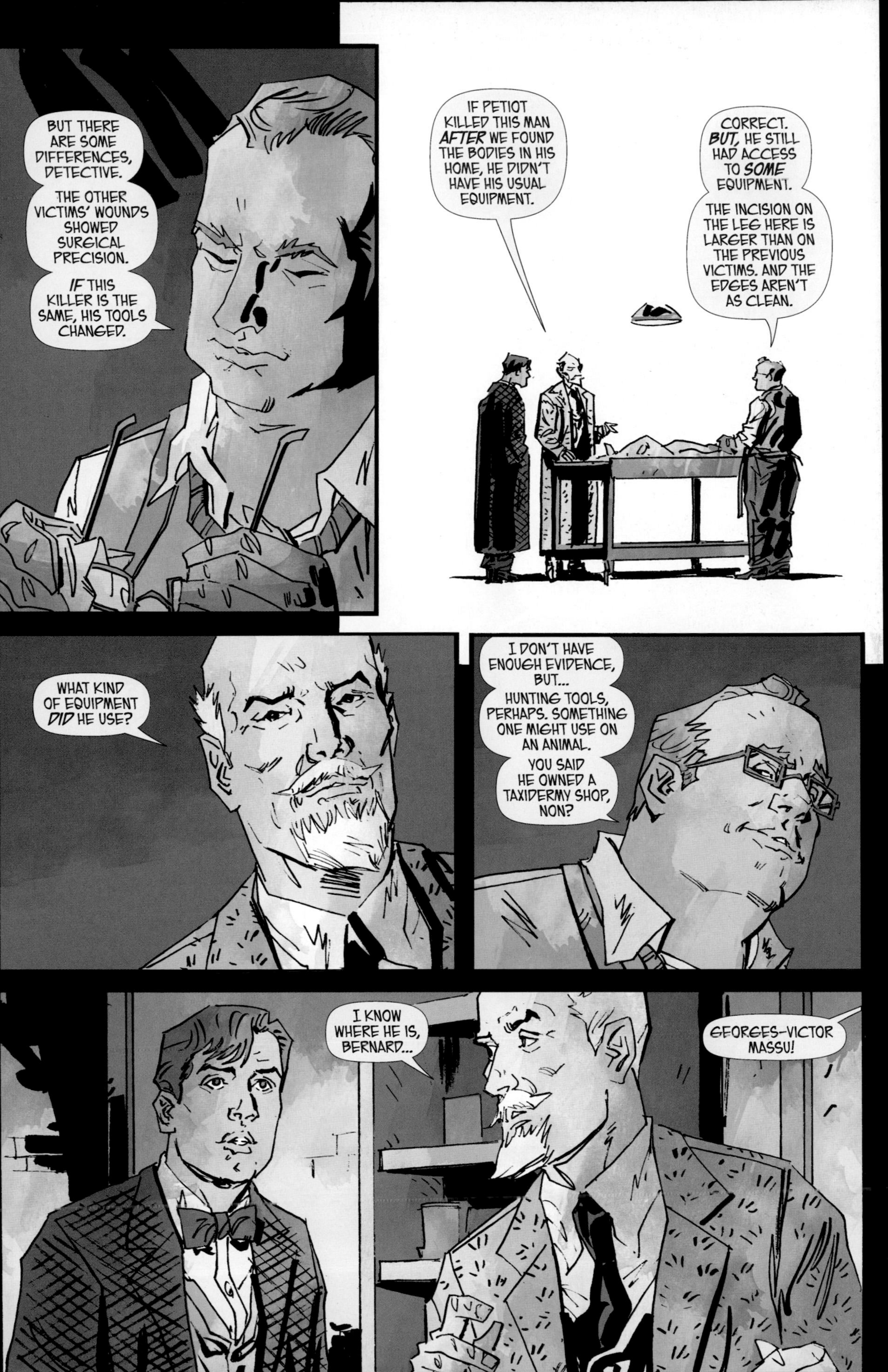
BUT THERE ARE SOME DIFFERENCES, DETECTIVE.
THE OTHER VICTIMS' WOUNDS SHOWED SURGICAL PRECISION.
IF THIS KILLER IS THE SAME, HIS TOOLS CHANGED.
IF PETIOT KILLED THIS MAN AFTER WE FOUND THE BODIES IN HIS HOME, HE DIDN'T HAVE HIS USUAL EQUIPMENT.
CORRECT. BUT, HE STILL HAD ACCESS TO SOME EQUIPMENT.
THE INCISION ON THE LEG HERE IS LARGER THAN ON THE PREVIOUS VICTIMS. AND THE EDGES AREN'T AS CLEAN.
WHAT KIND OF EQUIPMENT DID HE USE?
I DON'T HAVE ENOUGH EVIDENCE, BUT...
HUNTING TOOLS, PERHAPS. SOMETHING ONE MIGHT USE ON AN ANIMAL.
YOU SAID HE OWNED A TAXIDERMY SHOP, NON?
I KNOW WHERE HE IS, BERNARD...
GEORGES-VICTOR MASSU!

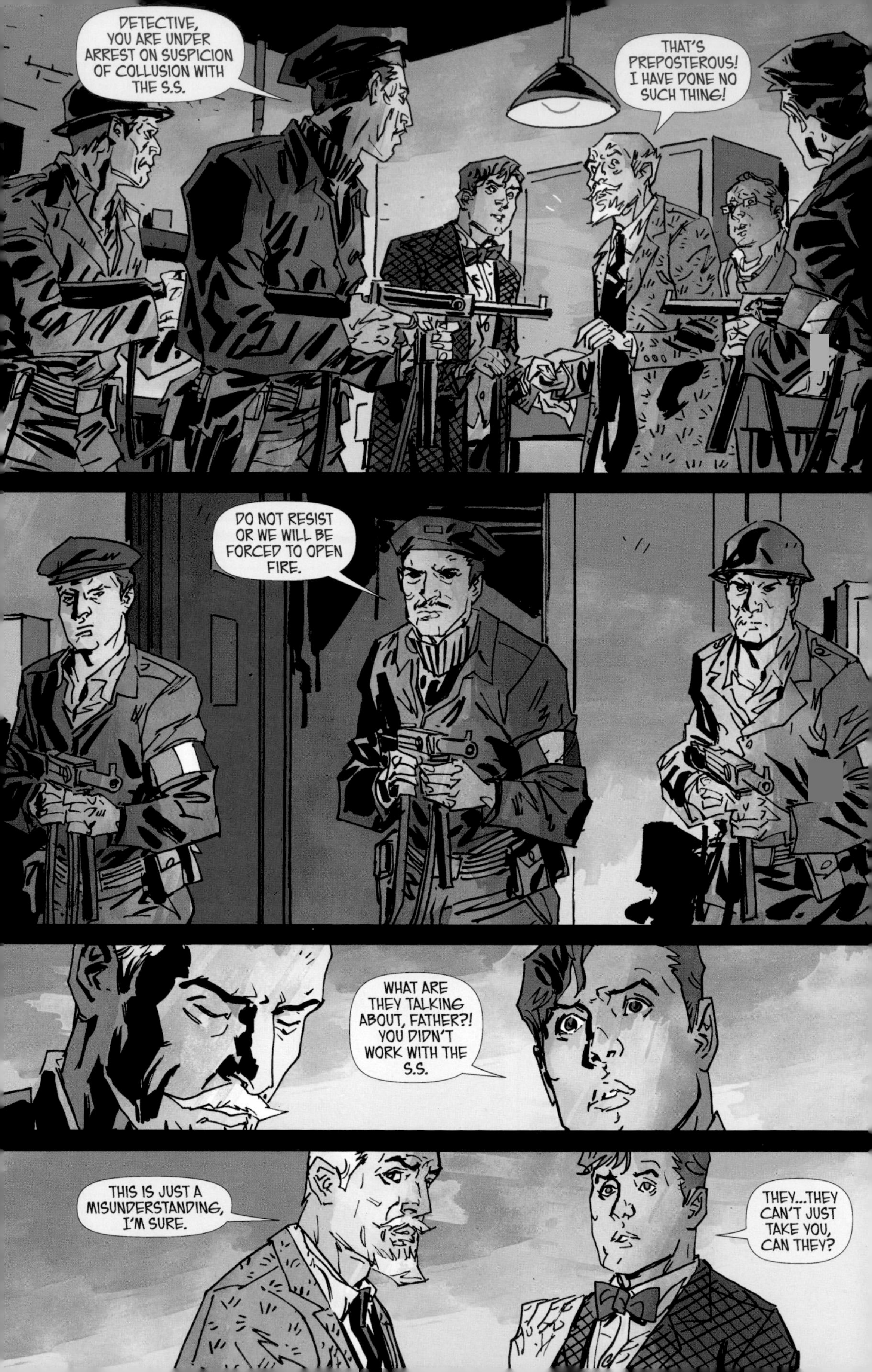
DETECTIVE, YOU ARE UNDER ARREST ON SUSPICION OF COLLUSION WITH THE S.S.
THAT'S PREPOSTEROUS! I HAVE DONE NO SUCH THING!
DO NOT RESIST OR WE WILL BE FORCED TO OPEN FIRE.
WHAT ARE THEY TALKING ABOUT, FATHER?! YOU DIDN'T WORK WITH THE S.S.
THIS IS JUST A MISUNDERSTANDING, I'M SURE.
THEY...THEY CAN'T JUST TAKE YOU, CAN THEY?

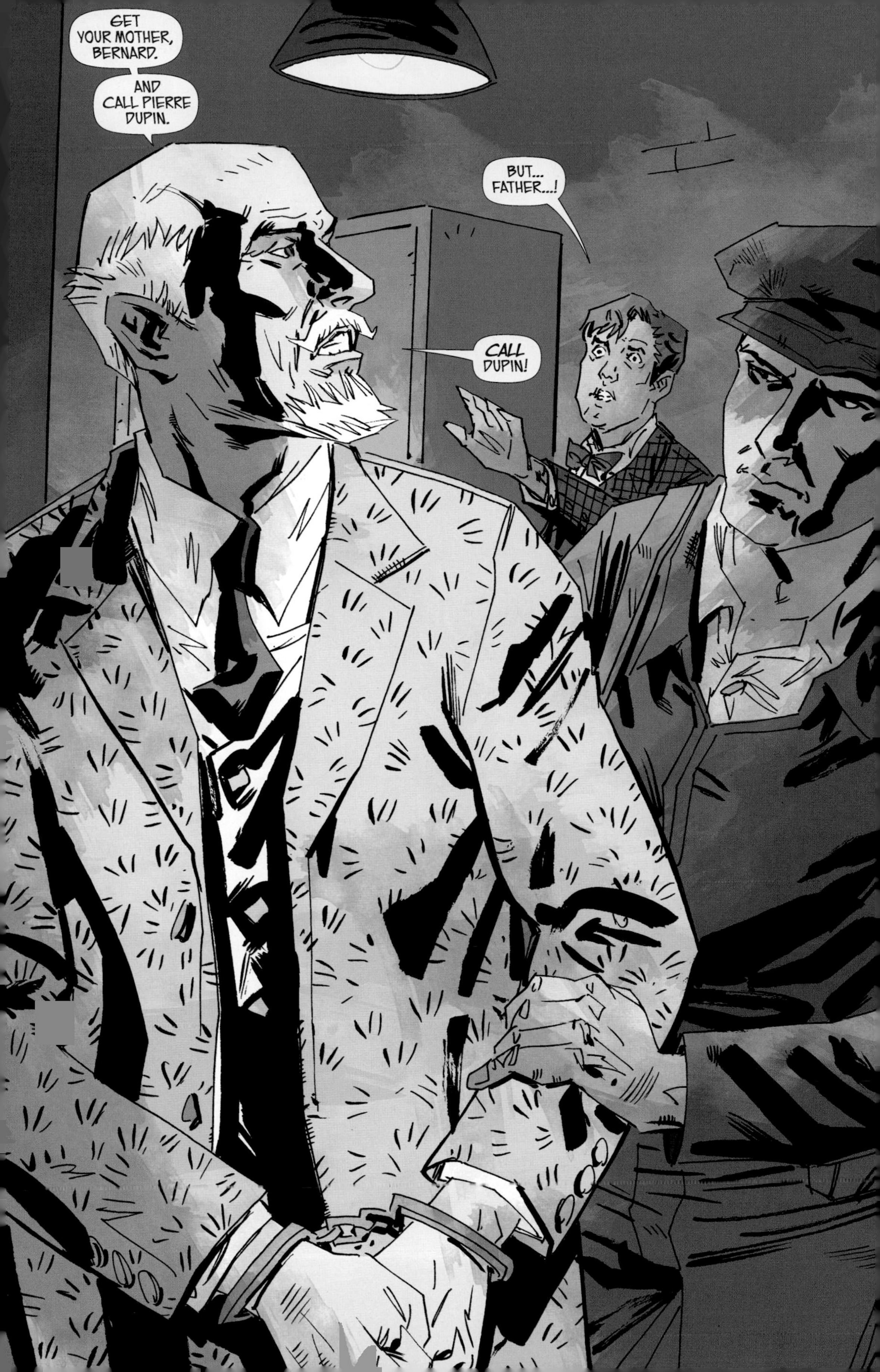
GET YOUR MOTHER, BERNARD.
AND CALL PIERRE DUPIN.
BUT... FATHER...!
CALL DUPIN!

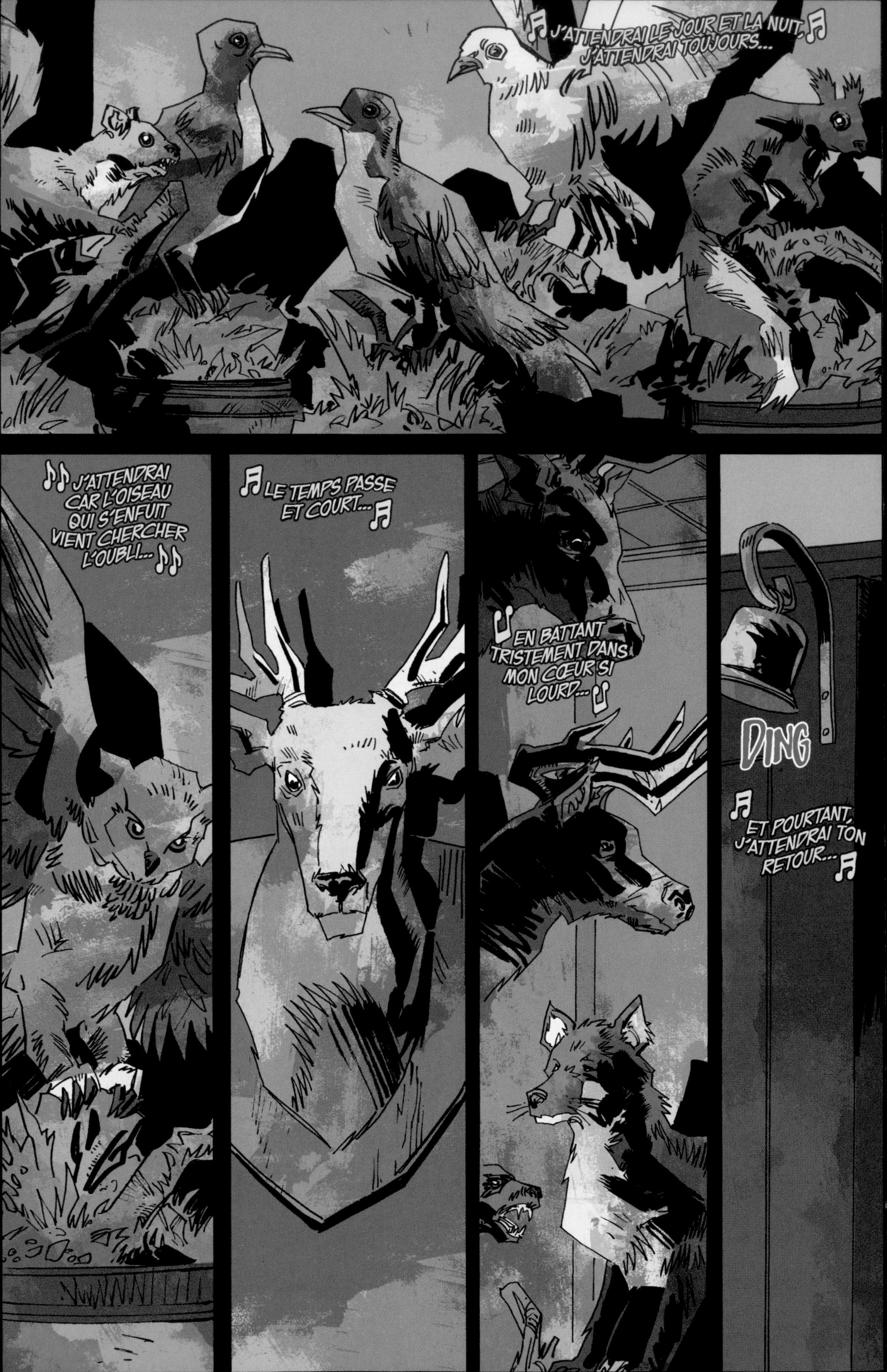
J'ATTENDRAI LE JOUR ET LA NUIT, J'ATTENDRAI TOUJOURS...
J'ATTENDRAI CAR L'OISEAU QUI S'ENFUIT VIENT CHERCHER L'OUBLI...
LE TEMPS PASSE ET COURT...
EN BATTANT TRISTEMENT DANS MON CŒUR SI LOURD...
DING
ET POURTANT, J'ATTENDRAI TON RETOUR...

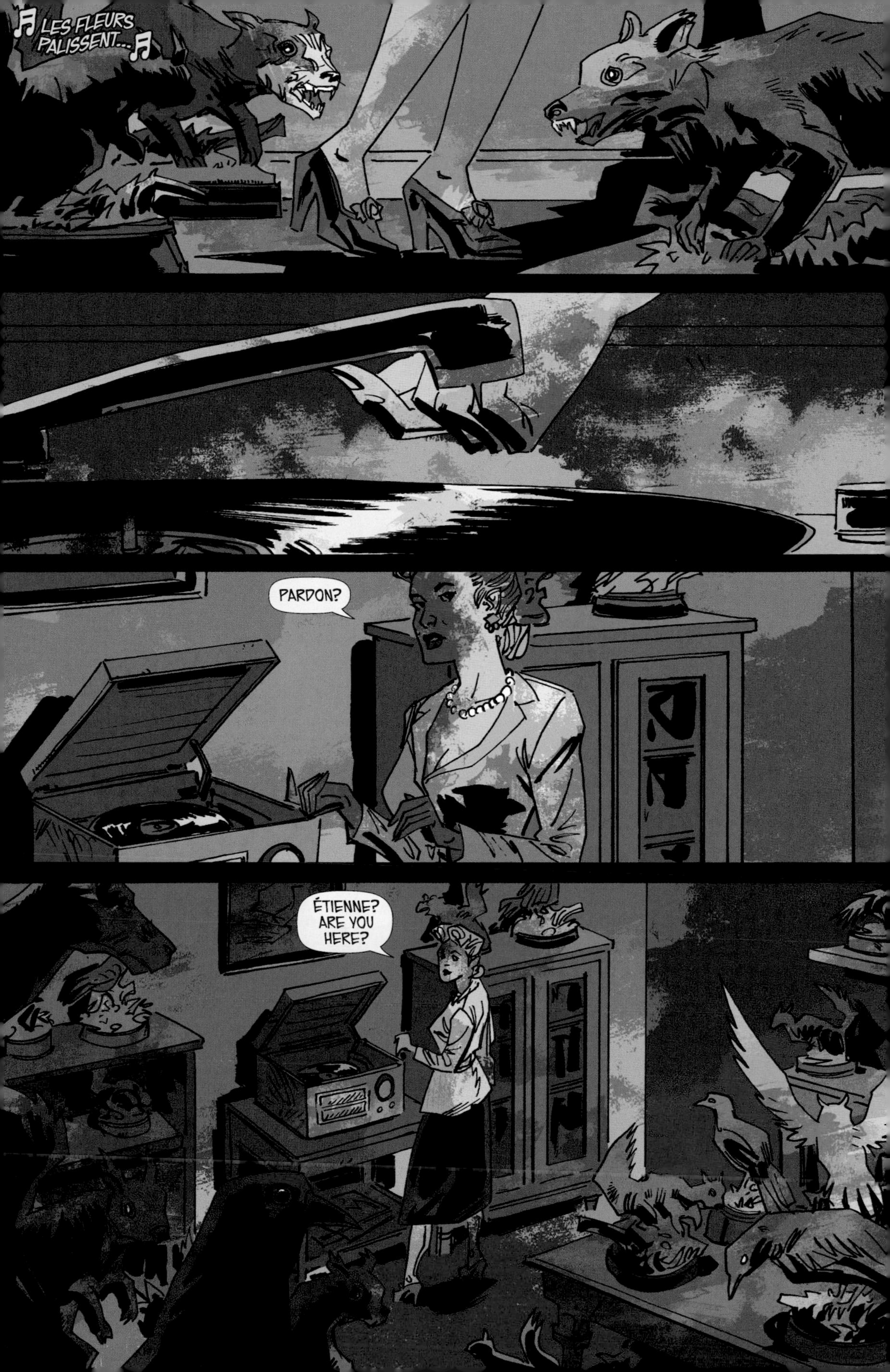
LES FLEURS PALISSENT...
PARDON?
ÉTIENNE? ARE YOU HERE?

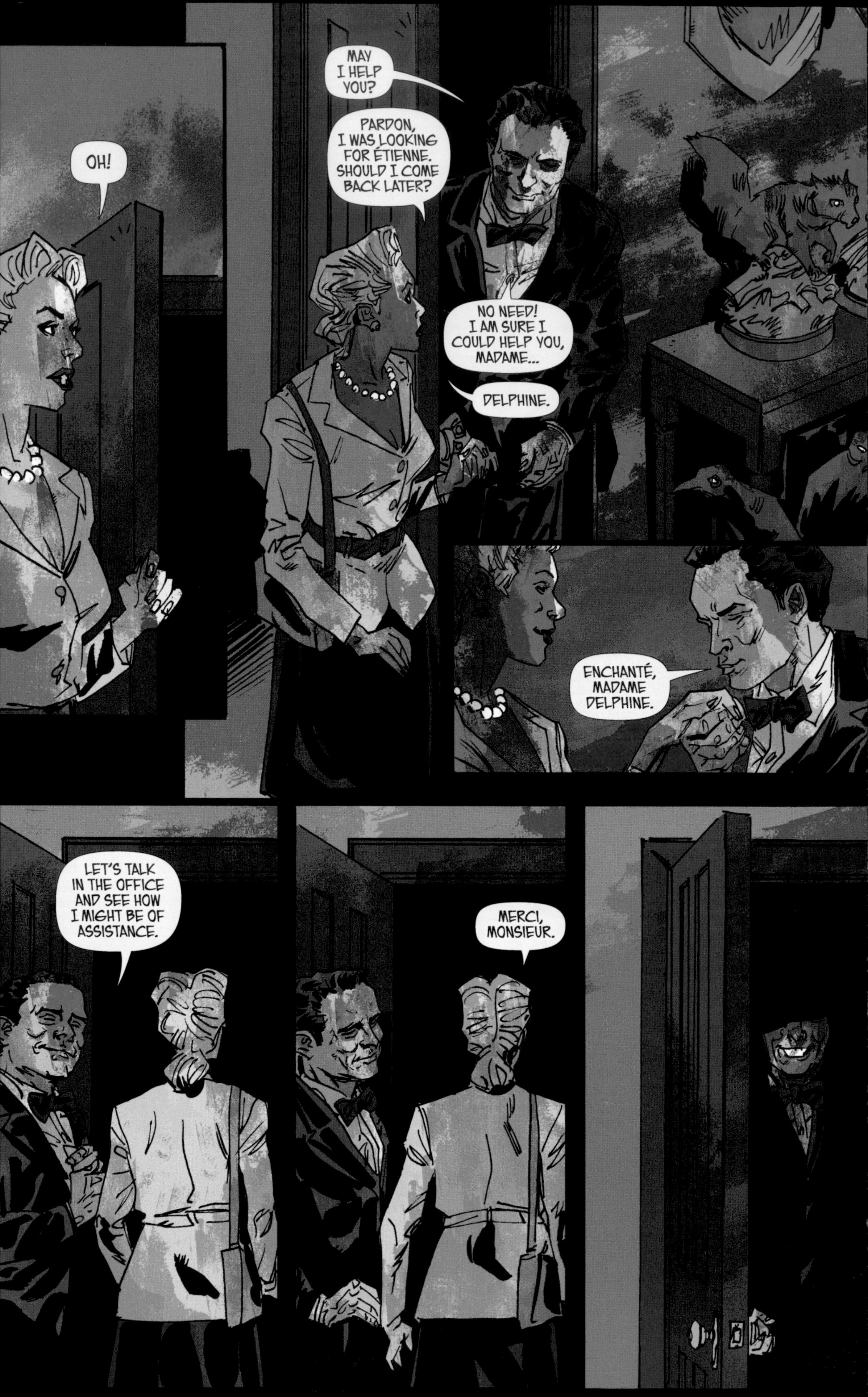
OH!
MAY I HELP YOU?
PARDON, I WAS LOOKING FOR ÉTIENNE. SHOULD I COME BACK LATER?
NO NEED! I AM SURE I COULD HELP YOU, MADAME...
DELPHINE.
ENCHANTÉ, MADAME DELPHINE.
LET'S TALK IN THE OFFICE AND SEE HOW I MIGHT BE OF ASSISTANCE.
MERCI, MONSIEUR.

Chapter 5: Le Hasard Vaincu (Beating Chance)

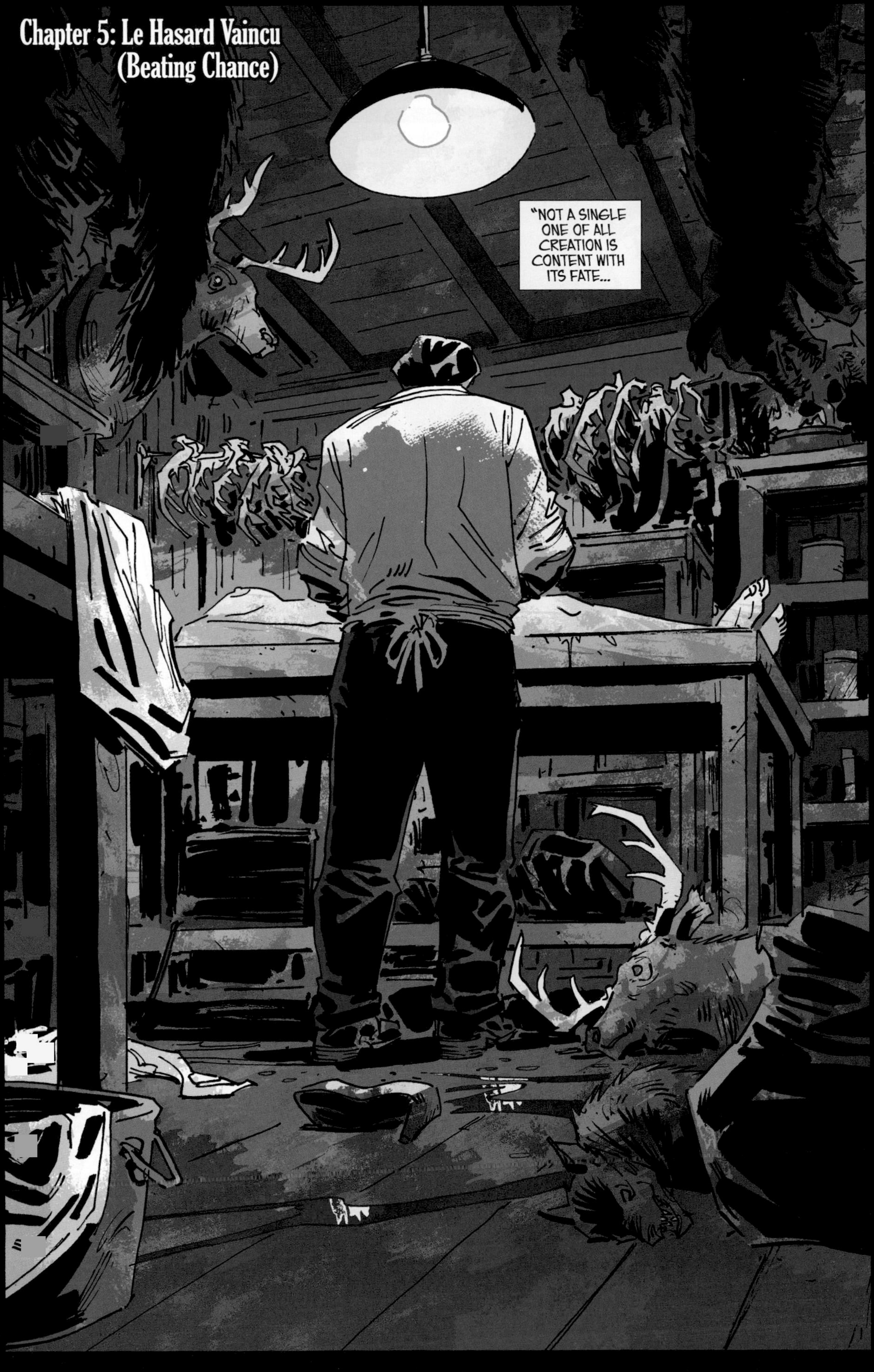
"NOT A SINGLE ONE OF ALL CREATION IS CONTENT WITH ITS FATE...

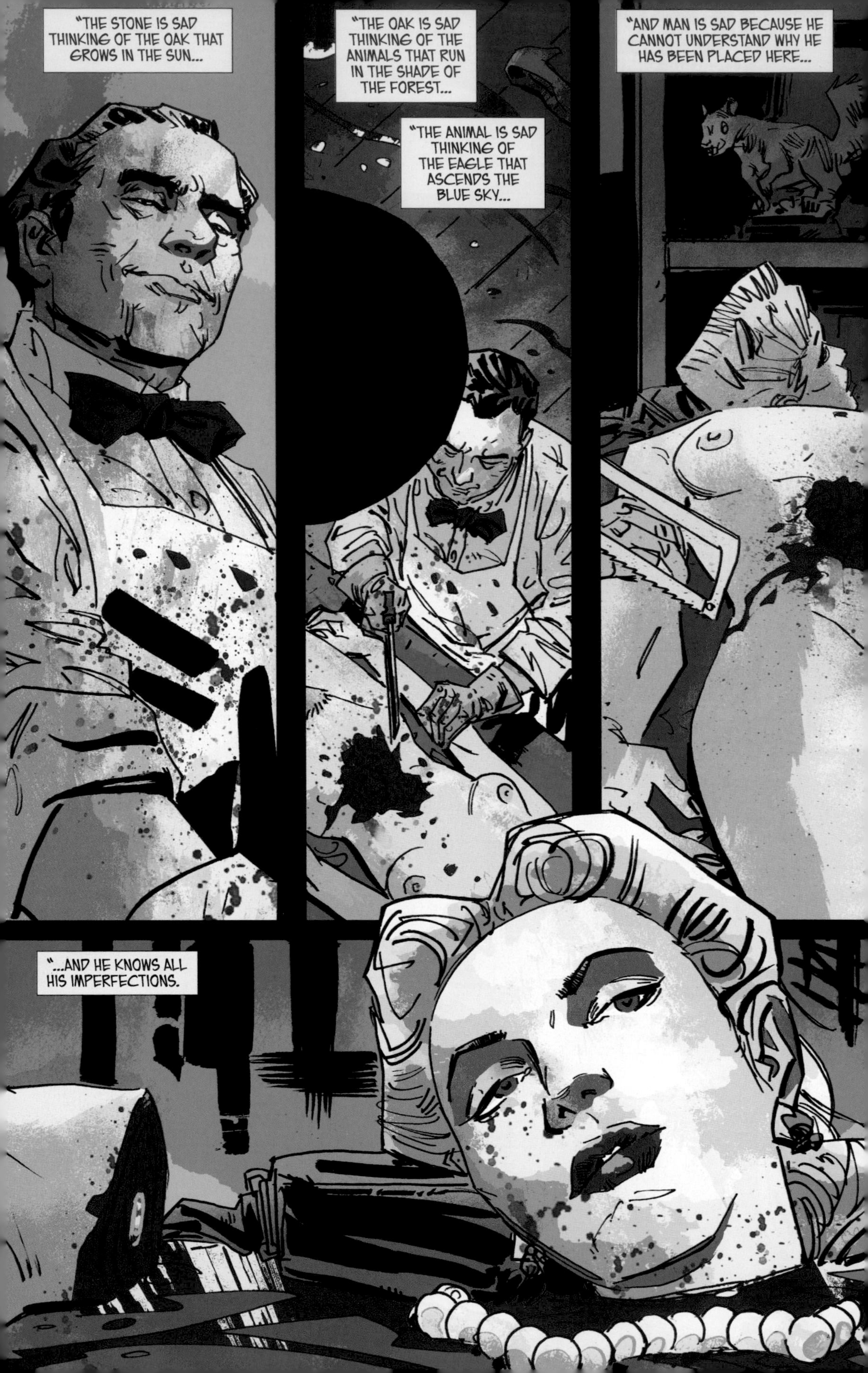
"THE STONE IS SAD THINKING OF THE OAK THAT GROWS IN THE SUN...
"THE OAK IS SAD THINKING OF THE ANIMALS THAT RUN IN THE SHADE OF THE FOREST...
"THE ANIMAL IS SAD THINKING OF THE EAGLE THAT ASCENDS THE BLUE SKY...
"AND MAN IS SAD BECAUSE HE CANNOT UNDERSTAND WHY HE HAS BEEN PLACED HERE...
"...AND HE KNOWS ALL HIS IMPERFECTIONS.

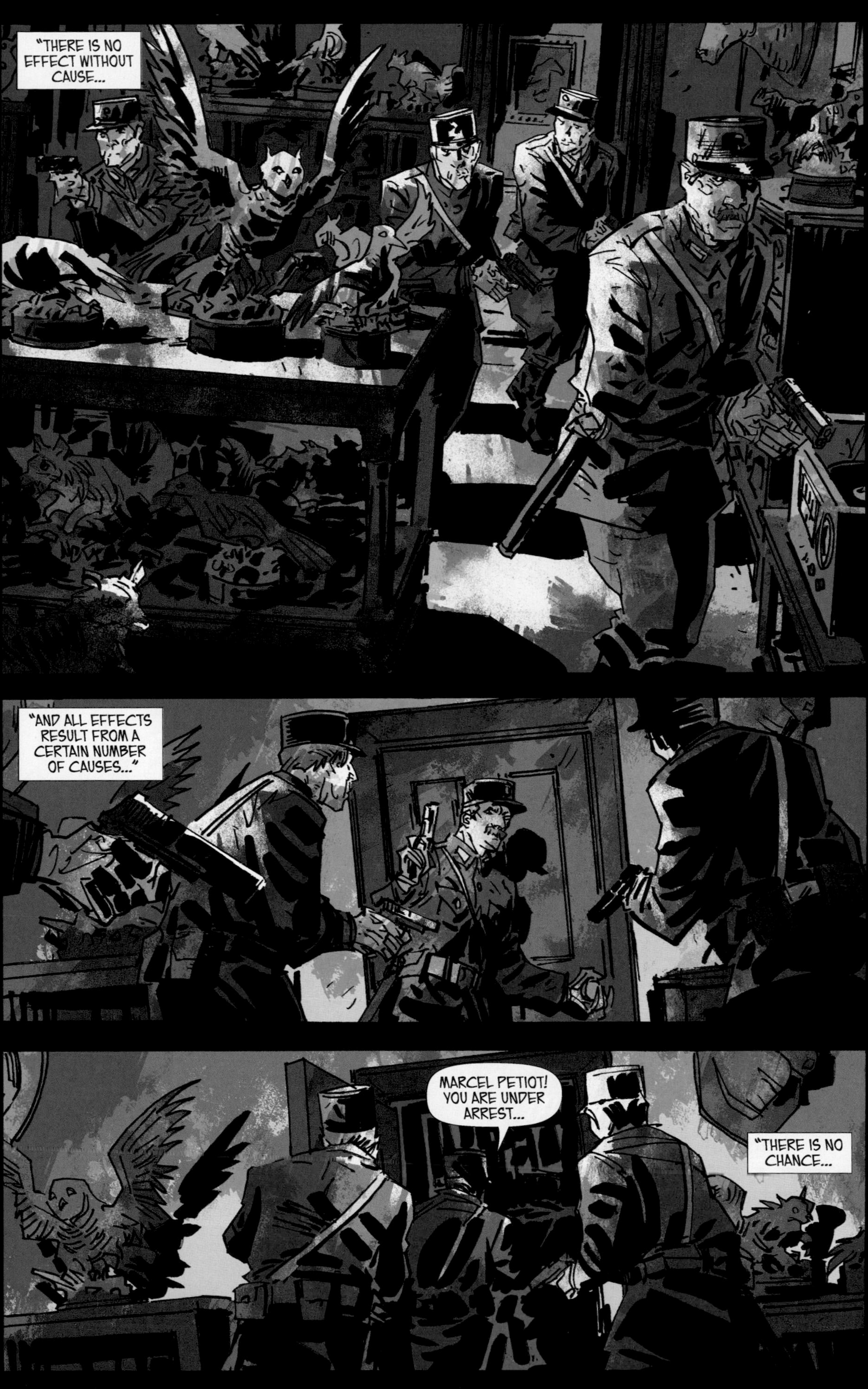
"THERE IS NO EFFECT WITHOUT CAUSE...
"AND ALL EFFECTS RESULT FROM A CERTAIN NUMBER OF CAUSES..."
MARCEL PETIOT! YOU ARE UNDER ARREST...
"THERE IS NO CHANCE...

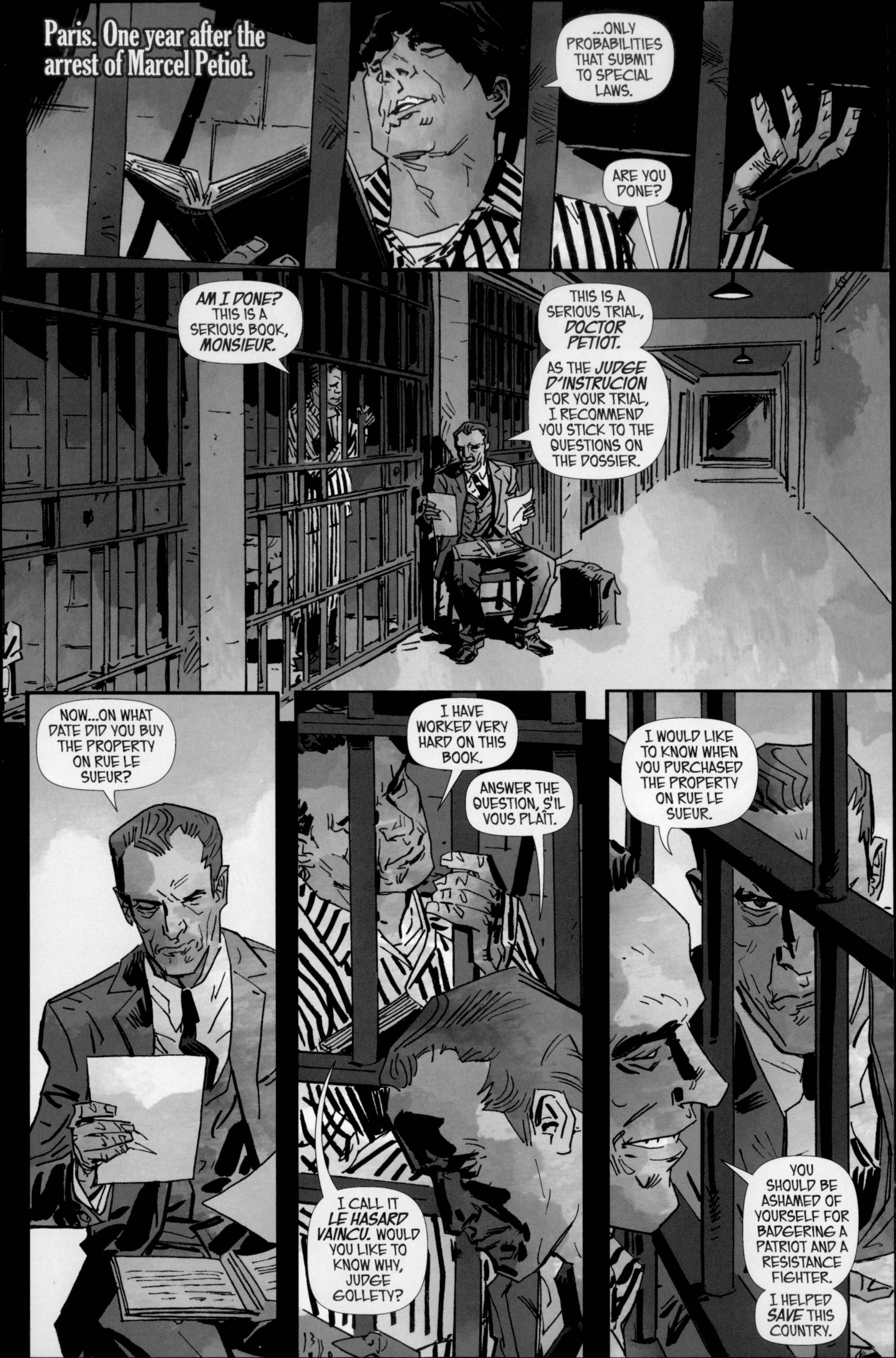
Paris. One year after the arrest of Marcel Petiot.
...ONLY PROBABILITIES THAT SUBMIT TO SPECIAL LAWS.
ARE YOU DONE?
AM I DONE? THIS IS A SERIOUS BOOK, MONSIEUR.
THIS IS A SERIOUS TRIAL, DOCTOR PETIOT.
AS THE JUDGE D'INSTRUCION FOR YOUR TRIAL, I RECOMMEND YOU STICK TO THE QUESTIONS ON THE DOSSIER.
NOW...ON WHAT DATE DID YOU BUY THE PROPERTY ON RUE LE SUEUR?
I HAVE WORKED VERY HARD ON THIS BOOK.
ANSWER THE QUESTION, S'IL VOUS PLAÎT.
I CALL IT LE HASARD VAINCU. WOULD YOU LIKE TO KNOW WHY, JUDGE GOLLETY?
I WOULD LIKE TO KNOW WHEN YOU PURCHASED THE PROPERTY ON RUE LE SUEUR.
YOU SHOULD BE ASHAMED OF YOURSELF FOR BADGERING A PATRIOT AND A RESISTANCE FIGHTER.
I HELPED SAVE THIS COUNTRY.

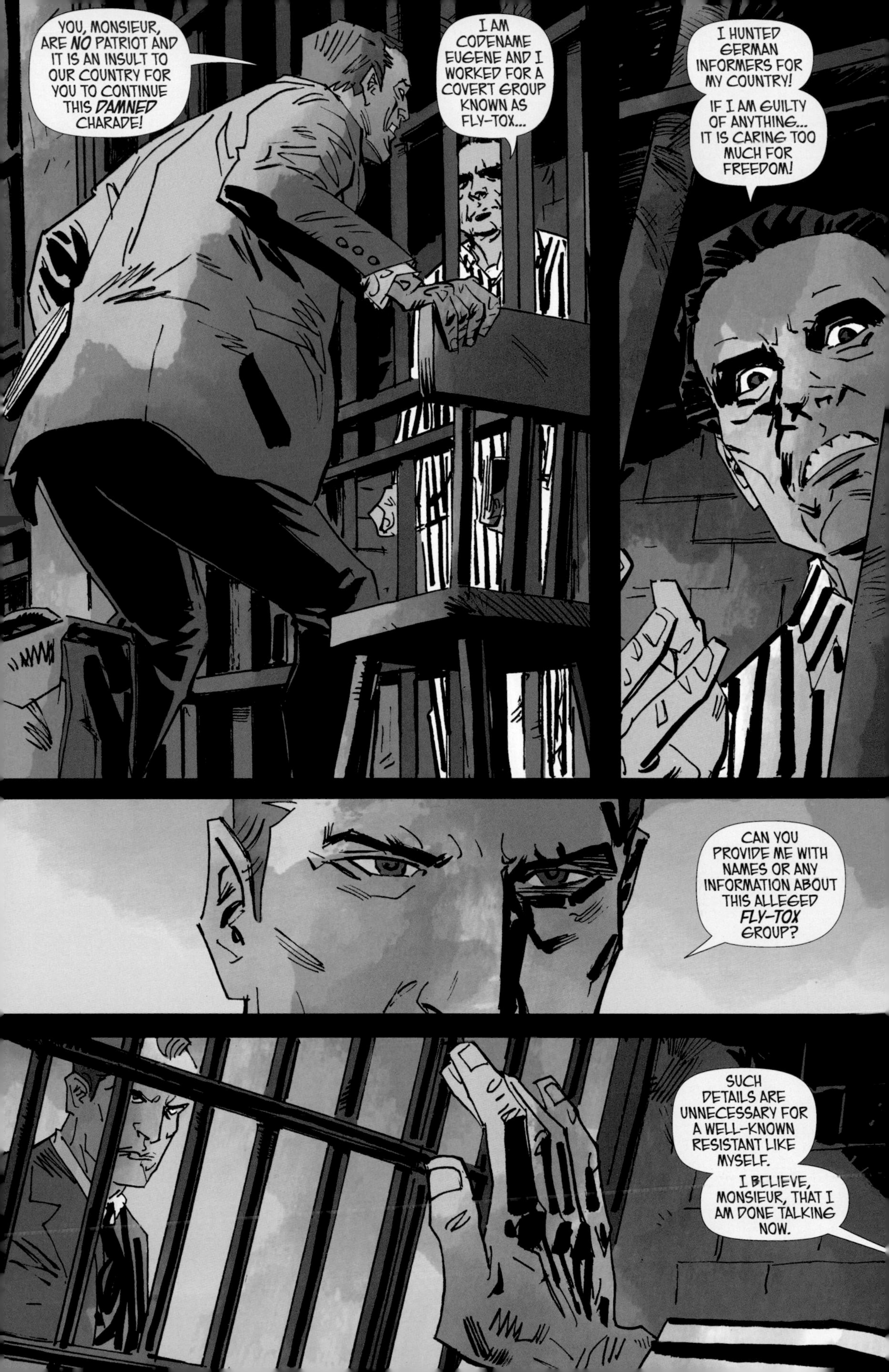

YOU, MONSIEUR, ARE NO PATRIOT AND IT IS AN INSULT TO OUR COUNTRY FOR YOU TO CONTINUE THIS DAMNED CHARADE!
I AM CODENAME EUGENE AND I WORKED FOR A COVERT GROUP KNOWN AS FLY-TOX...
I HUNTED GERMAN INFORMERS FOR MY COUNTRY!
IF I AM GUILTY OF ANYTHING... IT IS CARING TOO MUCH FOR FREEDOM!
CAN YOU PROVIDE ME WITH NAMES OR ANY INFORMATION ABOUT THIS ALLEGED FLY-TOX GROUP?
SUCH DETAILS ARE UNNECESSARY FOR A WELL-KNOWN RESISTANT LIKE MYSELF.
I BELIEVE, MONSIEUR, THAT I AM DONE TALKING NOW.

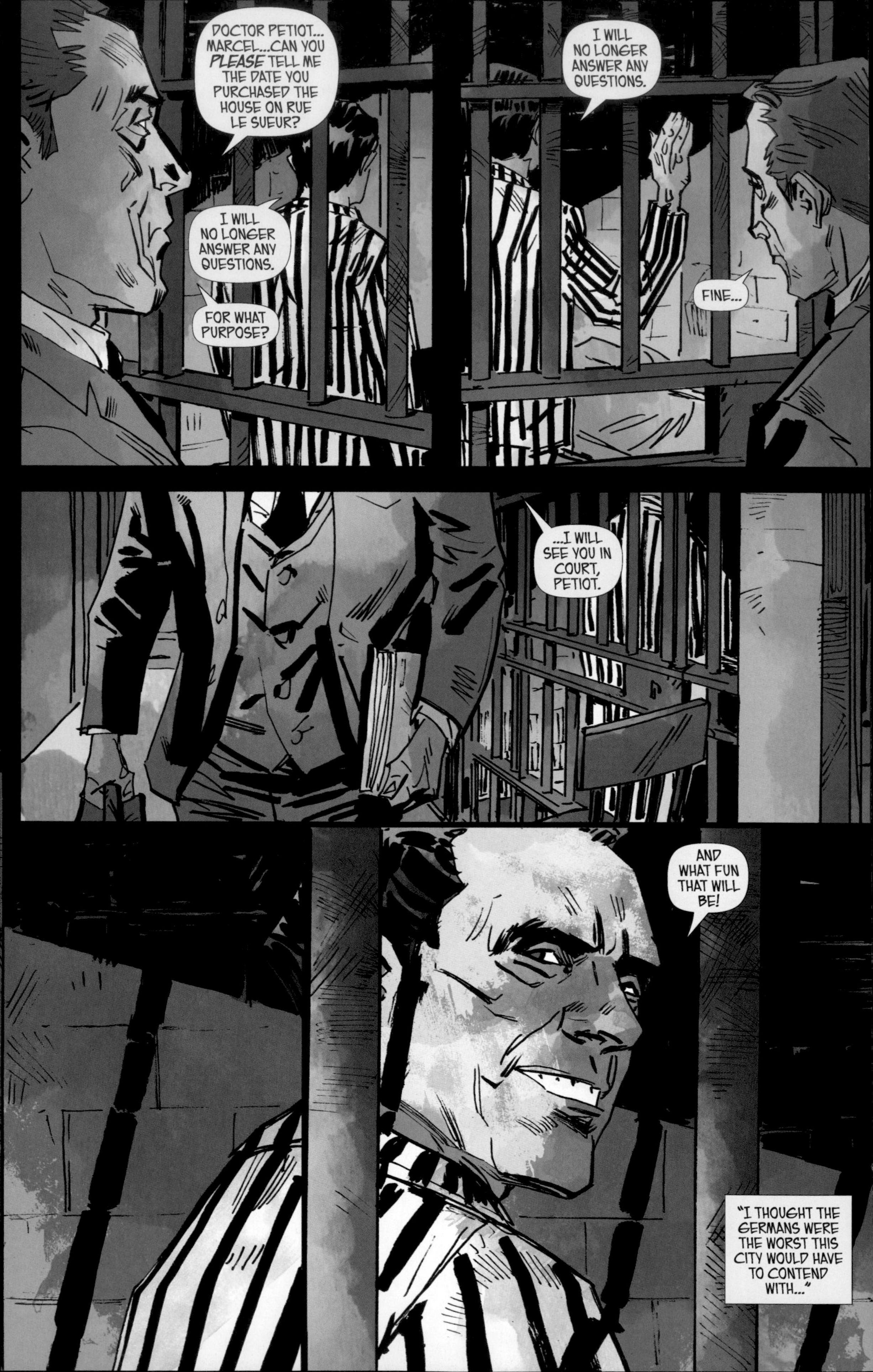
DOCTOR PETIOT... MARCEL...CAN YOU PLEASE TELL ME THE DATE YOU PURCHASED THE HOUSE ON RUE LE SUEUR?
I WILL NO LONGER ANSWER ANY QUESTIONS.
FOR WHAT PURPOSE?
I WILL NO LONGER ANSWER ANY QUESTIONS.
FINE...
...I WILL SEE YOU IN COURT, PETIOT.
AND WHAT FUN THAT WILL BE!
"I THOUGHT THE GERMANS WERE THE WORST THIS CITY WOULD HAVE TO CONTEND WITH..."

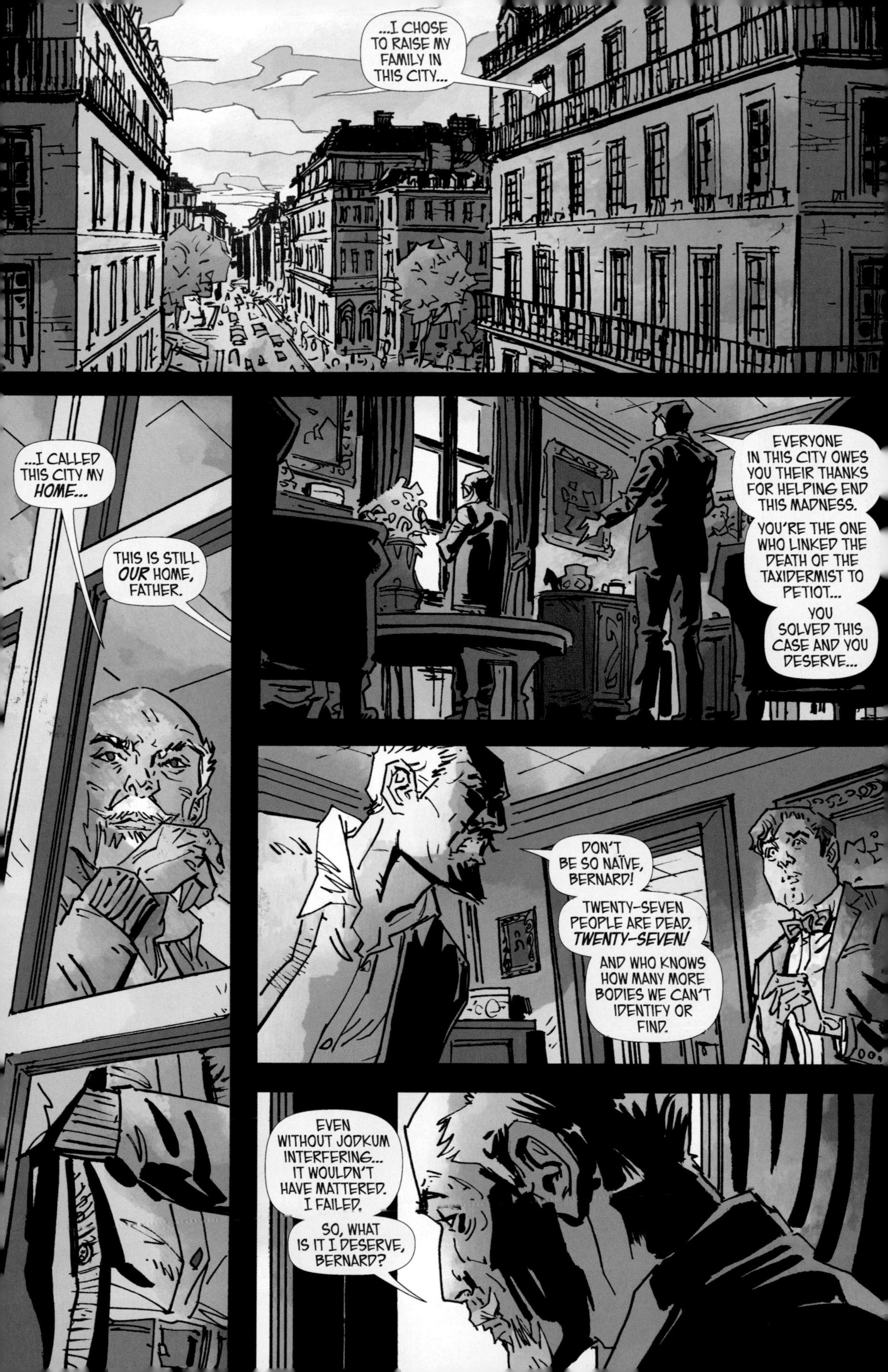
...I CHOSE TO RAISE MY FAMILY IN THIS CITY...
...I CALLED THIS CITY MY *HOME*...
THIS IS STILL *OUR* HOME, FATHER.
EVERYONE IN THIS CITY OWES YOU THEIR THANKS FOR HELPING END THIS MADNESS.
YOU'RE THE ONE WHO LINKED THE DEATH OF THE TAXIDERMIST TO PETIOT...
YOU SOLVED THIS CASE AND YOU DESERVE...
DON'T BE SO NAÏVE, BERNARD!
TWENTY-SEVEN PEOPLE ARE DEAD. *TWENTY-SEVEN!*
AND WHO KNOWS HOW MANY MORE BODIES WE CAN'T IDENTIFY OR FIND.
EVEN WITHOUT JODKUM INTERFERING... IT WOULDN'T HAVE MATTERED. I FAILED.
SO, WHAT IS IT I DESERVE, BERNARD?

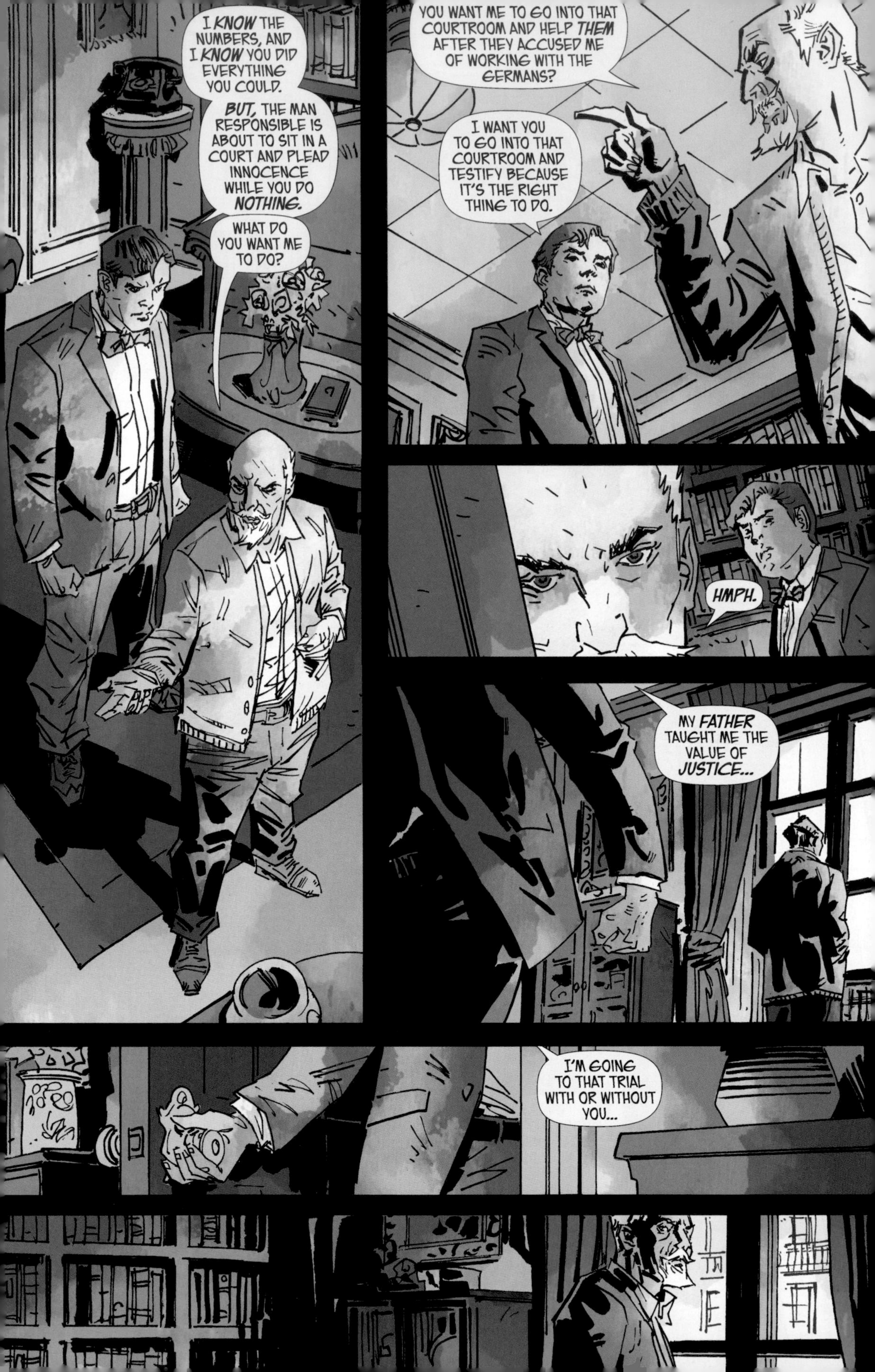
I KNOW THE NUMBERS, AND I KNOW YOU DID EVERYTHING YOU COULD.
BUT, THE MAN RESPONSIBLE IS ABOUT TO SIT IN A COURT AND PLEAD INNOCENCE WHILE YOU DO NOTHING.
WHAT DO YOU WANT ME TO DO?
YOU WANT ME TO GO INTO THAT COURTROOM AND HELP THEM AFTER THEY ACCUSED ME OF WORKING WITH THE GERMANS?
I WANT YOU TO GO INTO THAT COURTROOM AND TESTIFY BECAUSE IT'S THE RIGHT THING TO DO.
HMPH.
MY FATHER TAUGHT ME THE VALUE OF JUSTICE...
I'M GOING TO THAT TRIAL WITH OR WITHOUT YOU...

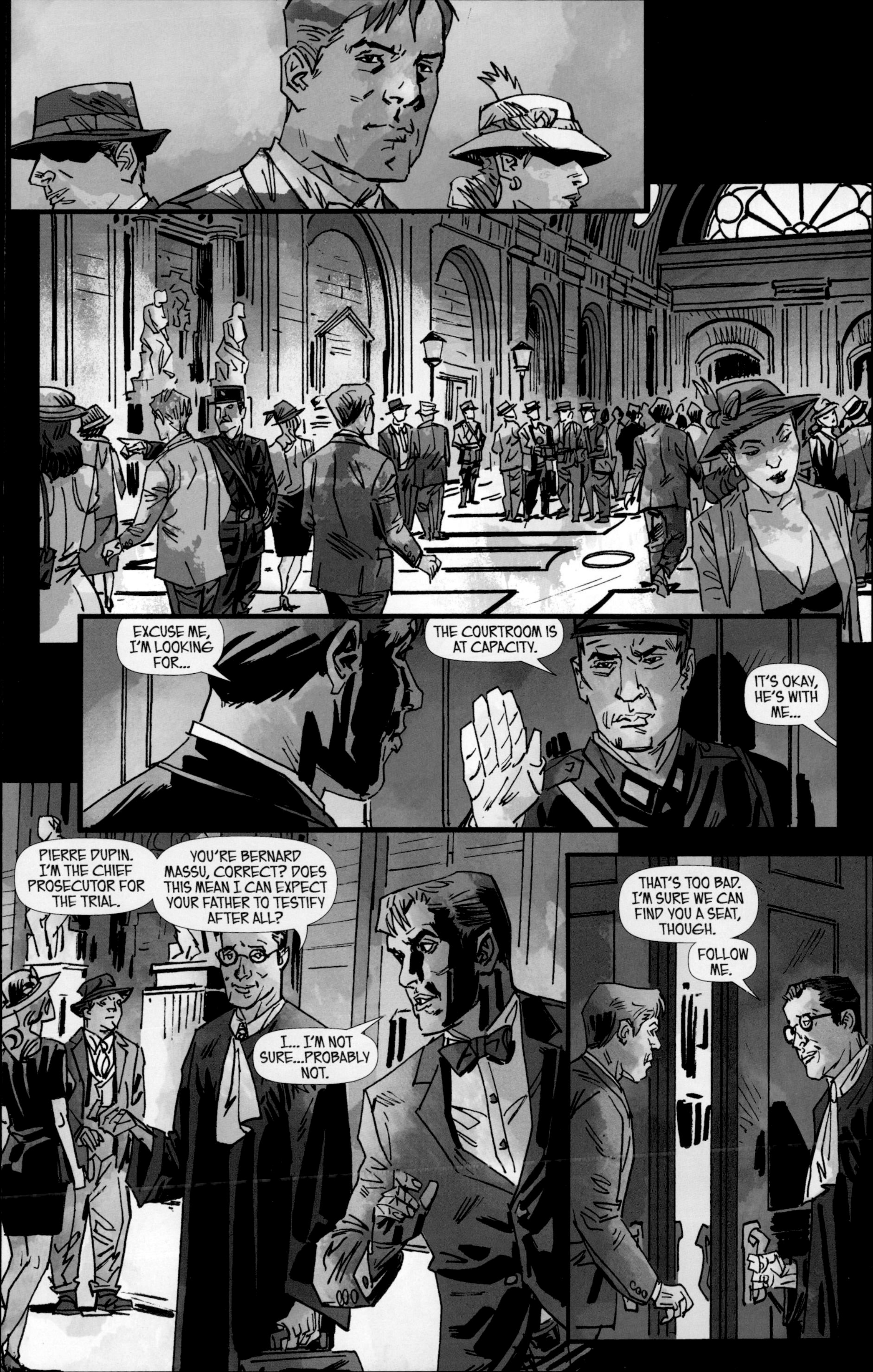
EXCUSE ME, I'M LOOKING FOR...
THE COURTROOM IS AT CAPACITY.
IT'S OKAY, HE'S WITH ME...
PIERRE DUPIN. I'M THE CHIEF PROSECUTOR FOR THE TRIAL.
YOU'RE BERNARD MASSU, CORRECT? DOES THIS MEAN I CAN EXPECT YOUR FATHER TO TESTIFY AFTER ALL?
I... I'M NOT SURE...PROBABLY NOT.
THAT'S TOO BAD. I'M SURE WE CAN FIND YOU A SEAT, THOUGH.
FOLLOW ME.

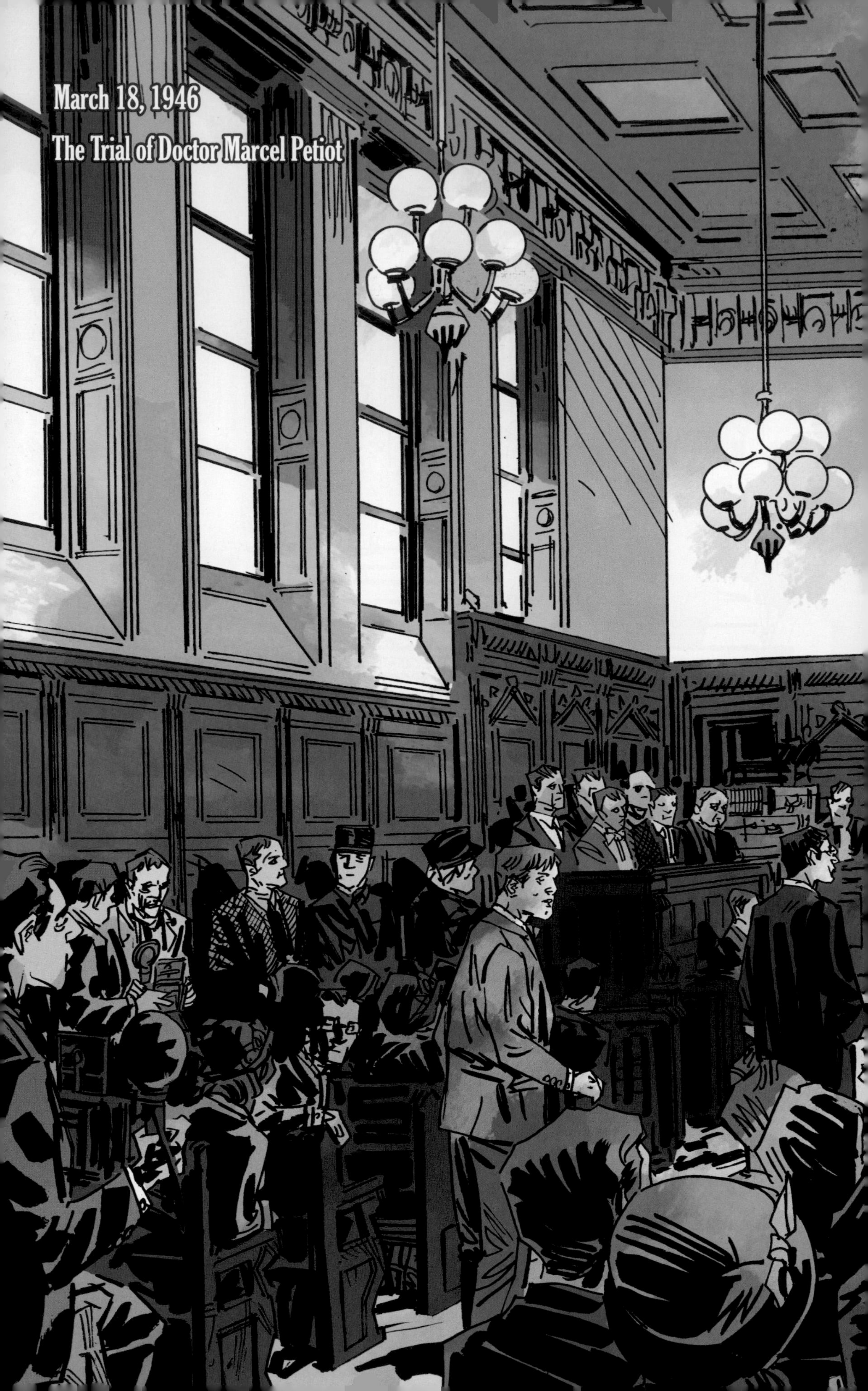
March 18, 1946
The Trial of Doctor Marcel Petiot

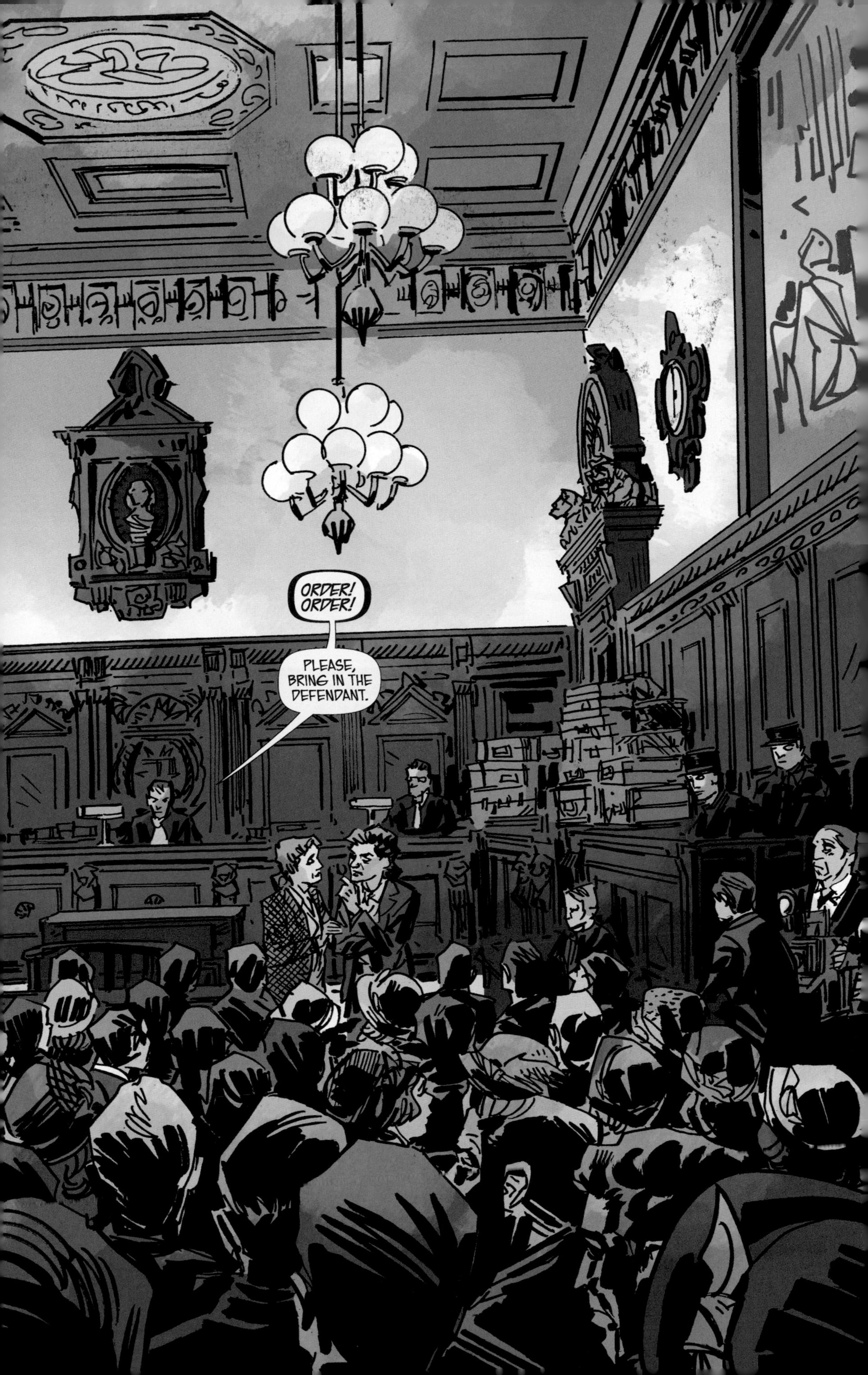
ORDER! ORDER!
PLEASE, BRING IN THE DEFENDANT.

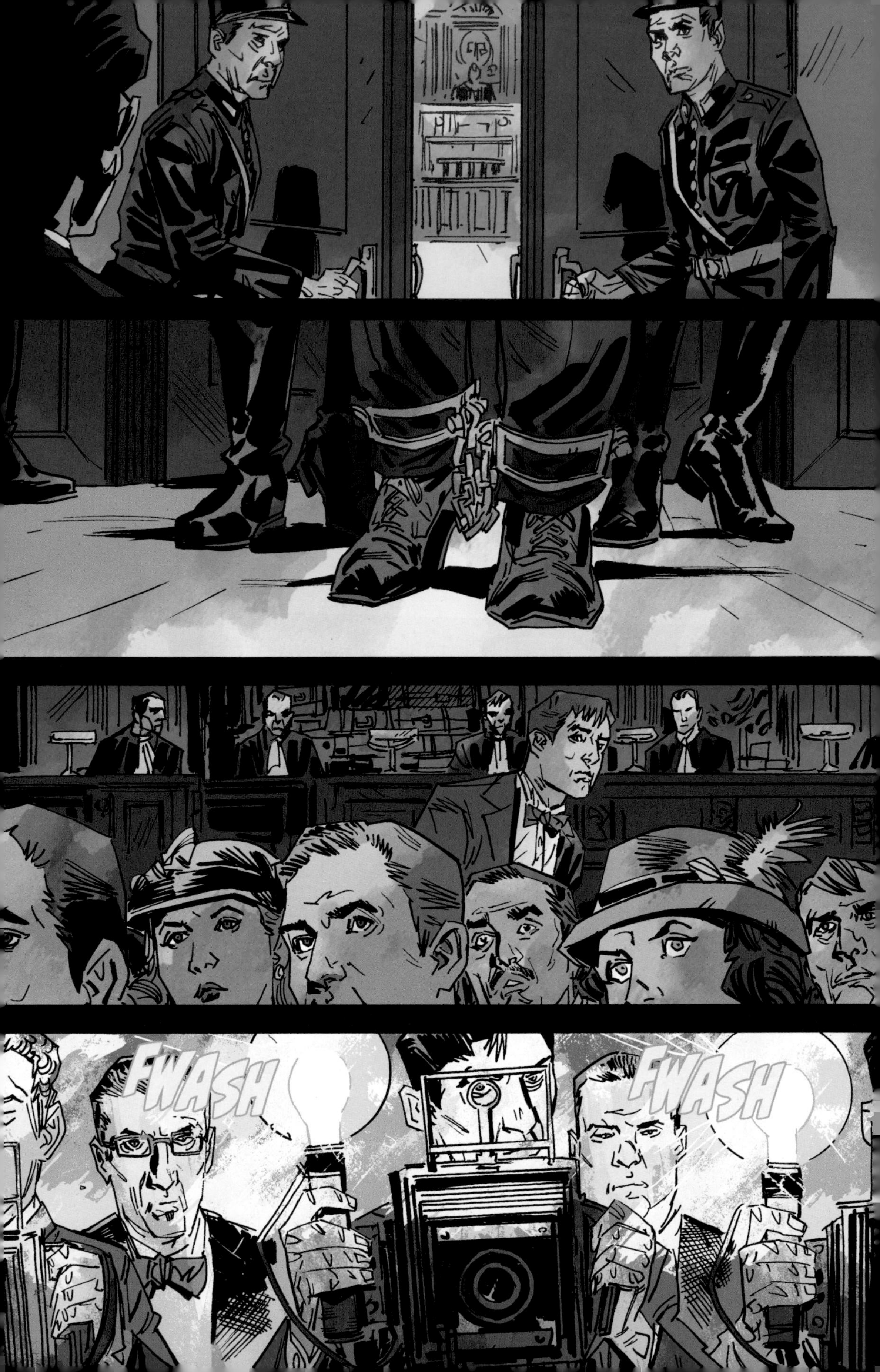
FWASH
FWASH

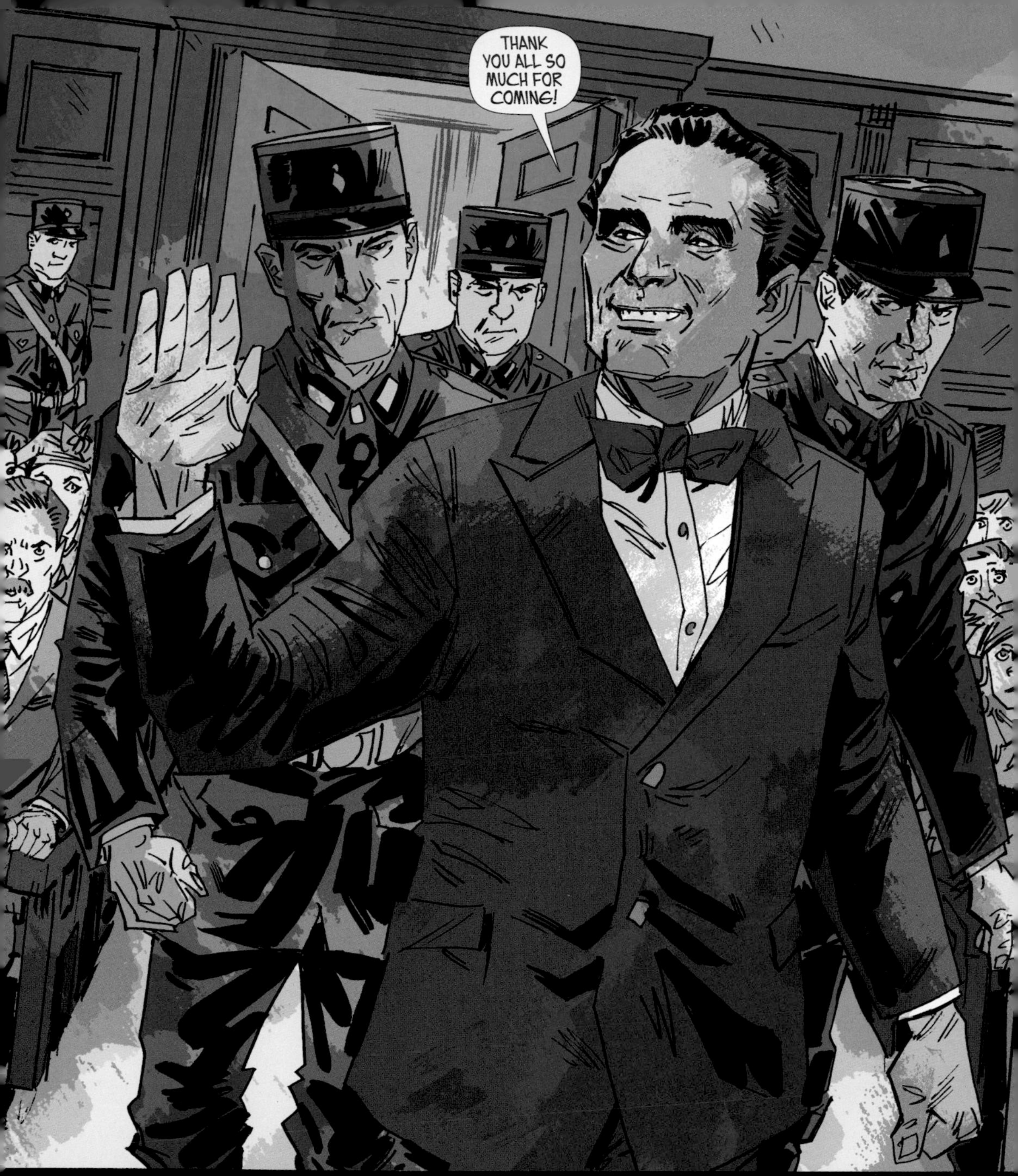
THANK YOU ALL SO MUCH FOR COMING!

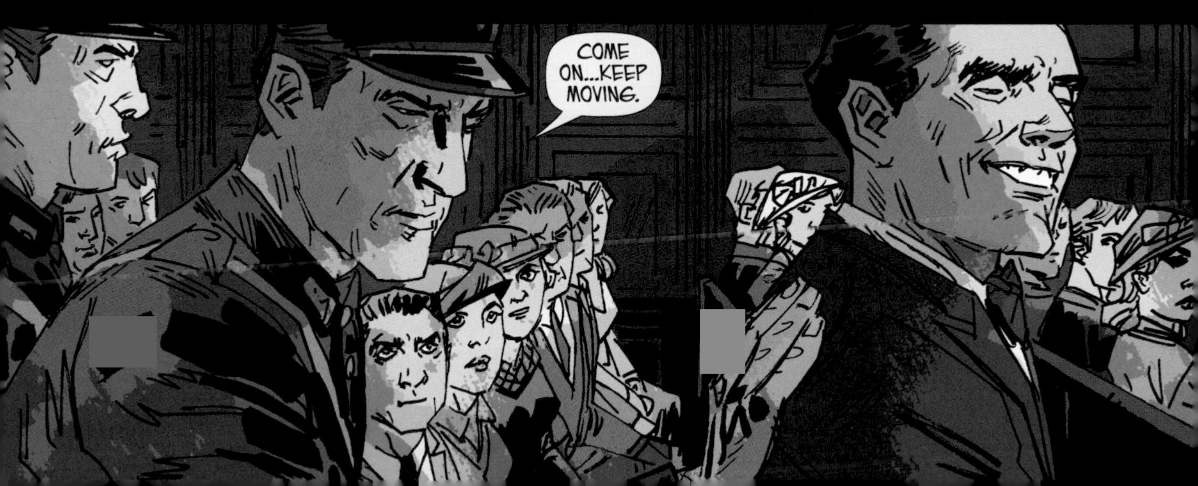
COME ON...KEEP MOVING.

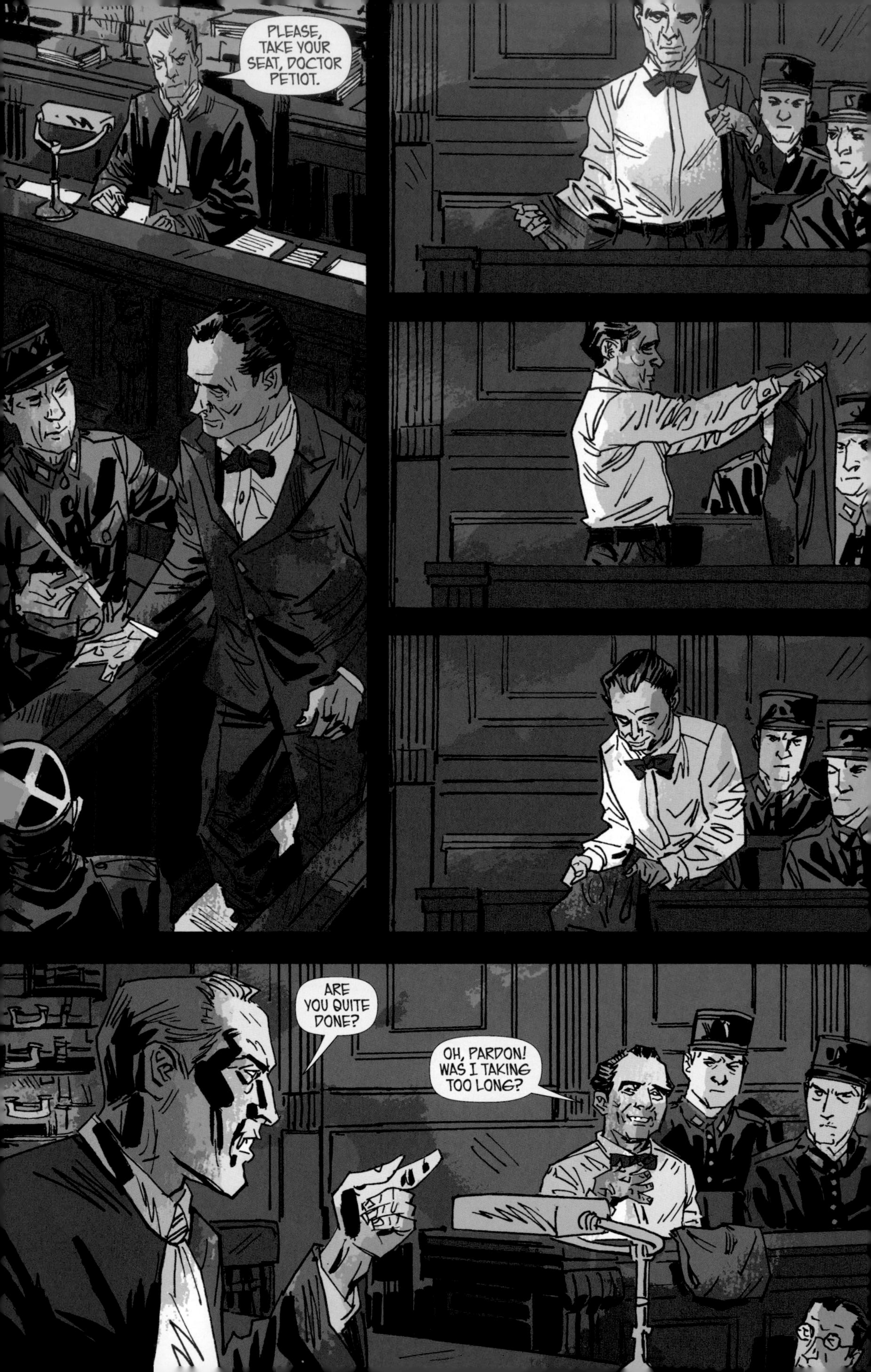
PLEASE, TAKE YOUR SEAT, DOCTOR PETIOT.
ARE YOU QUITE DONE?
OH, PARDON! WAS I TAKING TOO LONG?

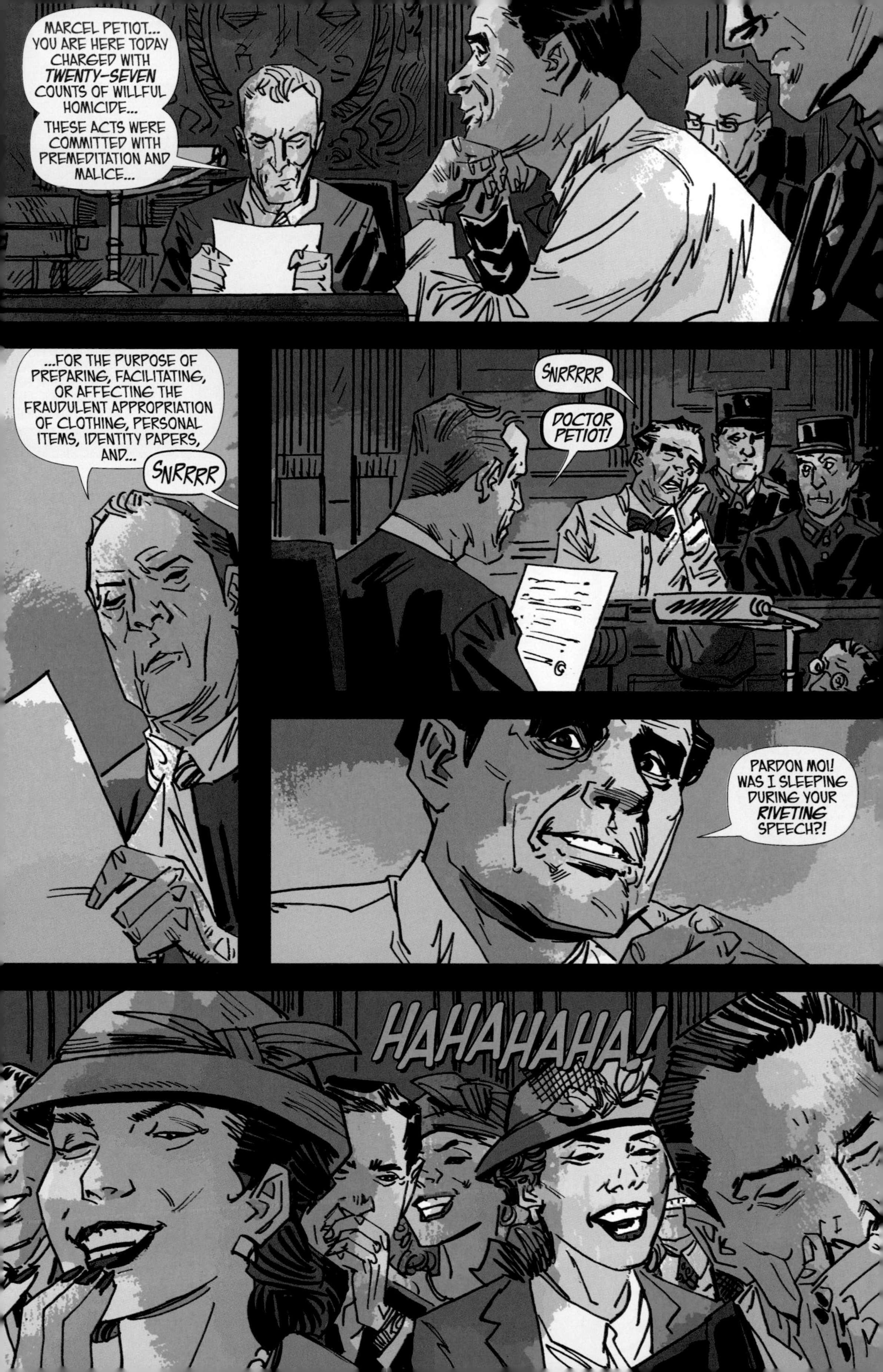
MARCEL PETIOT... YOU ARE HERE TODAY CHARGED WITH *TWENTY-SEVEN* COUNTS OF WILLFUL HOMICIDE...
THESE ACTS WERE COMMITTED WITH PREMEDITATION AND MALICE...
...FOR THE PURPOSE OF PREPARING, FACILITATING, OR AFFECTING THE FRAUDULENT APPROPRIATION OF CLOTHING, PERSONAL ITEMS, IDENTITY PAPERS, AND...
SNRRRR
SNRRRRR
DOCTOR PETIOT!
PARDON MOI! WAS I SLEEPING DURING YOUR *RIVETING* SPEECH?!
HAHAHAHA!

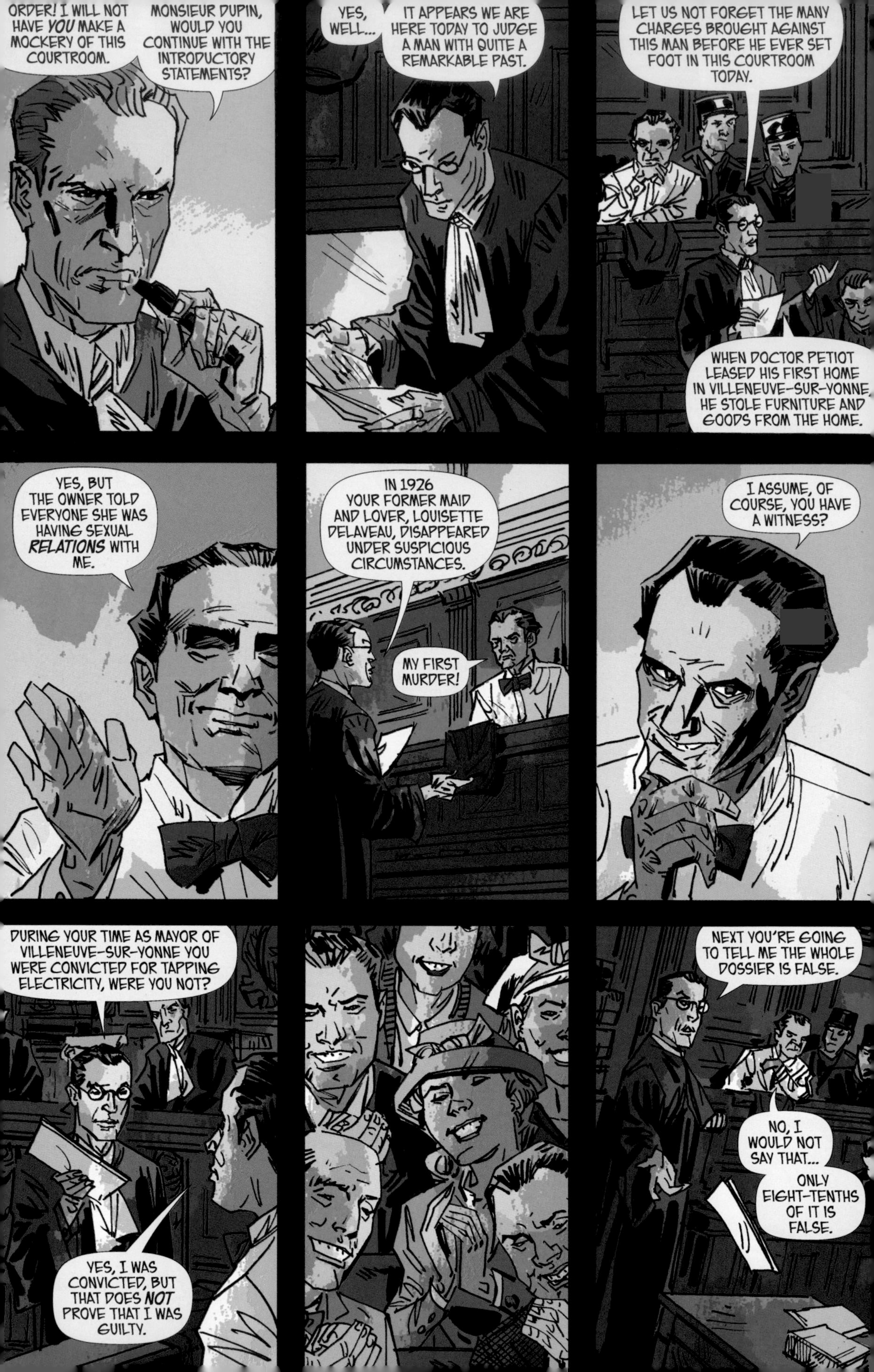
ORDER! I WILL NOT HAVE *YOU* MAKE A MOCKERY OF THIS COURTROOM.
MONSIEUR DUPIN, WOULD YOU CONTINUE WITH THE INTRODUCTORY STATEMENTS?
YES, WELL...
IT APPEARS WE ARE HERE TODAY TO JUDGE A MAN WITH QUITE A REMARKABLE PAST.
LET US NOT FORGET THE MANY CHARGES BROUGHT AGAINST THIS MAN BEFORE HE EVER SET FOOT IN THIS COURTROOM TODAY.
WHEN DOCTOR PETIOT LEASED HIS FIRST HOME IN VILLENEUVE-SUR-YONNE, HE STOLE FURNITURE AND GOODS FROM THE HOME.
YES, BUT THE OWNER TOLD EVERYONE SHE WAS HAVING SEXUAL *RELATIONS* WITH ME.
IN 1926 YOUR FORMER MAID AND LOVER, LOUISETTE DELAVEAU, DISAPPEARED UNDER SUSPICIOUS CIRCUMSTANCES.
MY FIRST MURDER!
I ASSUME, OF COURSE, YOU HAVE A WITNESS?
DURING YOUR TIME AS MAYOR OF VILLENEUVE-SUR-YONNE YOU WERE CONVICTED FOR TAPPING ELECTRICITY, WERE YOU NOT?
YES, I WAS CONVICTED, BUT THAT DOES *NOT* PROVE THAT I WAS GUILTY.
NEXT YOU'RE GOING TO TELL ME THE WHOLE DOSSIER IS FALSE.
NO, I WOULD NOT SAY THAT...
ONLY EIGHT-TENTHS OF IT IS FALSE.

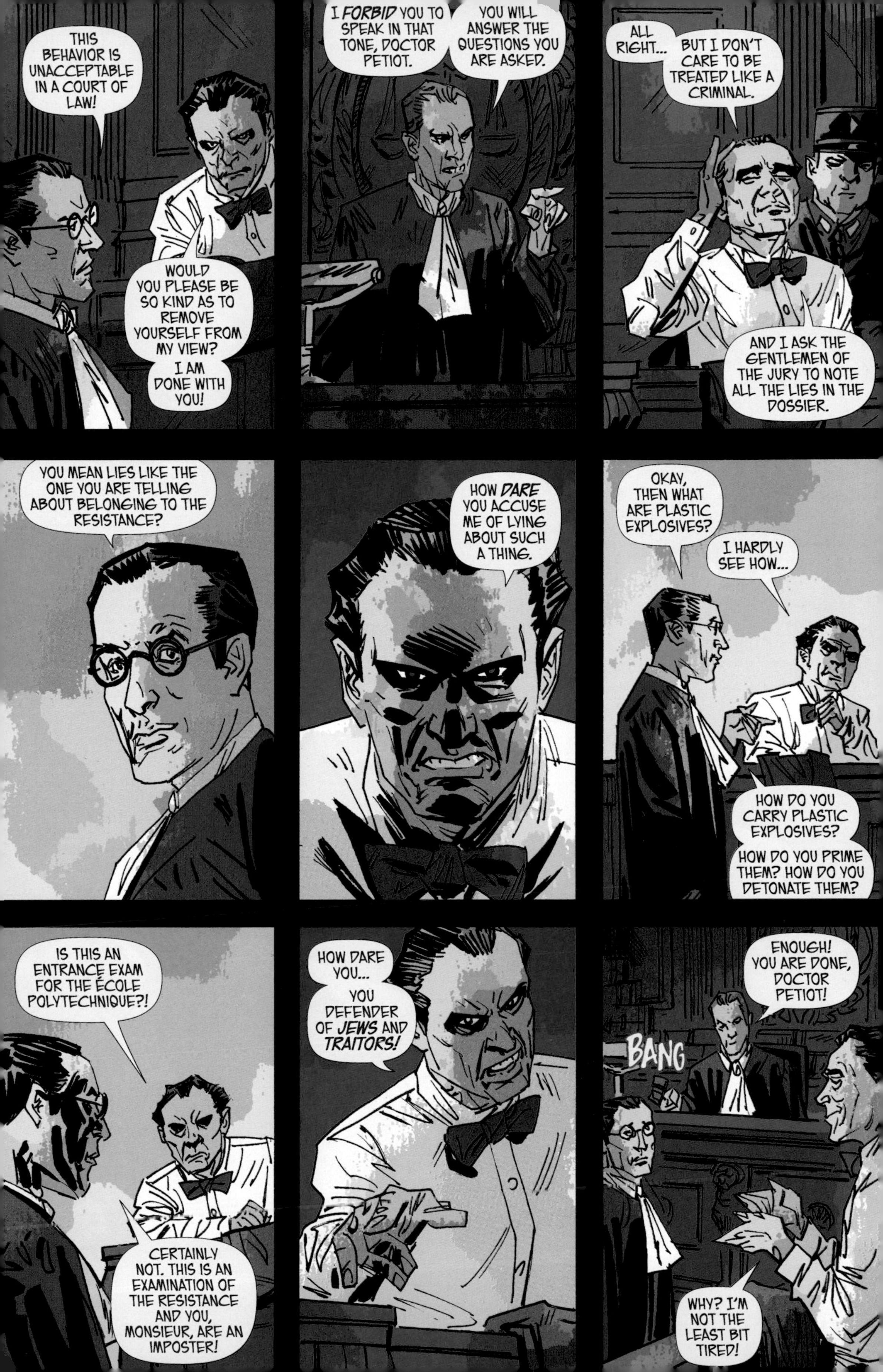
THIS BEHAVIOR IS UNACCEPTABLE IN A COURT OF LAW!
WOULD YOU PLEASE BE SO KIND AS TO REMOVE YOURSELF FROM MY VIEW?
I AM DONE WITH YOU!
I *FORBID* YOU TO SPEAK IN THAT TONE, DOCTOR PETIOT.
YOU WILL ANSWER THE QUESTIONS YOU ARE ASKED.
ALL RIGHT...
BUT I DON'T CARE TO BE TREATED LIKE A CRIMINAL.
AND I ASK THE GENTLEMEN OF THE JURY TO NOTE ALL THE LIES IN THE DOSSIER.
YOU MEAN LIES LIKE THE ONE YOU ARE TELLING ABOUT BELONGING TO THE RESISTANCE?
HOW *DARE* YOU ACCUSE ME OF LYING ABOUT SUCH A THING.
OKAY, THEN WHAT ARE PLASTIC EXPLOSIVES?
I HARDLY SEE HOW...
HOW DO YOU CARRY PLASTIC EXPLOSIVES?
HOW DO YOU PRIME THEM? HOW DO YOU DETONATE THEM?
IS THIS AN ENTRANCE EXAM FOR THE ÉCOLE POLYTECHNIQUE?!
CERTAINLY NOT. THIS IS AN EXAMINATION OF THE RESISTANCE AND YOU, MONSIEUR, ARE AN IMPOSTER!
HOW DARE YOU...
YOU DEFENDER OF *JEWS* AND *TRAITORS!*
BANG
ENOUGH! YOU ARE DONE, DOCTOR PETIOT!
WHY? I'M NOT THE LEAST BIT TIRED!

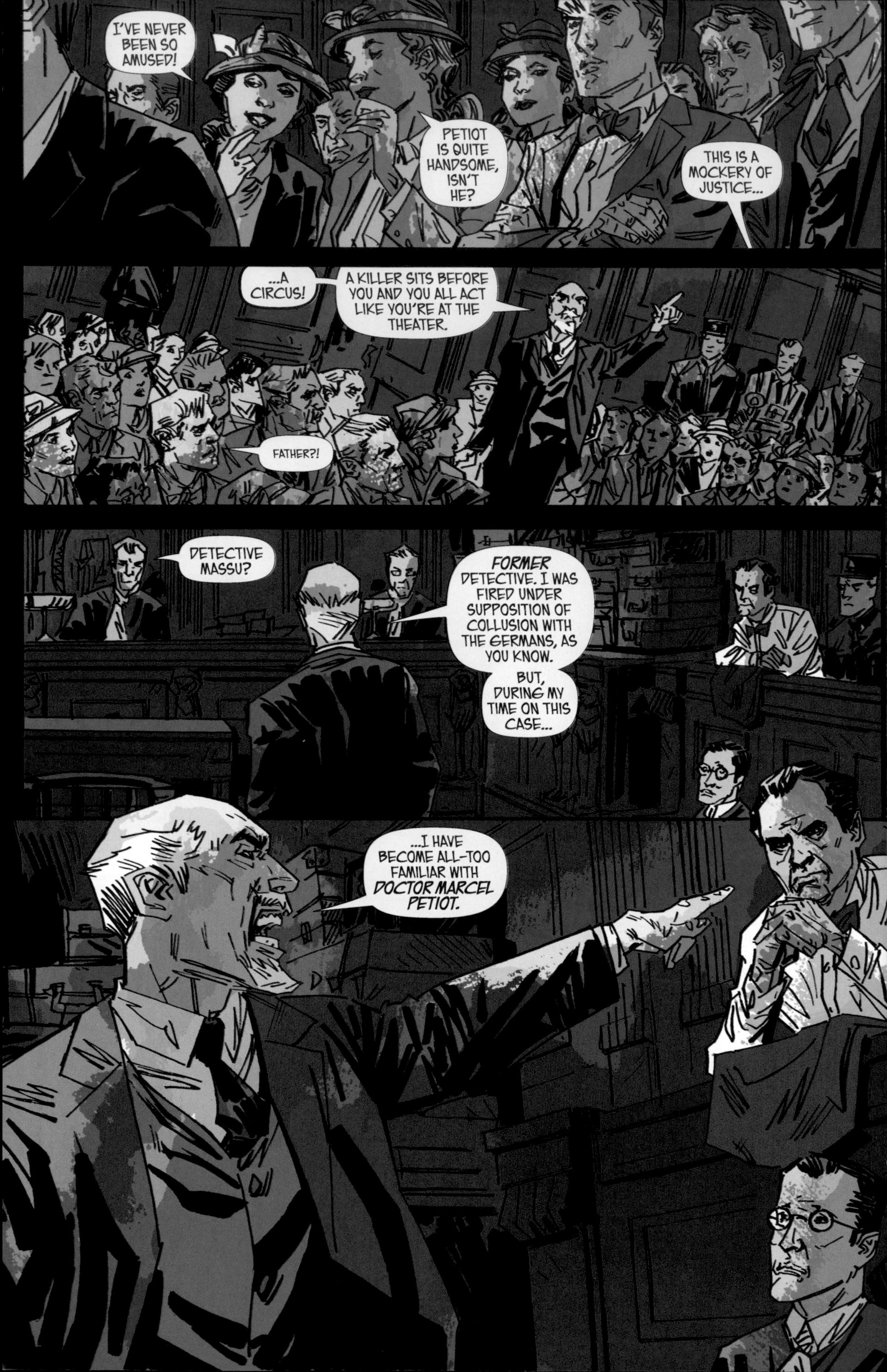
I'VE NEVER BEEN SO AMUSED!
PETIOT IS QUITE HANDSOME, ISN'T HE?
THIS IS A MOCKERY OF JUSTICE...
...A CIRCUS!
A KILLER SITS BEFORE YOU AND YOU ALL ACT LIKE YOU'RE AT THE THEATER.
FATHER?!
DETECTIVE MASSU?
FORMER DETECTIVE. I WAS FIRED UNDER SUPPOSITION OF COLLUSION WITH THE GERMANS, AS YOU KNOW.
BUT, DURING MY TIME ON THIS CASE...
...I HAVE BECOME ALL-TOO FAMILIAR WITH DOCTOR MARCEL PETIOT.

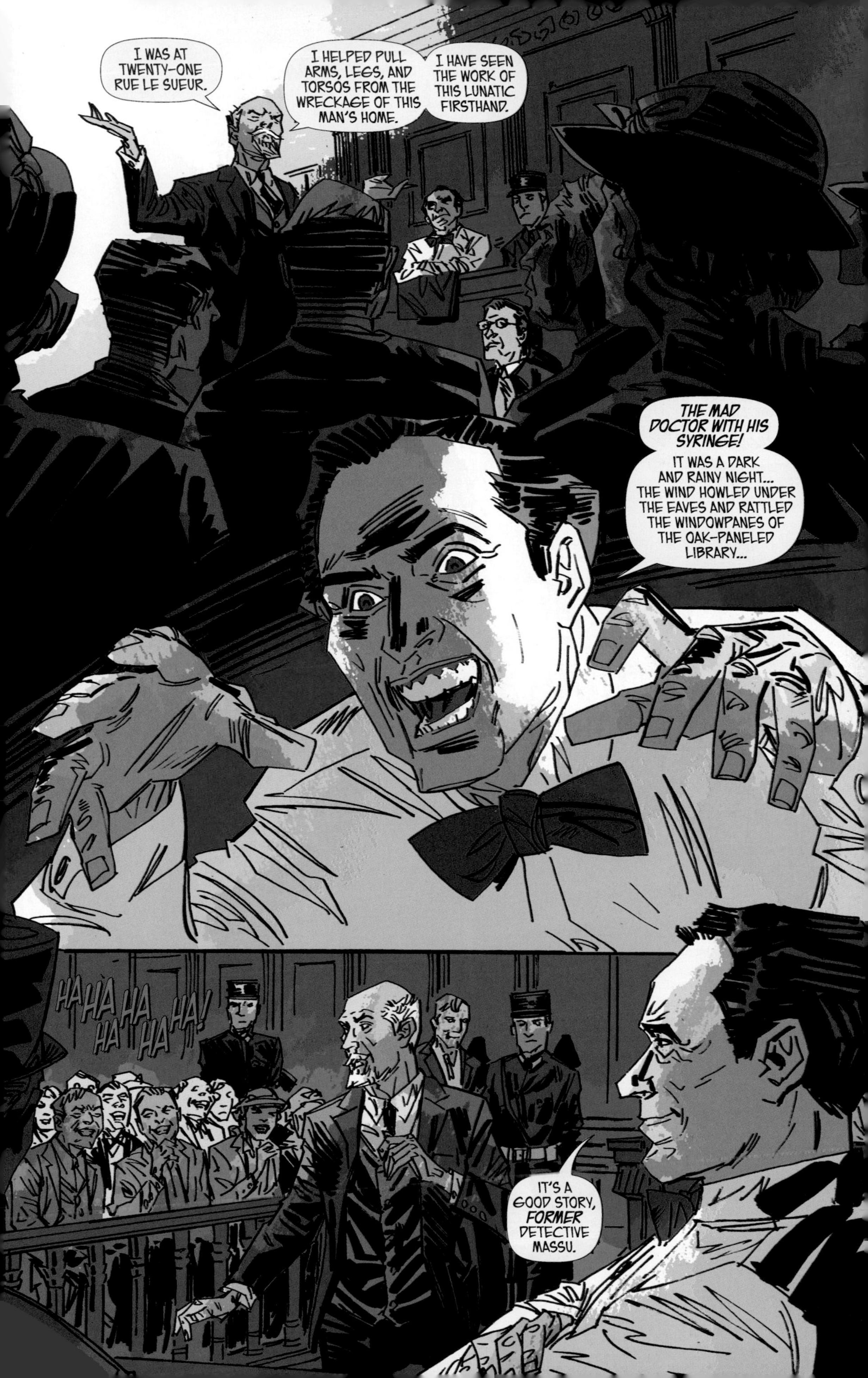
I WAS AT TWENTY-ONE RUE LE SUEUR.
I HELPED PULL ARMS, LEGS, AND TORSOS FROM THE WRECKAGE OF THIS MAN'S HOME.
I HAVE SEEN THE WORK OF THIS LUNATIC FIRSTHAND.
THE MAD DOCTOR WITH HIS SYRINGE!
IT WAS A DARK AND RAINY NIGHT... THE WIND HOWLED UNDER THE EAVES AND RATTLED THE WINDOWPANES OF THE OAK-PANELED LIBRARY...
HA HA HA HA HA! HA HA
IT'S A GOOD STORY, ***FORMER*** DETECTIVE MASSU.

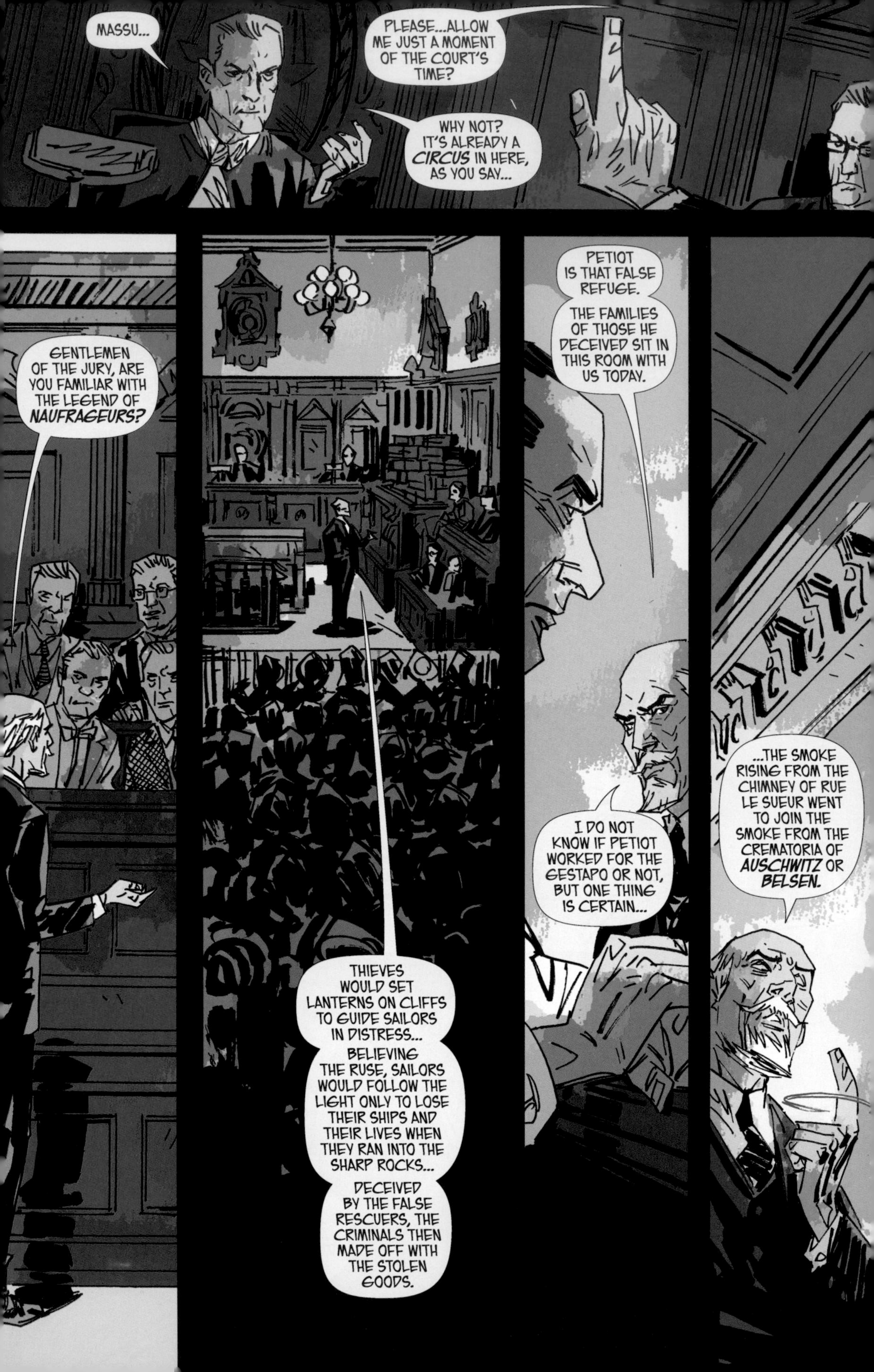
MASSU...
PLEASE...ALLOW ME JUST A MOMENT OF THE COURT'S TIME?
WHY NOT? IT'S ALREADY A *CIRCUS* IN HERE, AS YOU SAY...
GENTLEMEN OF THE JURY, ARE YOU FAMILIAR WITH THE LEGEND OF *NAUFRAGEURS?*
THIEVES WOULD SET LANTERNS ON CLIFFS TO GUIDE SAILORS IN DISTRESS...
BELIEVING THE RUSE, SAILORS WOULD FOLLOW THE LIGHT ONLY TO LOSE THEIR SHIPS AND THEIR LIVES WHEN THEY RAN INTO THE SHARP ROCKS...
DECEIVED BY THE FALSE RESCUERS, THE CRIMINALS THEN MADE OFF WITH THE STOLEN GOODS.
PETIOT IS THAT FALSE REFUGE.
THE FAMILIES OF THOSE HE DECEIVED SIT IN THIS ROOM WITH US TODAY.
I DO NOT KNOW IF PETIOT WORKED FOR THE GESTAPO OR NOT, BUT ONE THING IS CERTAIN...
...THE SMOKE RISING FROM THE CHIMNEY OF RUE LE SUEUR WENT TO JOIN THE SMOKE FROM THE CREMATORIA OF *AUSCHWITZ* OR *BELSEN.*

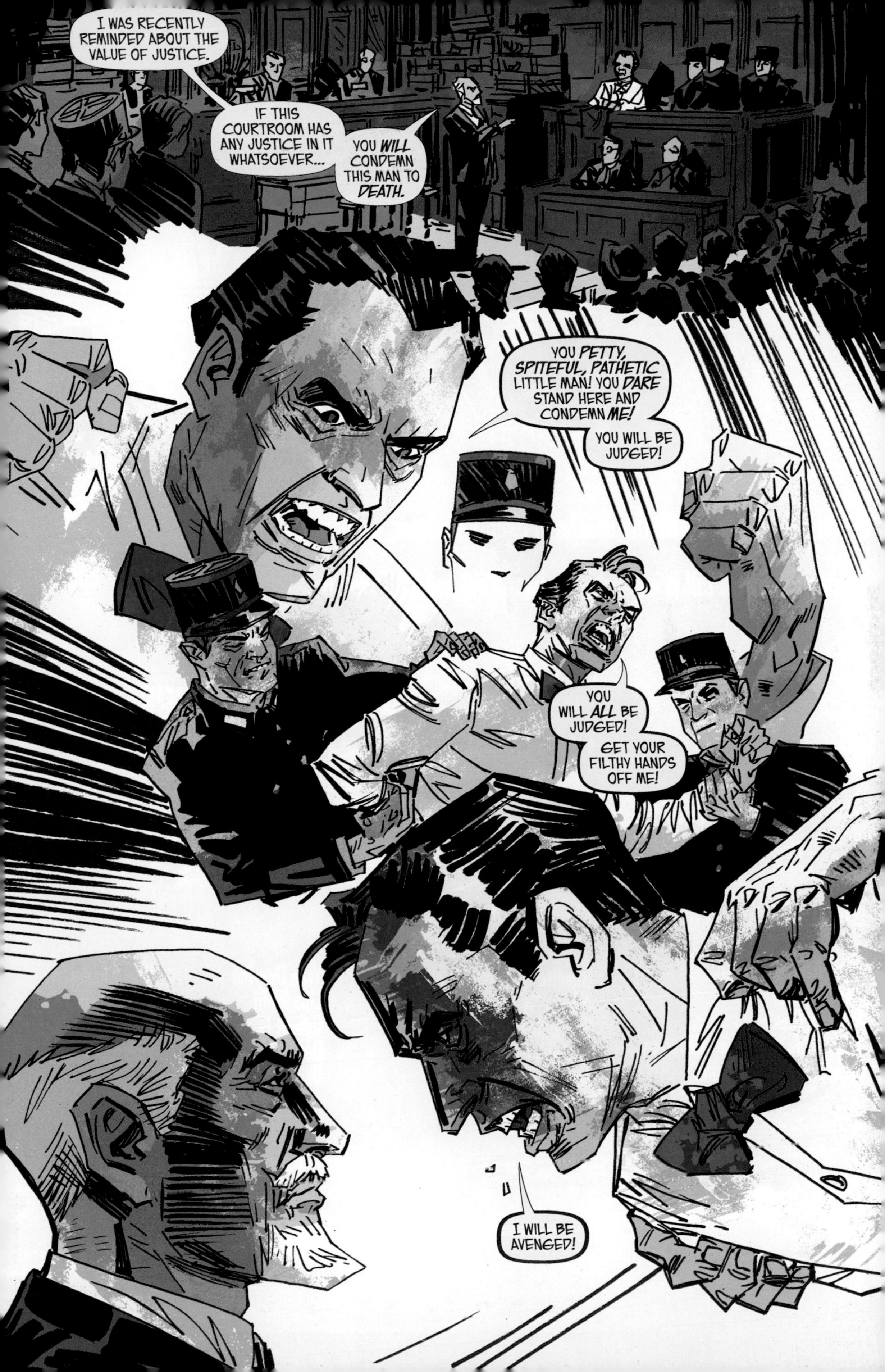
I WAS RECENTLY REMINDED ABOUT THE VALUE OF JUSTICE.
IF THIS COURTROOM HAS ANY JUSTICE IN IT WHATSOEVER...
YOU *WILL* CONDEMN THIS MAN TO *DEATH.*
YOU *PETTY, SPITEFUL, PATHETIC* LITTLE MAN! YOU *DARE* STAND HERE AND CONDEMN *ME!*
YOU WILL BE JUDGED!
YOU WILL *ALL* BE JUDGED!
GET YOUR FILTHY HANDS OFF ME!
I WILL BE AVENGED!

Marcel Petiot was sentenced to death and roused from his cell on the morning of May 25, 1946.

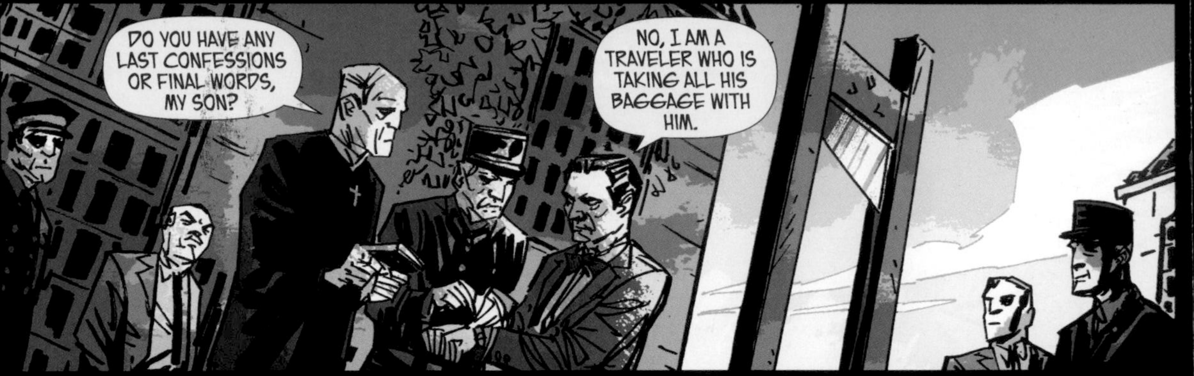
DO YOU HAVE ANY LAST CONFESSIONS OR FINAL WORDS, MY SON?
NO, I AM A TRAVELER WHO IS TAKING ALL HIS BAGGAGE WITH HIM.

Petiot was charged with the deaths of twenty-six men, women, and children.

The actual death toll is estimated between 60 and 200 victims.

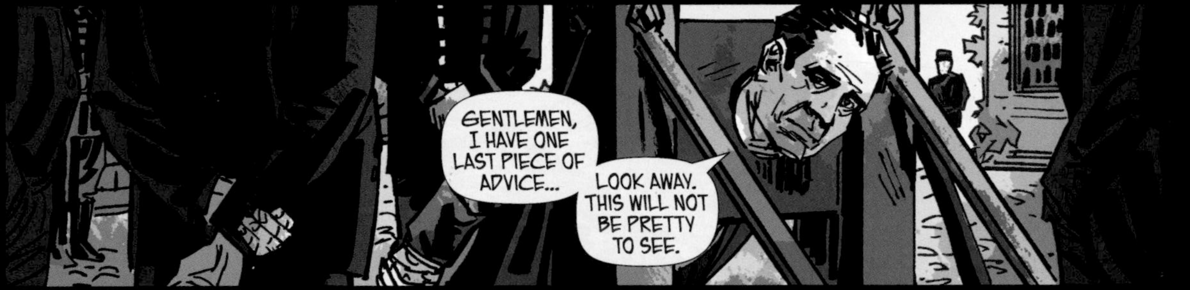
GENTLEMEN, I HAVE ONE LAST PIECE OF ADVICE...
LOOK AWAY. THIS WILL NOT BE PRETTY TO SEE.

Some of Petiot's confirmed victims include:

Jean-Marc Van Bever
Marthe Khaït
Joachim Guschinov
Jospeh "Jo le Boxeur" Réocreux
Claudia "Lulu" Chamoux
Annette "la Poute" Basset
Adrien "le Basque" Estébétéguy
Gisèle Rossny
Joséphine Grippay
Jospeh "Zé" Piereschie
Yvan Dreyfus
Lina Wolff
Gilbert Basch
Denise Hotin
Dr. Paul Braunberger
Kurt Kneller
René Kneller
Margeret Kneller
François Albertini

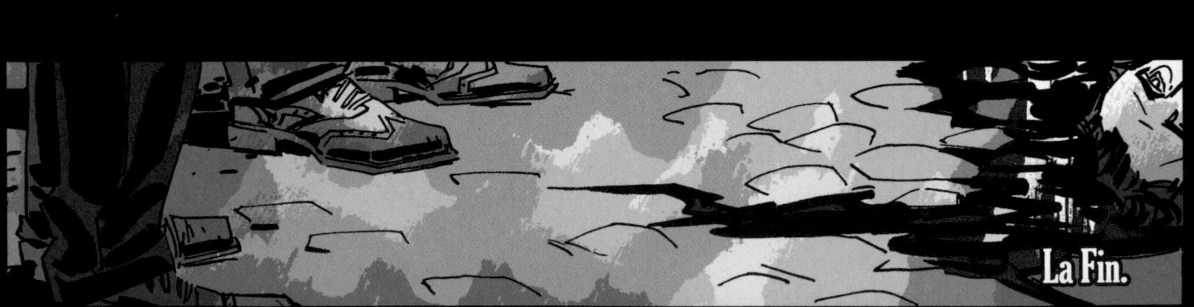
La Fin.